To Betty Smuller
From
Shin Williams

ALASKA SOURDOUGH

BOOKS BY RICHARD MORENUS

Alaska Sourdough

Crazy-White-Man

Frozen Trails

The Hudson's Bay Company

Northland Adventure

ALASKA SOURDOUGH

The Story of Slim Williams

By RICHARD MORENUS

RAND McNALLY & COMPANY
New York • Chicago • San Francisco

The author wishes to thank Dodd, Mead & Co. for
their permission to reprint excerpts from the poems of
Robert W. Service which introduce each chapter.

When I finished writing ALASKA SOURDOUGH, I asked
Slim Williams about a dedication for the book. He
cocked his head sort of sideways, squinted at the match
flame as he lighted a brown-paper cigarette he had just
rolled, took a puff, and said:

"I wouldn't know much about a dedication, Dick,
'less it might be to the partners I had in Alaska, fellows
I'll never forget." Slim puffed, tossed the cigarette
away, and began rolling a new one. "But I guess Gladys
would be first in a dedication. Gladys an' me been married a long time, an' I wouldn't change it." He lighted
the cigarette. "Then, I guess about the best friend me
an' Gladys ever had is Carl Backman. Carl's managed
me ever since I started lecturin' in 1934. There's only
one Carl." Slim thought a moment. "Then I guess a
book about me ought to be dedicated to the Indians and
Eskimos who were kind to me in the thirty-two years I
roamed Alaska. Good friends, them fellows. And above
all . . . a dedication to my dogs . . . the best in the
world."

There is Slim Williams' dedication, and mine is
added, to Nora, my wife.

ALASKA SOURDOUGH

· 1 ·

If only you'll let me spin my yarn . . . .
and seeing as how it's you,
I'll tell you the tale of a Northern trail,
and so help me God, it's true.

Slim Williams was hungry and tired. He had eaten almost nothing for the past two days; he had hardly slept at all for almost two weeks; besides, in spite of the fact that for fifteen days he and some three hundred other humans, all male, and a weird assortment of animals had been crowded onto a ship whose passenger capacity was one hundred, he had spoken to no one. All this was very serious to a normal, friendly six-foot-three-inch, 160-pound, eighteen-year-old boy.

This morning was raw and cold. Slim leaned on the bow rail, staring gloomily ahead into the cold, clammy predawn mist, and tried hard to recapture the enthusiasm that had caused him to spend $31.00, practically every cent he had in the world, for passage to Alaska. In Seattle it hadn't bothered him in the least that he didn't know where Alaska was, nor that all he did know about it was waterfront talk. The talk had been of gold, newly discovered there, and that to Slim meant a bright promise of adventure. Right at the moment, however, sixteen hundred miles later, his future seemed as dull and dismal as the fog around him.

The ship's whistle blasted, then in a moment it blasted again. This had been going on regularly for some time, an hour or more. Slim listened to twin echoes, one from the right and one from the left. The sound was obviously bouncing back from invisible cliffs along the shore. The ship moved forward with bare steerageway. Slim reasoned that the pilot was *hearing* his way through a channel, and the ship was safely in the middle as long as the echoing sounds reached it simultaneously. Now the echoes took longer and longer to return, and as they grew fainter, Slim guessed that they had reached the open water of a bay. He was right. A moment later the ship slithered onto bottom sludge left almost bare by low tide. Bells clanged and men shouted. The propeller beat a futile reverse, but the ship dug into the mud, listed slightly, and settled. There she would stay until the rising tide would lift her free.

As if this were a signal, men poured from cabins and the innards of the ship until the deck was jammed. Hell literally broke loose. Poker games, drinking parties, and fights had stopped for the first time during the trip. Most of the passengers were getting their first breath of fresh air and sight of daylight in many days.

The mist had begun to thin, and the dim outline of shore became visible about a half-mile ahead. There was no physical danger, but the men ran about in near panic. Lifeboats were cut free and lowered, rope ladders went overside, and in the hurry more men fell off into the water than reached it by climbing down. The freight doors along the ship's sides opened and horses, dogs, burros, even goats, were shoved overboard into the bay, with their owners holding the lead ropes and splash-landing with them. Soon the ship was empty except for the officers and crew.

Slim grabbed his packsack, which held his only possessions, and went overside with the others. The ship became a dim shadowy hulk as he waded shoreward through knee-deep gummy ooze and icy water. When he stopped to rest, men appeared as dark cursing specters, looming out of the haze and sloshing past him. They carried bags, boxes, some even had trunks on their backs; others were tugging or towing their resentful animals. Ahead Slim saw the yellow flicker of fires along the shore. At least these promised warmth, and, he hoped, food. He hunched his packsack to a more comfortable spot and slogged on after the others.

When he reached the shore, Slim stood and looked about dazedly. There was neither form nor arrangement in the temporary encampment. The ground along the shore was a morass of freezing mud that had been tracked out of the bay, and beyond that lay snow. The town, if it could be called that, was Valdez. Located on a glacial mud flat, it was ringed in, to the water's edge, by mountains. Through these, glacier passes afforded entrance to the land beyond. Gold had been discovered near Fairbanks, Alaska, and Valdez and her glacier passes were to Alaska what Skagway and the Chilkoot were to the Dawson Creeks in Canada's Yukon Territory. Valdez Harbor, because of the Japan Current, was ice free the year round, but the town, the passes, and the mountains received no such protection. Winters were long, snow was measured by the foot, and the blizzard winds and searing cold of the passes were known by the lives they took.

Hundreds of men, in groups or singly, milled around. They hugged fires, drying out; others looked after their outfits; some were putting up tents or caring for their animals. These men were far too occupied with their own misery to bother over the troubles of a lone, wet, hungry kid. Each group Slim tried to join either shoved him aside or ignored him.

Being alone was nothing new to Slim. He had been on his own ever since he could remember, from the time when, barely big enough to sit a saddle, he had ridden herd on his father's small cattle setup in South California. Afterward, through the years, he had roamed the Southwest and West, sometimes living with the Indians, but more often by himself. Slim had always been self-sufficient and had never learned to be lonesome. He had never known what it was to feel sorry for himself. Even now it wasn't the fact that these men paid no attention to him that bothered him. His need was not for companionship, it was for food.

He walked past the buildings of the town. Most of them were log, but some were of whipsawed lumber. But none of these offered him any relief. The gambling joints, dance halls, saloons were all well populated, but they reminded him too strongly of the ship he had just left, for it was this same stench and noise that had spoiled his appetite and ruined his sleep. One lighted window showed a sign, "Meals." He hurried over and was stopped by a placard in the window, "All you can eat $5." He dug in his pocket and took out his money, and looked morosely at the $1.30 he held in his hand.

Finally he walked over to where a man was sitting well apart near the shore on an upturned packing box. He was warming his hands over the small fire on the ground before him. "What place is this, mister?" Slim asked.

The man who looked at Slim wore a dirty, shaggy beard, his eyes were red-rimmed and unsure, his hands shook. He stared first at Slim's sopping oversized boots. Then he slowly lifted his head taking in the details of the tall, gaunt youngster until he looked into the boy's clear, smiling hazel eyes. The face was generously featured, high cheekbones, and large nose, and mouth rather like Lincoln's, and big ears. It was a good face and already starting to show the characteristics of strength and humility. Black hair showed from under Slim's cap.

The man shrugged, and turned again to face his fire, and said, "Get some wood and build up this fire, and dry out before you freeze." His voice was low and raspy.

"But where can I get something to eat, mister? I'm hungry," Slim insisted.

"You walk around that way you'll freeze, you crazy kid; get some wood and fix the fire first."

Slim got busy scrounging wood, and with the fire burning higher he was grateful for its warmth. Again the man studied the boy. "You just come off that boat out there, didn't you?" This was more a statement than a question, yet Slim nodded.

"You started for Alaska when you left Seattle, didn't you?" Again Slim nodded. "Well, that's where you are—Alaska." The man spat in the fire and rubbed his hands together over the flame. "If you're hungry, the grub shack's over there," he motioned by a backward jerk of his head, "but you get dry before you go walkin' around. How many on that boat this time?"

"About three hundred," said Slim.

The man stared out over the harbor. "Three hundred on a dirty tub built to carry a hundred. Just like it was when I come up two years ago in '98." He looked quickly up at Slim. "This is 1900, ain't it?"

Slim nodded.

"Wasn't sure. You lose track o' time up here," the man said. "I come up two years ago in '98."

Slim freshened the fire and rubbed circulation into his legs. "But you didn't tell me what the name of this place is," he said.

"I told you, it's Alaska."

"But what town?"

"You call this lousy place a town? When I come here two years ago it was called Copper City. A few tents, there was, and the biggest one was the saloon. Then I went north over the glacier looking for gold, stayed two years, and come out as broke as I went in. When I come out they tell me they changed the name o' the place to Valdez.

"They got a few more tents and some log shacks, but the biggest ones is still joints and saloons. If the North don't break you, them hell dives will. If you got any sense, kid, you'll get back on that tub like I'm goin' to do, an' you'll go back where you come from. I got a fellow goin' to take me out in a rowboat, an' you can go too if you're smart, if you got money enough to pay your way. I sold my outfit to pay mine. This ain't no country for kids."

"I sort of think I can take care of myself, mister," Slim said confidently.

"Don't be so smart, kid," the man mumbled. "That's what *I* thought. That's what they all think when they come up here. I wasn't much older'n you a couple o' years ago when I come up, and look what it done to me. Burned me out, that's what it done. 'Gold!' they said. 'Go to Alaska and get rich!' they said. 'Gold for pickin' it up—you'll be a millionaire!' That's what everybody said, and me an' a few thousand other fools believed 'em." The man squinted up at Slim and studied his face for a moment. Then he turned and pointed north. "Look over there," he said, "see those?"

The mist had fully lifted and the air cleared, and Slim had his first glimpse of the full regal magnificence of Alaska's mountains. These seemed to start at his very feet and rise straight upward five, six, seven thousand feet to where their towering snowy peaks were gold crowned by the morning sun against an icy blue sky.

"Ever see anything like 'em before?" the man asked.

Slim shook his head. He had seen mountains before, in his native California, and in Oregon where he'd worked in mines and in lumber camps, but he had never seen mountains like these.

"Them ain't mountains, kid, them's the teeth o' the devil." The man pointed toward the base of one of the peaks. "You see that tongue of ice stickin' out there? That's just one o' the glaciers, miles o' crawlin' ice. Thirty-five miles to the top o' that one before you can get past the teeth o' the range, an' they'll cut you, an' tear you, an' crush you, an' spit you out broken an' smashed like it's done to thousands of others. One bad step over that trail o' ice and it's cold, freezin' death. You never worked in your life until you cross one o' them glaciers, then you'll know what work is. An' when you get on the other side, you think you'll find gold?" The man coughed and spit in the flames at his feet.

"Maybe I ain't even looking for gold," said Slim.

The man looked up with a start. "Not lookin' for gold? Then what did you come for?"

"I don't know exactly, maybe for adventure," Slim spoke quietly as he stared at the mountains and slowly shook his head, "but one thing I'm sure of, I got this far, so I'll go see for myself what's on the other side of them. It may not be gold, but it'll be what I'm looking for."

"You're a fool, kid. Alaska'll kill you in a year. You're nothin' but a fool! Now go and get some grub." The man swore disgustedly, coughed, and spit.

Slim thanked the man for sharing his fire and walked back to the food shack. The sign was still in the window. Slim stared at it sadly for a moment, then looked around. He had never acquired the habit of asking favors and had no intention of trying to get a free handout. There was only one way he knew to get the things he needed: work. So he went job hunting. Every establishment which could rightfully be called a business, whether in a tent or a log shack, seemed to be a one-man operation, and there were no odd jobs or chore work to be had. Then Slim saw activity at the edge of town and went to investigate.

He saw two columns of men. One column, made up of two, three, and often four abreast, was headed out of town toward the glacier in the distance, and stretched out as far as Slim could see. These men were newcomers like himself, but already on the march, "going in" on their search for gold. The other column, just as long, but single file, were old-timers, the ones "coming out." He had no more than arrived at where the ingoing column was forming than a heavy voice called out of the crowd, "Hey, you! Slim!" He looked quickly around and saw a man waving and motioning to him. The man was a big fellow, about an inch taller than Slim, and a hundred pounds heavier. He wore a full bushy beard and was a moose of a man. Surrounded by prospectors, he was obviously carrying on a profitable business, buying from one and selling to another almost as fast as he could talk. Slim hurried to where he was, and when he got there the man looked up and said, "You want a job, Slim?"

Slim, amazed that anyone could possibly know him, said, "How'd you know my name?"

"Anybody that's as long, tall, and drawn out as you are has got to be 'Slim.' You want a job?"

Slim nodded, and accepted the explanation that had given him this name years before and wherever he went. "What do I do?" he asked.

"Start neckin'!" and the man went back to his bargaining. After a few moments he looked up to find that Slim was still there. "Thought you wanted a job," he bellowed, "then get neckin'!" And when Slim still made no move, the man started to laugh. "All right, kid," he said, "you're a cheechako all right, but I'll take you on."

Necking, Slim painfully learned, consisted of towing a sled with an average load of 200 to 250 pounds by a rope which passed from the back under the armpits and up around the nape of the neck. It was a sort of rope yoke; heavy loads could be hauled in this manner more easily than by the hands or a shoulder harness. "I buy the outfits from these sourdoughs comin' out," the man explained. "They have no more use for 'em, an' I sell 'em to these cheechakos goin' in, because most of 'em have nothin' to start with. Your job is when I buy an outfit you neck it followin' me along this line o' cheechakos until I get it sold, then we come back an' get another. My name's Big Ed, an' I'll pay you the goin' rate of a dollar an hour. Now grab that rope and get neckin'."

Slim necked. He necked for four hours, then tossed off the neck yoke. "I'll take my four hours' pay," he told Big Ed.

"You're like 'em all!" Big Ed roared. "Quittin' before you get started. What did you come up here for if you're afraid o' a little work?"

Slim clamped his jaws and balled his fists, but hunger and fatigue caught up with him. "Tomorrow I'll pull that sled with as big a load as you can buy and just as far as you want, but now I want my pay," he said. "I ain't had anything to eat for two days, and all I worked for now was a feed, so pay me so's I can eat. And I'll be on the job in the morning."

Big Ed threw his head back and laughed, then he counted out bills and handed them to Slim. "Slim," he said, and there was admiration in his voice, "you're all right even if you are a kid. Go get your belly full o' grub, an' my camp is right back there," he pointed, "an' you go there an' get yourself some sleep."

The next morning on his way to work, Slim passed along the line of saloons which operated on a twenty-four-hour basis. The smell, the carnival sounds of laughter, curses, and fights were continuous. In front of one of these a man was kicking a dog. The creature cowered and cringed as the heavy mukluks thudded into his ribs. Slim loved dogs. It took about two strides of his long legs for him to reach the scene. He clamped one of his big hands on the man's shoulder and spun him around.

"What d'you think you're doin'?" the man snarled. He was a small man, hardly reaching Slim's shoulder. His parka hood was thrown back uncovering a head of fiery-red hair.

"I want you to quit kicking that dog," said Slim quietly.

"Listen, kid," the man warned, "it's my dog and I'll kick him if I want to."

"Don't kick that dog again, mister." Slim almost surprised himself at the firmness of his tone.

The redhead stepped back and looked Slim over from his feet up. "Listen, sonny, I'm old enough to be your poppa. I don't like little boys tellin' me what to do, so instead o' takin' you acrost my knees an' whalin' you like I should, I'll just slap you so's you'll know better next time." With which he stung Slim's cheek with a resounding smack of his flat hand.

The crowd which had gathered around laughed and waited to see what Slim would do. The wait was short. Slim folded one hand into a malletlike fist and swung at the little man's jaw, but he missed. For this effort he received another hard slap on his face.

Slim never fully remembered the next few minutes. Before him was a dancing redhead with a leering face. He swung with both fists, but all he met was air. Fists came out of nowhere and from every angle, and every time they hit they hurt. His body hurt, his face hurt, and he tasted blood. The red head popped in and out of Slim's vision and he flailed at it but never once hit it. It was like fighting a lightning-filled cloud. Slim's focal point, the redhead's face, became more and more vague until one final sharp shock on his chin removed it and everything else from his vision.

When Slim regained consciousness he was flat on his back, the redhead was sitting on his chest rubbing snow in his face. He sputtered and tried to get up. The man astride him rose, and helped Slim to his feet.

"Now, sonny," the redhead said without even breathing hard, "suppose you go on home and tell your momma you don't know anything about fighting." With that the man calmly walked away, called to the dog who followed him meekly.

Slim looked around. The men in the circle turned and went about their affairs. Then he took stock of himself. He was a bleeding mess. He had just had the living daylight pasted out of him by a small redheaded phantom who had walked away without a mark on him.

Slim walked down to the shore and did the best he could with the cold water. Later when he showed up for work, Big Ed looked at him but showed no surprise at the puffed purplish eyes and split swollen lips. He even grinned.

Slim spat a bit of blood and grinned back. "Guess I opened my big mouth too wide," he said.

"You're a good lad, Slim. You got guts, and I like you, but maybe you learned a lesson to mind your own business."

Slim nodded. "I wasn't tryin' to pick a fight, Ed, but that fellow was kickin' a dog, an' one thing that boils me red inside is anybody beatin' a animal."

Ed nodded. "I know how you feel, but don't forget, Slim, it's his dog he's kickin'." Then abruptly, "Feel like goin' to work?"

"That's what I come for," said Slim.

All that day Slim's necking was an unpleasant process, but he had learned one of the cardinal rules of that golden country, mind your own business. He decided upon it as one of man's greater virtues.

The next day he went seriously into his job of necking. He was conscientious and a hard worker. He made a temporary deal with the restaurant cook to cut down the price of meals if he would cut down the amount he consumed. He also took advantage of Big Ed's invitation to share his camp until he could set up one of his own. In this way, after a twelve-hour work day, Slim was able to show a profit. Before many days he was able to buy his own little Yukon stove, a stewpot and a frying pan; so, with his own tent and blankets, he set up house-keeping for himself. Next he bought warm socks, a pair of moccasins, a parka, wool shirt, and heavy pants. From the be-ginning he had felt he belonged to the North, but now he began to look the part.

After each day's work he spent as much time as he could stay awake asking Big Ed questions, and listening attentively to the answers.

"Yes, Slim," Ed told him one night after supper, "I been here four to five years now. I seen thousands of cheechakos come in, just like they're doin' now. Every one of 'em as sure as sin they're goin' to strike another Klondike. An' just as many thousands of 'em comin' out. Sourdoughs, who gambled their souls with the devil an' lost, just like you see 'em every day now."

"Where do they go when they cross the glacier, Ed?" Slim asked.

"Who knows?" Ed rolled himself a cigarette and lighted it. "You've been neckin' 'em up to the foot o' the glacier back there, an' they climb it and go through the pass to the other side. Slim, no man alive today knows how much country there is in back of those mountains there. These cheechakos go in and crawl around God-knows-where, they'll never tell, and most of 'em don't even know where they been. One out o' thousands may find gold. The rest of 'em come out like you see 'em, broken, cryin', snivelin' wrecks. Everyone goin' in is sure he's the one that's goin' to make it. An' they don't know where they're goin', how they're goin' to get there, or how they're goin' to stay alive when they do."

Every day Slim was up at daybreak, necking. He pulled sledloads of supplies for the cheechakos the five-mile distance from town to the base of the glacier. There they began the hard climb over the treacherous mountain pass. Slim began to recognize the things Ed had told him. He could see that these men were exaggeratedly noisy—talking, shouting, cursing—a column of hundreds following the trail that thousands had taken before. Their physical equipment was haphazard and shabby. Some had sleds, some had carts, and a few even had wagons made of boxes, bicycle wheels, or any makeshift available. About half the men had animals of one sort or another harnessed to their outfits. There were horses, one man had three goats in harness; and there were dogs of every description —fox terriers to Newfoundlands, full bloods and mongrels. Some men had no outfits at all except the clothing they wore, a little food, a gun, and a knife. But Slim helped them all. With him it was a job.

On the return trip he necked for the sourdoughs going out. Their loads were light, and their outfits scant. These men were silent. They walked with heads down, looking only where their next step took them.

Some few of the sourdoughs actually had gold, precious pokes of dust they had panned. If they planned to go home, it was almost a certainty that they would never reach the ship with more than enough gold to pay their fare. Few of them would resist the smiles of the dance-hall girls, or pass the bars or gamblers unscathed. Some would return up north to refill their empty leather pokes, others would count the cost too high and go home penniless. Slim had never seen men cry. He had always attributed tears to weakness, but he knew these men were not weak. They were men who had come to conquer and were going home in defeat, and their defeat was more than they could stand.

Finally when Slim felt he had sufficient capital, he went to Big Ed with his proposition that he go into business for himself.

"I got thirty dollars," Slim reasoned. "These fellows will sell to me and buy from me, just like you, and there's plenty for both of us."

Big Ed laughed, and slapped Slim on his shoulder. "Been in Alaska, let's see, less'n three weeks, got yourself a bobtail outfit and thirty dollars, and you're on your own. One thing I'll say for you, Slim, for a kid you got guts aplenty. Good luck, Slim, and when you go broke, call on me."

Slim was in business. He had also made his first friend.

Slim was a natural trader. He was busy. He bought, sold, and traded sleds, outfits, tents, dogs, guns. He was working every minute of the day. Supply and demand were continuous. It seemed that just as the line going over the glacier to the north began to dwindle, another ship would arrive in the harbor and discharge its overload into the mud of the bay, and the line took proportions again. The line coming out seemed endless.

At the end of about three weeks Slim took stock. He had never worked so hard in his life, but he had not increased his capital. His ability to trade goods he had proved, but he was a very poor business man. All his trades had turned out to be even swaps, dogs for sleds, stoves for blankets, rifles for tents, but very little gold or cash in the bargains. The result was that his net gain was experience. He gave up this venture, and Ed never raised a question when he came back and went to necking again—this time on his own.

From then on, for the fee of a dollar an hour he necked sleds hour after hour up the steep glacier trail thirty-five miles to its crest, and down again. It was tedious, almost unbelievably hard work, backbreaking, and every step of the way was dangerous, any misstep was death. In this way he planned to buy a better outfit for himself, complete with dogs, and follow the trail beyond the mountains.

Slim loved dogs. He had always loved them, but once he saw a team of Malemutes, he lost his heart completely to these aristocrats of the dog world. His ambition was to own and drive the finest dog team in the North.

After a month of this independent necking Slim had acquired two things: a better outfit and an insatiable curiosity about the country beyond the mountain. His curiosity was complete, but his outfit lacked two essentials, a gun and a team of dogs. These were both expensive, especially dogs that were practical for hours of daily work on frozen trails, but Slim was determined to get his own team. He therefore kept on necking and saved his money.

One time he had a heavy load, over two hundred pounds, and every foot of the way up the glacier trail was a tragedy of effort. As he was nearing the top, he stopped for another rest and saw a group of men huddled together. He sensed trouble. It wasn't at all unusual for an occasional fight to start between partners who a few days before had been avowed friends; and the cause was always the same, one partner claiming he was doing most of the work. Such brawls went unnoticed. But this was no fight. There had been an accident. Slim braced his sled and went to investigate.

Four men stood at the lip of a crevasse looking down. Slim joined them. The crevasse was about four feet wide at the top. For the first few feet the glacier showed the white of the packed surface snow and the frost crust, then deeper inside it became ice, first light blue, then darker and darker, turning to lavender, purple, then black. No one could guess how far down this crack might go, for at that point the depth of the glacier was not known. Slim heard the bottom was at least a half-mile down, lost in the blackness of millions of tons of ice that had existed for ages.

One of the men standing there had let a lighted coal-oil

lantern down into the opening by a rope. The light flickered eerily against the shining faces of ice. Another of the men cupped his hands to his mouth and leaned forward and yelled into the opening, "Can you hear me, Tom?"

From the crevasse came an answer like a voice through a megaphone. "Yes, I can hear you plain. I can see the light of the lantern, too."

Slim understood the situation immediately. "Let me try to get him out," he suggested. "I haven't got this name 'Slim' for nothin'." He was already peeling off his parka and fastening the noose of rope under his arms.

As Slim sat on the lip of the crevasse giving his instructions, one of the men said, "Hope you can make it, Slim. We couldn't get to him, but you're thinner'n any of us. Tom was a little fella, skinnier'n you even, by a lot. He wasn't much bigger'n a kid."

"Well, I'll go as far as I can," said Slim hopefully. "There may be side cracks or something that he could o' slipped into if he was a little fella. Can't tell. You keep the rope tight and let me down slowly. If I find I'm gettin' wedged, I'll tell you and you pull me up. Now, let me down."

He slipped off the edge, and the men paid the rope out gradually. At about twenty feet down he called to them to stop. He was almost six feet deeper than the others had been able to go.

Slim talked with the imprisoned man. He could hear him clearly, and he learned why he could not see him. Just as he had feared, there was a side crack, which he could feel with his feet. Without a doubt the man had fallen directly down, then his body had slipped through this opening. There was no knowing how far or how deep he had fallen, but Slim knew that rescue was hopeless. He called to the men above to pull him up.

The four waiting men spoke almost at one time, "How about it, Slim? Did you get to him? Can we get him out?"

Slim slipped out of the rope noose and into his parka before he answered. Then he looked at the four hopeful faces and slowly shook his head. "There's a side crack down there he somehow slipped into. I talked with him, and his voice was like he was in a big hall. I was almost wedged so tight I couldn't move, and I wasn't even anywhere near him, so I don't see any way to get to him."

"He'll die!" said one of the men. "We can't let him die down there like that."

Again Slim shook his head. "Nothin' anybody can do. It won't be bad. He'll just get cold, and finally he'll go to sleep. I'm awfully sorry, fellows. I wish I could've done more."

Slim went back to his work, completed his haul to the glacier summit, and by dusk was back where the accident had taken place. One man was still there. "The others went on," he told Slim, "but I stayed and talked with him until a couple of hours ago when he said he didn't feel any pain or anything and he was getting sleepy and was going to take a nap. He hasn't said anything since." Nor would he ever speak again. Cold, numbness, sleep, then frozen death: a pattern of northland tragedy.

Slim continued his way until night forced a camp. The moon and the millions of stars transformed the glacier into a glade of shimmering white fire, licking its way between the sheer towering mountains whose peaks pierced the purple-black of the sky. The ice whispered its resistance to the deep cold. This magic of the subarctic night transformed the glacier into a living thing.

With his tent up, and in his sleeping bag, Slim closed his eyes and his thoughts went to the man on the trail and his lonely vigil.

·2·

In the hush of my mountained vastness . . . .
Natheless I suffer them thrive,
Crushing my Weak in their clutches,
that only my Strong may survive.

The next morning Slim was about five miles from the foot of
the glacier when he took special notice of a small tent pitched
far to one side of the trail. It had been there a few days before.
Three dogs were tied in front of it, but they were the only
signs of life. Slim veered off his trail for a closer look. The
dogs were friendly little fellows, two small collies and a bull
dog, and they wiggled and jumped as Slim talked with them.
Then he straightened up and called, "Hello! Anybody in
there?"

From the tent a thin shrill voice answered, "Come in!"

Inside, Slim found a little wizened man all rolled up in a
bearskin robe. His face was chalky white, his hair was white,
and so were his mustache and goatee. When he saw Slim, he
smiled, and squeaked, "Glad you come. Glad somebody come.
I been sick two, three days. I ain't been able to get up. It's
this gol-hanged cold! A fellow can't get warm." The little
man shivered until his teeth chattered.

Slim went to work. A warm fire in the stove, hot tea, and
a warmed-up bowl of mulligan did wonders. Slim next looked
after the dogs and gave them a good feed. Then he sat down
with the old man who told him he had done well in business

in the States, and could have retired, but that he longed for adventure. As he read newspaper reports of the gold strikes in Alaska he yearned for one bit of excitement in his life. He had gotten this far and decided that time was against him. It was a young man's country, and all he wanted now was to go home.

"If I can get well enough to get my strength back, that's what I want," he concluded his story, "just to get home."

"I can get you down to Valdez where the boat is," Slim offered, and went to work clearing the man's sled, and packing the equipment and outfit. Then he harnessed the dogs. He picked the man up like a baby and wrapped him in his bearskin robe and tied him to the sled. He even propped him up, with snowshoes for a back rest, so he might at least enjoy a short part of his Alaskan adventure.

Slim felt proud driving the dog team into Valdez. He waved jauntily to Big Ed as he passed. This was his first time driving dogs. It wasn't the greatest team in the North, but at least they were dogs, eager and willing.

By good fortune a ship was in the harbor. Slim found a man with a skiff and arranged for his charge to be put aboard. When time came to say good-by, the little man held out a scrawny hand no bigger than a child's and shook hands with Slim.

"All I wanted to do was get aboard a boat going home," he said. "I got the money, and more when I get there. I'm giving you my outfit. You been good to me, Slim. You keep it for your kindness and care. Good luck, boy."

When the skiff was a few yards off shore, Slim suddenly realized what had happened. "Thank you, mister," he shouted. The little man waved. "Hey," Slim yelled again, "what's the names o' the dogs?"

A tiny squeaky voice came back across the water, "Brownie, Blue, and Fat. Good-by, Slim." After that the little man just seemed to disappear inside his bearskin robe.

There Slim stood, possessor of two trail outfits. He had two sleds, two tents, enough food to last him about nine months, a gun, a team of three dogs, and all Alaska before him.

For the first time Slim felt really secure. About all he could remember of his boyhood was work and hunger. At ten he was punching cattle on his father's ranch in Southern California. By fourteen he had trailed to Texas and back, lived with Indians and learned from them how to get by when there was almost no food available. At fifteen he was slugging it out with a double-bitted axe in Oregon lumber camps. He had sledged and mucked in mines. Privation and hunger and hard work were no strangers to him. The memory of his mother was of tenderness, and the only love he had ever known. From her he had received a heritage of patience and honesty, an understanding that right was right in which there was no room for wrong. About his only gift from his father was a restless spirit, the urge to see what no one else had seen. Slim himself supplied an ingenuous faith that he would somehow be cared for. The melding of these promised an unusual future for this unpredictable boy. His one thought now was to cross the mountains and explore the great country to the north.

Slim turned to his new dogs.

"How about it, boys, shall we go and see something of Alaska? But first we better get acquainted," he said. "One of you is Blue, one Brownie, and one Fat. Now which one o' you little fellows is which?"

There was no doubt. As Slim spoke each name, a dog answered by lifted head and ears, by a look of its eyes, a flap of the tail. With the unerring understanding of dogs, these three recognized friendship and immediately offered their complete loyalty.

First they had to transport the two outfits over the glacier. Slim found out he had good dogs on his first trip up the trail. They worked fine, and made up in effort what they lacked in size. He lifted, pushed, and boosted the heavy sled to help them over the rougher, harder spots of the trail. When they reached the top, he cached this first load, and after a rest started back to Valdez for the remainder of the supplies.

On the return trip with the empty sled, Slim was in a hurry. The trail somehow seemed extra long, and he was anxious to get through the mountain pass to the other side as soon as he could. At one place the trail made a long loop and doubled back on itself, dropping about a hundred yards in so doing. The loop was a mile out and back. Slim had often wondered why he couldn't make the short cut across this narrow spot. It was too steep to climb, but he might be able to make it going down. Up to that time he had never been in such a hurry, but now he wanted to make time. He yelled "haw" to his dogs, and they obediently swerved off the trail and plunged down the glassy slope, the sled and Slim after them. Prospectors along the trail stopped and stared.

The dogs' feet barely touched the ice, the sled slithered and skidded, and Slim hung onto the handle bars with all his strength. It was too late when he saw the danger, and he was helpless to avoid it. He had almost reached the bottom and safety when he saw directly ahead a slitlike break in the ice. A crevasse! With a split second to think and act, Slim tipped his sled over. At the same instant he lost his hold, slipped and fell directly into the opening of the crevasse. He felt a crushing blow on his side, then blackness.

Slim came to slowly, to the accompaniment of a steady stream of the most vivid cussing he had ever listened to. He heard himself being damned as the most unspeakable fool from Valdez to Barrow, and Dawson to Nome, with the United States thrown in for good measure. When his eyes began to focus, he looked up into the bushy face of Big Ed who cussed him all the more when he found out he was conscious and could hear him. This made Slim mad, so mad he couldn't move and couldn't talk, which was about as mad as he ever got. The next thing he knew, Big Ed reached down and grabbed him under the arms and pulled him out, talking all the while. When Slim was once more on his feet, he said, "Now what in the name of Borealis were you tryin' to do, you crazy lunkhead?"

Slim had missed death by a fraction. He looked down at the crack in the glacier, then back to Big Ed.

"You see that side opening down there?" Big Ed pointed to a widened portion in the crevasse. "If you'd slipped in there you'd been a goner. That's why I had to keep cussin' at you so's you'd wake up mad. When most people first get mad they don't move. Like you didn't. If you'd started to wiggle before I grabbed you, you might be out o' sight by now. You smashed your sled, but we got your dogs and they're all right. You want to do any more slidin' down ice banks you better pick a safer place, 'cause maybe I won't be around to pull you out. Slim, you're the luckiest, lankiest, durnfool I ever saw. Now you go down to my camp and rest up before you try the glacier again." Which Slim did. He was badly bruised but not seriously injured.

While his side was mending, Slim had some good visits with Ed. Mainly, Ed talked to Slim. "You goin' over again, Slim?" he asked.

Slim nodded.

"Sure you know what you're up against?"

"As much as the others that go over," said Slim.

"Just remember one thing, Slim. Like this time I pulled you out of the ice crack, you were takin' a chance. Now, don't do that when you get out there on your own. Don't take chances. You're eager to go, and I don't blame you for that, but nobody knows what you're goin' to run into, so nobody can tell you anything about what to do. Only you lived with Indians, so do like the Indians do. They never take a chance."

Slim grinned and nodded. "I'll remember, Ed," he said.

Ten days later his side had mended. Then with the rest of his outfit and his other sled, he climbed the glacier again. This time, however, he stuck strictly to the well-traveled trail.

Slim had never actually crossed the mountains. During the months he had worked, his hauling chores had stopped at the top of the glacier. From there on the prospectors had taken their own loads. It was only up the hard, steep icy climb to the 7,000-foot crest that they needed Slim's help. From there the trail passed through a narrow boxlike canyon whose sheer walls seemed to meet high above. Only a slit of sky showed through. At the far end Slim stopped and had his first look at the Alaska beyond the coastal Chugach Mountains. At the bottom of an almost sheer 1,000-foot bluff, a valley sloped away to the north. There, about a hundred miles away, along the horizon, was the jagged snow-topped ridge of the Alaska Range dominated by Alaska's regal Mt. McKinley, America's highest peak.

Slim was almost mesmerized by the sight he saw. The valley as far as he could see was white, splashed and liberally spotted with the heavy deep green of spruce, threadlike courses of streams, and open surfaces of frozen lakes. Although it was May, the North had not yet broken up. But when he looked to the east, beyond a large river, the sight made him actually hold his breath. He knew he had never seen beauty until then. These were more mountains, they were the Wrangells; but each peak stood independently, as though striving for single mastery over the others—Mt. Drum, Mt. Wrangell, Mt. Sanford, 12,000, 14,000, 16,000 feet of rugged perfection. A column of smoke rose lazily from the top of Mt. Wrangell. This first sight of an active volcano fascinated Slim. Around him, at his feet, was a country where a man could travel forever and never see it all; could live a lifetime and never know all its secrets. Let others hunt their gold, thought Slim. Theirs were paltry riches compared with what he had. He would make these very mountains his own. His riches would be the adventures this country held. It was his. All his for the taking.

Almost directly below him lay Klutina Lake which he guessed to be perhaps fifteen miles long and about five wide. Tiny wisps of camp smoke lifted from a point where the Klutina River left the lake to flow eastward to join a larger river flowing south. This, Slim learned later, was the Copper River. This prospector camp was his first objective.

It was a tough descent. The trail seemed almost straight

down and it was narrow. Slim studied it, realized it would take more than one trip to move all his outfit, and said to his dogs, "Those fellows at that camp made it down all right, but they only had one trip to make, and we got three. But we'll do it." The dogs wagged their tails in agreement.

The trail was a hard one, and it took over an hour for Slim to make the trip down. After he reached the bottom there was another fifteen-mile haul before he arrived at the prospectors' camp. This trail led along the shore and was heavy with brush and windfalls. The sun had already thawed the brush snow, so much of the trail was over bare ground, making the pull doubly heavy for the dogs. Only a day or so earlier he could have used the trail the prospectors had made on the lake ice. But the May sun had begun to turn the lake ice to slush, and it was no longer safe for sled work. It was dusk when he finally reached the camp. He set up a tent, and after a night's rest returned for the remainder of his outfit.

The trail back to the base of the cliff took him almost half the day, even with the empty sled, and by the time he had made the climb and brought down the balance of his outfit, it was dusk.

It would have been foolish to attempt the brush trail at night, so he camped where he was. The night was clear and cold. The temperature took a quick drop at sundown, and was close to zero within a space of two hours. Slim cooked his supper and crawled into his bedroll. When he awoke it seemed like daylight. He got up. The dogs were still asleep and took no notice of him as he went to the shore to get water to boil his coffee. The lake was frozen. He looked at the sky. Bright stars and the moon full overhead made the night as day. Then Slim looked at his watch. It was two o'clock. What had wakened him he didn't know, but there he was up and fed, and it was the middle of night. The quick dip of the temperature had crusted the slush on the lake. He tested it, walking up and down and stamping. It held his weight. It was good ice. He was sure it was safe to travel, and the fifteen-mile haul to the camp would be easier on the ice than over the shore trail. He ate a good breakfast and broke camp. He packed, loaded his sled. It was big, and the load was heavy, close to a thousand pounds. Finally he wakened the dogs. They weren't too anxious to have their sleep disturbed, but once they were in harness and found their footing secure on the lake, they went to work and were away.

Slim watched the miracle of dawn as the sun tinted the gray in the east first a delicate pink, then the shades of salmon through to flame red, finally rising over the Wrangell peaks in blazing gold. Slim stopped the dogs so he could appreciate the fullness of what he saw. Inwardly he glowed with the thrill of his new-found freedom.

As the sun got higher the crust of the lake began to chip and crush under the weight of the load, then noticeably soften into slush. The air was still cold, yet the sun's rays carried thawing heat. Then Slim saw the prospectors' camp, and this sight quelled the momentary uneasiness he had felt. Even though the sled runners threw out twin sprays of water, the ice underneath felt firm to his feet. Besides, it had been worth a chance to save himself a whole day of drudging trail work. He waved to a few prospectors who were watching him from the campsite on the shore.

During the drive Slim had kept about 150 feet from shore, thinking that that far out the ice would surely be secure, and also that he would be close enough to land in case of emergency. He had guessed wrong on both counts, for just as he turned his team toward the camp, he saw clear water between him and shore. The dogs were in full run and there was no chance to stop them. About thirty feet from shore there was a crash. The heavy sled broke through as the ice gave way, dragging the dogs in after it. Slim followed, and came to the surface choking and almost paralyzed from the cold of the water. He floundered and beat frantically with his arms. Every bit of ice he touched crushed or crumbled under his weight. Suddenly, a rope splashed alongside him. He made a quick lunge for it, luckily caught it, and hung on.

When the men pulled him ashore, they carried him to a fire to dry out. They brought him fresh clothing from the tent where he had cached part of his outfit. They gave him hot coffee, bannock, and a slab of meat. The men—there were six of them—were not effusive or even talkative, but they were generous with whatever they had that Slim might need. At first he searched their faces to see if there was any suggestion of ridicule because of his accident, for it seemed now, in the face of events, that he had done a foolhardy thing. But all he saw was friendly understanding.

These men were old-timers in the North, who, after their first year, had dropped the freshman title of "cheechako" for the rugged name of "sourdough." Slim had known of sour dough. In fact, years before his mother had given him his first bit of this yeasty leaven culture to carry for his bread-making. Since it required about a year to develop this yeast substitute to its practical stage, the name "sourdough" became a synonym for those who had lived through their first year in Alaska and remained.

When the men were satisfied that Slim was well cared for, they took their shovels, picks, and pans and went about their own business of hunting for gold. One older man stopped and laid a hand on Slim's shoulder. "That was a tough one, kid," he said, "but we all had 'em one way or another. Don't let it get you. My tent's that last one over there. Help yourself."

Then Slim was alone, sitting before the fire on a length of log, staring at the lake, but even if there had been anyone to see, it wouldn't have mattered. He could no more have controlled the tears that wetted his cheeks than he could have brought back the dogs he had learned to love. He blamed himself for their drowning. He thought of the trust they had placed in him, and fool that he was, how he had led them into danger because of his inexperience. His dogs were gone. Most of his outfit was gone. All he had left was what he had brought down on his first trip—a tent, his gun, and a scant month's supply of food. He had made a most expensive mistake.

A sharp breeze had come up from the west. Slim built up the fire and sat again, trying to make some sort of structure out of the remnants of his plans. All at once he was aware of movement on the lake. The whole surface of ice was turning. The combination of sun and wind had broken the ice mass into smaller segments, and these were slowly being ground to pieces. From a half-mile to the west, where the lake emptied into the Klutina River, came a sound like rumbling thunder, caused by huge masses of ice being flung by tons of force into the funnel of the river's channel. The rotten, honeycombed ice, such as had given way under Slim and his team, actually disintegrated as he watched. The rocks along the shore, where floes were forced in by the wind, soon bore the only evidence that the lake had been frozen over. The lake itself, freed of its icy restraint, came alive; the blue of the water, the white froth of waves, the sound of splashing against the shore, were vivid signs that breakup had arrived. Sleds and dogs would be of no more use until freeze-up again in the fall. From now on transportation would be by water. And Slim had no boat.

This was the challenge Slim needed to pull him out of his well of self-pity. He would build a boat, Indian fashion, as he had learned years ago in the States. He collected saplings of shore willows for the framework, weaving lengths of this pliant wood to form the hull. He secured the joints with strips of spruce root be boiled and split. When the frame was finished it was canoe-shaped, sturdy and firm, about twelve feet long and four feet at the beam. Where the Indians used skins as cover, Slim used the canvas of his tent. He stretched the canvas and secured this to the framework by over-and-under wedging it onto the gunwale. It gave a tight service-able covering. Among the supplies the old man had given him were cans of lard for dog food. This now served the practical purpose of waterproofing the improvised craft. Finally, a pair of oars was no problem for a boy who had served his apprenticeship in a lumber camp.

After building his boat, he went back up the trail toward the glacier. All along, the way was strewn with sleds and equipment that men had discarded either going in or coming out. There were many impractical, fantastic contraptions they had brought with them. Slim examined these castoffs until he found what he was looking for, strips of iron. He took these back to camp and fashioned a grappling hook. For the next four days he dragged the bottom where he judged his dogs and sled had gone down. At the shore the water dropped off to about a twenty-foot depth, and out where he had gone through it was at least forty feet down. He hoped he might hook onto the sled and salvage some of his outfit, but luck was against him.

Notwithstanding his lack of supplies, he never once thought of going back. Now that he had taken his first step toward exploring the Alaska beyond the mountains, he would go on, not back. He knew there were outfitting posts beyond, where he could get supplies, but he would need money or gold, and he had spent all his cash for his final purchases before leaving Valdez. So, at the moment he had nothing to trade, and certainly no gold.

It was his appetite that again came to his help. He wanted a good meal of meat. Therefore he decided to go hunting. He knew he could get game, and since he was the only one who had a boat, he might find a stream on the far shore which no one else had seen, whose bottom possibly might be gold instead of sand. He took a shovel and a pan, just in case, and his rifle; certainly all of his luck couldn't be bad.

With thaws becoming the daily rule, the prospectors spent more and more time scrabbling along creek beds, panning sand for the show of "color," the heavy dust of gold. They returned to their tents to sleep, the rest of the time they spent abroad in their search. They paid no more attention to Slim than they did to each other. There was no visiting, no conversation. They all had the same purpose in mind, and secrecy was part of their plan.

Slim figured if he just happened to find gold his worries would be ended; if not, he would have game and could sell the meat to the men at camp who were too busy to hunt their own food. In his little boat he followed the shore about fifteen miles around the east end and along the north shore. He was surprised that there was no snow. Even in the few days of thawing the ground snow had melted. On the other side of the mountains, on the Valdez side, there had been twenty feet of snow when he left. It was a trick of the air currents that gave heavy snowfalls on the south slopes of the coast range, and very little precipitation to the north. Slim saw robins, big, fat, and perky, and clusters of crocuses already in bloom with blossoms at least two inches in diameter. Spring indeed had arrived.

Slim explored the shore, and several small creeks that fed into the lake. He panned a few samples of sand, but there were no nuggets that he could see. He did, however, get food. He shot three goats, and this fresh meat was as good as gold. When he returned to camp he traded it at fifty cents a pound for the grub staples he needed to replenish his outfit—flour, cornmeal, salt, lard, baking powder, sugar, matches, tea, coffee, and the like. He also traded for traps, rope, anything that he could transport and that he might need.

When this meat was gone, he got in his little boat and went to his hunting grounds again. This time a young moose brought him more for his outfit. On another trip he bagged two more goats. He decided he had all the outfit and supplies he needed, so he told his friends he planned to set out down the river to work his way farther toward the interior, with his goal Copper Center, about forty-five miles away.

The prospectors, too, had planned to move. These men, well equipped with tools and supplies, made their boats of wood. Slim helped them down trees, whipsaw the logs into planks, and fashion sturdy flat-bottomed boats.

Slim was a day ahead in leaving. His boat, heavily weighted with almost five hundred pounds of supplies, was not too easy to handle. The Klutina River was high, the current a millrace. Every foot of the way was treacherous with submerged rocks. It was a continuous fight to stay upright and off the rocks. There was no chance to make shore for a rest, therefore he plied his oars until he thought he couldn't hold out another moment. But somehow he kept the bobbing craft afloat. He was near exhaustion when the stream broadened and the current slowed to join the Copper River. He gratefully pulled ashore and made camp for the night.

The morning broke into another beautiful day. The river too was as gentle as the warmth of the sun. Slim guessed that he had about ten miles yet to go to reach Copper Center. The Copper River was thaw-swollen to about a quarter of a mile in width. It slithered oily along the high clay banks. It was fast but it did not present the dangers of the Klutina's rapids. Slim's little boat rode it smoothly. His business at the oars now was more to keep his boat headed with the current and to prevent its turning broadside. He kept close inshore. A more seasoned river man would have kept to the middle to be free from the swirling shore eddies and such danger as Slim suddenly saw immediately ahead of him.

A big spruce had lost its shore rooting and spread its length almost half the width of the river, not over fifty feet directly ahead. Slim pulled with all his strength, but he only succeeded in turning his boat crossways of the current. He leaned his back into every stroke and was still fighting when he hit. As his boat went over, he grabbed one of the tree's outstretched branches and, hand over hand, pulled himself to shore.

By the time he waded up on the bank, the current had freed his boat from the sweeper. There he stood and watched his boat bobbing downstream, keel up. Somewhere along the bottom of the Copper River was strewn everything in the world that Slim owned. There he stood, wet and bedraggled, without a thing on earth except the clothes he wore.

·3·

There's a whisper on the night-wind,
there's a star agleam to guide us,
And the Wild is calling, calling . . . .
let us go.

Slim took stock. At the moment he was a pretty sick-feeling boy. What he had experienced since he had arrived in Alaska was not too firm a basis on which to build self-assurance and confidence. But he was young, and resilient, and although his immediate prospects did not appear too brilliant, he knew it was all his own fault. Mistakes to Slim were things that happened because you let them happen. He never threw the blame on the other fellow, the country, or the weather. He absorbed each mistake onto the profit side of his experience, determined he would never make the same one twice.

Slim sloshed up and down the clay along the river picking up bits of dry wood. He collected enough to make a good fire. He was grateful at least that an old Texas cowpoke had showed him the trick of keeping his matches dry by carrying them in a capped shotgun shell. As he dried out, he emptied his pockets to see what his assets really were: a bandanna, this he hung over a bush to dry; two rifle shells, these were no longer of any use so he tossed them into the river; his supply of matches, which he set on the ground; and finally a wad of sticky green paper which he started to toss into the fire, then stopped. He wondered as he flattened it out what it was. He grinned. He had forgotten that one of the prospectors had taken ten pounds of moose meat and had paid for it with a five-dollar bill. He wasn't bad off at all, he thought. He had money. All he needed was some place to spend it. Finally he felt his hip, and his sheath knife was still secured to his belt.

When he was dried out and comfortably warm, he climbed the river bank, which rose steeply some hundred feet to level ground, to see what the country was like around him. There was very little timber on the floor of the valley and he had a good view. In the distance, in every direction, was the encircling ring of mountains. There the green of the timber showed clearly up to the line where it gave way to the rocks and snow of the heights. Downstream about two miles he saw a cabin and several tents. That, he assumed, was the settlement of Copper Center. He didn't know, but he felt sure he would find supplies there. The only trouble was, it was on the opposite bank of the river and Slim had never learned to swim. Nevertheless, he started off, and when he got opposite the cabin, he yelled, whistled, and waved his arms until he attracted attention. A prospector rowed a flat-bottomed scull across and picked him up.

When they reached the other shore, the man, who said his name was Waycross, said, "You look tired, muddy, and hungry, son. Come on in the shack, and such as I got I'll feed you."

Over a piled-up platter of sourdough batter cakes and sirup, Slim told his story.

"And I got nobody to blame but me," he concluded.

Waycross nodded. "But you ain't the only one, son," he said. "I put my shack up here two years ago and I bet I seen a hundred dumped out there in the Copper. Like you, most of 'em stayed close to shore. In high water, always stay in midstream, shores is dangerous. Eddies an' sweepers'll get you ever' time. Main thing is ever'time anything like this happens to you, learn what you done wrong, so's it won't never happen again. It's the only way you'll learn to stay alive in this country. Ever'body makes mistakes. The ones who learn by 'em is still alive. Them that don't, ain't.

"Now that Copper River, she's a mean one. Sometimes she's just like a kitten, but most times she's a hellcat. I'd like to have the outfits that's been scattered along her bottom. Want some more wheat cakes?"

When Slim's empty plate was again steaming and dripping, the man asked, "And what are you goin' to do now?"

"Go to work, I guess," said Slim between mouthfuls. He wiped a dribble of sirup from his chin.

"Where?"

"Right here's as good a place as any."

The man shook his head. "No, it ain't."

Slim looked up sharply. "Why not?"

"Because there ain't no work here," Waycross said quietly. "It's spring, and ever'body in Copper Center will be in the creeks. Look out there on the river."

Slim could see men in flat-bottomed boats poling their way upstream. Then he recognized the three new boats in the middle of the river, floating downstream with the current. He was glad his friends had safely run the rapids.

"Most o' the population o' Copper Center will be in boats like that before long goin' some place else," Waycross said. "No work here because there's nobody to work for. Best thing for you to do is go back over the glacier the way you come. I'd grubstake you if I could, but you're eatin' just about the last flour I got. My partner's outside now for more grub, an' soon's he gets back we'll be leavin' for the creeks. I can give you a fishhook and a piece o' line an' some matches, a little salt, an' that's about all I got to spare. An' I can fix you up with a can an' a pan to cook in, then you better take my advice and get out of here, Slim."

"Not until I get to see all I want of those mountains over there," Slim pointed toward the east. "I sort o' got my heart set on that."

"The Wrangells?"

"Is that their name? Then I'm not going to leave this country until I travel in those mountains. I never see anything in my life I wanted to do so much."

"It's your life, son," the man shrugged. "You can kill yourself any way you want to. For a kid like you, goin' it alone in Alaska, I won't give you a year before you do something you don't know anything about and get yourself killed. But if you're so hell-bent to tackle them Wrangells, you better go back outside and get yourself a good grubstake before you do."

That night Slim caught a mess of grayling and had a good feed of fish by the river bank. Waycross offered him his partner's bunk in the shack. The next morning he talked with another of the Copper Center prospectors and received the same advice and lack of enthusiasm for his plan to explore the Wrangell Mountains, or even to stay in Alaska. By afternoon most of the tents were down and there were no more than half a dozen men left at the settlement. The rest were searching the sands of the side creeks for gold, or going deeper inland toward the rumored strikes at Fairbanks, about 275 miles to the north.

Slim walked to the river bank and contemplated his prospects. He was more than a hundred miles by trail from Valdez, and all he had in the way of supplies and equipment for the return trip was a fishhook and line, his knife, a pan, a pail, some matches, the few supplies Waycross had given him, and a five-dollar bill he couldn't spend. His prospects were not good. The Copper River was once more free of traffic except for one lone Indian. Slim watched him paddle his canoe to shore, just about where he was standing. The two regarded each other a moment. The Indian bobbed his head in greeting. Slim did the same. The Indian got out of his canoe and came toward him, and handed him what appeared to be a roll of white fur. "You buy," he said, and it was no question.

Slim undid the roll. He had seen rabbitskin sleeping robes

before and had wanted one. In making them, the squaws sewed tanned hides of rabbits into long strips, one skin in width. They wove these strips, matlike, to form a solid blanket of fur. This one Slim held was approximately seven by eight feet in size. It was an exceptionally fine one, and he wanted it badly. In fact, it was something he critically needed on his long walk back to Valdez.

"You buy," the Indian repeated.

Slim knew States Indians. He had been raised with them in California, had lived and traveled with them in New Mexico and Arizona, and had learned much of their ways and habits. Somehow he felt sure that all Indians thought alike. They would trade as long as there was anything to trade with and for. But Slim had nothing to trade. He shook his head sadly and handed the robe to the Indian.

The Indian shoved it back and repeated, "You buy."

Suddenly it dawned upon Slim that the Indian had said, "buy." This Indian, therefore, had been exposed to white men and currency and knew what money was for. Slim reached in his pocket and brought out his five-dollar bill, flattened it out, and held it up in front of the Indian. The Indian stared at it, looked into Slim's eyes, then, pressing the robe into Slim's hands, snatched the bill. In another minute he was into his canoe and paddling off. Slim had his robe, light in weight and equal to two blankets in warmth. He laughed a little when he thought that the five-dollar bill had sort of taken care of itself.

The next morning early he took to the trail. Waycross rowed him back across the river, and as they shook hands the old man said, "Wish I could help you more, Slim, but somehow I think you'll make it."

"I will," Slim said confidently, "and I'll be back to see you when I get myself another outfit. I still got to find out what's in them Wrangell Mountains."

Waycross studied him quizzically for a moment. "Damned if I don't think you will at that," he said. "You're a crazy kid,

but for a kid you sure got guts. So long, Slim, and good luck."
With that he shoved his boat off the shore and began to row.

Slim faced north and began to walk. It was about noon when he reached the junction with the Klutina which he would follow westward. He stopped, caught some fish, and ate. Almost at his feet he saw a canvas sack in the water, caught among some shore rocks. It was a part of some other unfortunate's loss. He investigated and found the sack still contained about three or four pounds of beans, now thoroughly soaked and swollen triple in size, but, nevertheless, beans. Slim scooped up a handful and added to his menu of fish, then rescued the remainder.

There was no trail to follow, but he had no fear of getting lost. He stayed with the Klutina River until he reached the lake, then along the lake shore. The familiar prospectors' campsite was now deserted. He scrounged the site thoroughly. When he turned up nothing that would be of any use to him, he went on for the final fifteen miles of the familiar trail along the shore. That night he camped at the foot of the sheer cliff up which he must go before he reached the glacier and then Valdez. For supper he had another fish stew, but saved just enough of his carefully rationed beans for breakfast. His feet hurt from the miles of rough walking; his hands were sore and cut from clearing his way through brush; and he was hungry for something besides fish and beans. But he was near the end of the trail. That night when he rolled up beside his campfire in his rabbit robe, he felt that the country hadn't been too rough on him. He'd learned some hard lessons, and had come through all right, and in one more day, or two, he'd be back where he could make ready for a fresh start.

The next morning Slim climbed the cliff, went through the boxlike canyon, and on familiar terrain started down the glacier. About a mile ahead of him was a string of some twenty men who had apparently camped the night on the glacier. They too were headed down, single file, going slowly. Before too long Slim caught up with them and passed them. As he went by the leader a familiar voice yelled at him. "Hey, you stringy idiot, where do you think you're goin'?"

Slim turned and looked at the bushy-bearded face of his friend, Big Ed.

"Thought you'd be at the North Pole by now the way you went streakin' out o' here, and what are you doin' back?" Big Ed had stopped the men who were following him and walked over to meet Slim. "All right, Slim," he said when he had heard all the details, "I'll help you out. The thaws and winds have been checkerin' up the glacier, and she's been crackin' and cavin' in here and there, so's the winter trail's no good, and she's real downright dangerous. I come up and guide a bunch like this down at a dollar a head. I'll split this bunch up and give you a few so you won't hit Valdez broke."

Slim followed Ed part way back along the line of discouraged sourdoughs. Ed stopped and pointed, "You take these last five, Slim, and keep 'em together and I'll learn you the safe way down."

Most of the men were sitting down, resting, but one in Slim's group was lying prone, his arms outstretched. Slim hurried to him and knelt down. The man was a big fellow, Slim judged he must weigh about 290 pounds. He seemed young and husky enough, but he lay there face down on the ice, crying.

"What's the matter, fellow, something wrong?" Slim asked with honest sympathy.

The man raised his head. "I'm sick," he said, "I'm just done in, that's all. I can't go on, I can't do any more, and that's all there is to it." His face showed pain, and was wet with tears.

Slim called Ed. "This man's sick, Ed," he said. "He just can't go on."

"Well," said Ed slowly, looking down at the prostrate figure, "that's too bad. I hoped we'd get all these fellows down safe, but I guess we won't. I wouldn't leave a dog here to die on this glacier, that would be one awful death. So, I guess there's just nothing else to do but to put him out of his misery quick and sudden. I've had it happen before, Slim, and I just hate to shoot 'em, but it's about the only thing to do." While he was talking, he had pulled his big revolver from its holster and weighed it in his palm.

Slim felt a cold shiver up his back. "Don't do that, Ed!" he pleaded, "I'll pack him down."

"No," Ed said quietly, "he's too much of a load, Slim, and the travel's too slippery and dangerous. This is about the only way." He lifted the revolver.

"But you can't just kill a man like that, Ed. You can't do it! I won't let you shoot him!" Slim reached for the hand that held the gun.

Ed shoved Slim away. "Get back, Slim, I've got to shoot him, it's the only way."

By this time the man was on his feet. He stood straight and grabbed Ed's arms. "I'm all right," he said. "Don't shoot, don't kill me, I'll be all right." And he was. He was suddenly healed, and from then on there was no more trouble.

During one of the rest stops Slim hunkered down alongside Ed. They were quiet for a moment, then Slim said, "You weren't goin' to shoot that fellow back there."

Ed looked at the lanky youngster. "Figured it out, did you?"

Slim nodded. "But he sure fooled me, Ed. I thought for certain he was sick, and all the time he was just a quitter."

Ed sighed and shook his head. "Funny, ain't it, Slim?"

"I guess I never expected to see 'em up here in Alaska. But I seen 'em in lumber camps back in the States. Big, husky fellows you'd think could stand an awful lot, and they'd go all to pieces."

"You'll find 'em up here too, Slim, and the only way to cure 'em I know of is to scare 'em, and the one thing they're scared of is dyin'."

Slim nodded. "I figured that, but you scared me too till I figured out just what it was you was doin'."

Ed chuckled. "You're all right, Slim. For a kid you got things pretty well in hand,"

"But it sure don't seem like it, Ed. I went over the glacier and a hundred miles in and come a hundred miles back, and all I got to show for it is I drowned my outfit and dogs. I got exactly what I landed in Alaska with more'n eight months ago when I crawled up on the beach there at Valdez—nothin'. Except now I got me this rabbit robe."

Ed nodded. Slim said quietly, "I told you what happened. Makes me out kind of foolish, don't it?"

The big fellow looked at his young friend, shook his head slowly. "Slim," he said, kindly, "remember before you went in I asked you if you thought you was ready to tackle the North, and you said you was? You was ready because you're young and maybe a little anxious, but I know you're no fool. Nobody could tell you what you'd find or what to do. You just count yourself lucky you're still alive. No, Slim, you weren't foolish, you were gettin' experience—sometime they may look the same, but there's a lot o' difference between 'em."

Slim thought a moment before he answered. "After I got dumped there in the Copper, Ed, I made up my mind if makin' mistakes was the way to learn, I'd learn my lessons good so I wouldn't make the same one again. I sure learned a lot."

Again Big Ed nodded. "Ever think o' goin' back to the States, Slim? You could work with me till you got passage money. You don't care nothin' about gold, and that's all this country's got to hold a man. Ever think maybe you don't belong here, kid, and you ought to go back?" Ed was giving the same advice Slim had heard from everyone else.

Slim looked sharply at Ed. "I'm no quitter, Ed. I came to Alaska, and I'm goin' to stay." Slim was more positive than he had ever been. "There's a lot of this country and I'm going to stay anyway until I see it. I already seen some mountains, the Wrangells, and I won't be satisfied until I know them like I know this glacier trail. Then there's mountains to the north and I want to see what's behind them. And I'm going to get dogs, Ed, and I'm going to have the best team of dogs in Alaska. I learned a lot, but you can't learn it all at once, and I'll work here this summer and by next winter I'll be ready to take the trail. You watch and see if I don't, Ed."

"Maybe you will, Slim." Big Ed studied the boy's face carefully. "I guess maybe you will. Maybe I'm wrong that you don't belong here. Maybe you're just the kind o' man the country needs, and maybe when you grow up you'll be the kind of a man Alaska can be proud of, the country could use a few. You can work the glacier with me as long as you like, Slim."

Slim nodded his thanks. He was beginning to feel the establishment of a plan in his thinking.

Ed and Slim delivered their charges safely to the bottom of the glacier and collected their fees. Slim's first stop was the food shack. The sign announcing the price of meals was still in the window, but this time Slim did not hesitate. He had $5.00 and he ate his money's worth.

Later he sought out Ed, who again had offered to share his tent and outfit until Slim could re-establish himself.

Slim worked hard that summer. Valdez was growing out of its slush-and-mud existence as a tent camp to a street-and-building town. Board sidewalks were laid, a sawmill was cutting lumber, and stores and houses were being built. Even a wharf was under construction. Slim, with his ability as a lumberjack, found his services in demand. He could work as many hours a day as he wanted at the usual rate of a dollar an hour.

But most important, this time Slim sought out and listened to advice. He talked with successful sourdoughs who were in for supplies and who would be going back to their gold diggings. He talked with men who knew dogs. He talked with trappers and learned what he could of the methods of trapping used in Alaska, and how they differed from those he had learned in the States. No one he talked with seemed to know too much about the country itself; directions and distances were vague and uncertain. But Slim asked questions and listened earnestly to the answers.

Families from the States began to arrive in Valdez. There was a lawyer and his wife and two children. The man who opened the clothing store had a family. A doctor opened an office. Slim knew all these people by sight, but the ones with whom he spent his spare time were the ones who knew the land beyond the mountains.

That summer Slim received a jolt from which he never fully recovered. In fact, he never really knew what hit him. Among the newcomers was a girl. She lived with her parents, and her father owned the sawmill. The girl appeared to be about Slim's age, perhaps a year or so younger. Slim saw her often that summer. She was small, and dainty, and beautifully blonde. He knew he had never seen anything so lovely. He wanted to meet her, and to talk with her, but he never dared to speak. Someone told him that her name was Linda and that she planned to teach school. This put another obstacle in his way. What would they have in common? Slim had never been to school.

Slim's social life had not been expansive. He enjoyed dancing. He danced with the girls in the dance halls, and paid for the privilege. They were young and beautiful too, and he could talk with them, for they knew the language of the lumberjack and the men of the creeks. But an occasional dance was the limit of his interest. Also, not drinking himself, he bought none for them, so he did not represent too great a commercial prospect.

But Linda was different. Her beauty was neither false nor feigned, but a fragile sort of thing such as Slim had never seen before. When she walked she wore her respectability with unobtrusive assurance. When Slim met her, he'd step aside, off the plank walk to let her pass. She even smelled different, clean like soap, different from the cologned aroma of cosmetics, tobacco, and whisky of his dancing partners. He wondered if he would ever touch her, and how far away from him she really was.

This was all a new and strange experience for Slim. When he thought of Linda, it was in a proprietary sense. He felt possessive, and possessed. When he looked at her it was as though he beheld some rare and beautiful thing that would always be beyond his reach, but eternally his. Slim hadn't the slightest realization that he had fallen in love.

But there was one emotion Slim could understand. During that summer's nights he would often walk out alone on the flats in back of the town, sometimes three or four miles, almost to the foot of the glacier. He'd stand transformed by the magic of the subarctic night and look up at the towering mountains, whose massive hulks were lost in blackness as they rose until their snowy caps appeared mystically silver in the moonlight. He listened to air currents, high above, play eerie minor melodies through the crags and caverns of the heights. These mountains to him were like people. They promised the adventure of all Alaska, and he stood in awe of their mystery.

· 4 ·

They range the field and they rove the flood,
And they climb the mountain's crest;
Theirs is the curse of the gypsy blood,
And they don't know how to rest.

With his earnings that summer Slim bought. Then he sold and traded until finally he acquired an outfit that just suited him. His pride was a team of nine Alaskan dogs. They were young animals, large for Huskies, about sixty pounds apiece, and had already been broken to harness. Slim practically slept with them, he loved them so. He fed them the choicest fish he could get, and although Slim was no talented conversationalist, and ordinarily talked only when he had to, he visited with those dogs.

Nights when he'd go back to look at his mountains, he'd take his lead dog with him, a brawny, blue-eyed brute, and he'd talk to him. "You see them mountains?" he'd say, and wait as if to give the dog time to answer. "They got trails in 'em that are upendicular, they go straight up and down. One time on the other side I shot a goat off one o' them crags an' it fell a full quarter of a mile straight out o' the sky. When it hit, all the fat was broke loose from the meat, an' I tell you, that was about as fine eatin' as a fellow ever had, except you, you'd rather have fish. But we're goin' into them mountains, an' we're goin' over 'em, an' we're goin' to see what the rest o' this Alaska looks like."

When fall came, with snow, Slim was the first in Valdez to harness his dogs. He worked daily with them on the flats behind town to become accustomed to the big team before starting over the glacier. He had heard talk of another trail through a notch 3,000 feet up. Anything new appealed to him, so he listened to arguments for and against the glacier trail and Thompson Pass. The Pass intrigued him. It was less dangerous, they said, but the snow, cold, and winds made up the difference. It was also a few miles longer. He even made a few exploratory trips to learn the trail.

While Slim was making up his mind where to go and which way to get there, somebody offered him a paying job. He accepted, and thereby became the first regular mail carrier between Valdez and Fairbanks, the new gold-rush town about 375 miles to the north. While he was being sworn into government service, a stranger came up. He was a slight man, dressed in trail clothes, with skin that was pale, evidence of having just arrived.

"Young fellow," he said, "I hear you're going to Fairbanks. I haven't got an outfit and I want to get there. How much do you want to take me along?" Slim made a deal.

Soon he had loaded his sled and lashed on his sacks of mail, wrapped his passenger in a bearskin robe. He started for Thompson Pass. The trail was well worked, and almost as crowded as the glacier trail. There were the same two lines, the hopefuls going in, the defeated coming out.

The Pass lived up to the rumors, a bare way over a jagged sawtooth range. Wind frothed the ground snow until the air was a blinding gray. It was almost impossible to see, and it was cold. Progress was foot by foot. Slim walked ahead of his dogs, straining to see the form of the man ahead in the line, praying that this man was following another ahead of him.

Over the crest of the pass Slim actually walked out of the wind on the descent. He stopped and looked back into the swirling gray from which shrouded figures emerged like wraiths. On the sled his passenger had drawn out of sight well within his bearskin covering.

When Slim left Valdez he worried, as much as he ever worried, about how he would find his way to Fairbanks, for his only knowledge of its whereabouts was a vague idea that it was about a two-week dog trip north. But in which direction north, he didn't know. There was no need for worry, however. The news of another strike in the Fairbanks area had resulted in a rush that established a well-populated trail. It led through Copper Center. Slim stopped, but his friend Waycross was no longer there.

Slim was a chatterbox compared with his passenger. They'd go all day without the interchange of more than a few necessary phrases. There was simply nothing to talk about, was Slim's reason for silence. Another deterrent was that he spent hour after hour running behind his team. The man with him was apparently well pleased to mind his own business.

Days were clear and cold. Nights were still and colder, with temperatures dropping to thirty and forty below. The trail was good, and Slim made excellent time over the rolling floor of the valley. Ahead was the Alaska Range and Mt. McKinley. The trail led through and over the Isabel Pass, higher than the Thompson, and a tougher one to take. Here again Slim went ahead of the dogs and more than once lent his strength to help them pull the load through drifted snow. Past this, the trail again dropped to the Tanana River Valley and a few days' drive to Fairbanks. As Slim delivered his mail, his passenger waved a farewell and went his way. Slim never saw him again, or ever knew his name; but neither mattered to Slim. After a day's rest, he was on his return way to Valdez.

For the next several winters Slim began to know and be known from Valdez to Fairbanks, to Fortymile, and from Dawson to Nome as he traveled the thousands of frozen miles of the mail routes. Each year he would summer where breakup found him, and with the snow he would take to the trails. He had long since learned that the most important thing he had was his transportation. Therefore, whenever an opportunity came to improve his team, he'd trade or buy to get a better dog.

He even developed a flair for the dramatic. When he'd drive into a town, his dogs were always at a full run, tails curled over their backs and yelping to announce that Slim Williams and the mail had arrived. He was not a bragger or a show-off, he just knew his dogs were the best and wanted all Alaska to know it. He was known and welcomed wherever he went. He gradually unfolded from a reticent, gangling, unknown kid to a man whose word was backed by a confident ability to make good. He was now a big man, six feet, four inches in his mukluks, and 180 pounds of well-co-ordinated willing muscle. He looked twice the size in his fur-hooded parka. He had a good word for everybody and everything, and a smile as broad and bright as the Northern Lights.

Slim tired easily, of any one job that is. He so liked variety and to be his own man that when the mail trails no longer intrigued him, he quit. So far he had seen nothing of the Alaska he really wanted to see. He worked because he had to, and he had been at this one job for almost four years. So, with his dogs and outfit and a few dollars ahead, he decided he would go to the country he had first fallen in love with, the Wrangell Mountains.

It was near spring in 1905 when Slim made this decision to give up mail hauling to take his chance at trapping. With breakup a month or so away it would be a good time for him to scout the territory while he could still use dogs, and to build himself a good camp from which to work the next fall. Then during the summer he could become acquainted with the new country and be ready when snow came. He also thought that he might take a partner on this new venture.

One of the friends Slim had made in Fairbanks was a man called "Corks." He had been a riverman on timber drives in the States before coming to Alaska, and his insistence that caulks, "corks" as he called them, were ideal for proper footing, gave him his name. After a few icy falls and the steel studs chewing out the webbing of several pairs of snowshoes, he discarded his hobnail boots for the more practical mukluks. But the name Corks remained.

Slim found him through the simple process of combing the crowded gambling joints. Corks was at his favorite pastime, shooting craps. Slim wedged his way through the reeking crowded room until he stood alongside his friend. He was just in time to see Corks pick up the dice, rattle them over his head, and toss a natural on the green-covered table. Corks smiled and nudged Slim with his elbow. "Seen you come in, Slim. You brought me luck, so I had to make this pass first."

Corks wasn't as tall as Slim, about to his shoulder, but he was chunky and heavier by about twenty pounds, broad-shouldered and bullnecked. His skin was as leathery and weather-beaten as Slim's, and his eyes had the same vacancy as if focused far in the distance. When he turned his head, his shoulders moved with it.

Slim motioned his head toward the door; Corks nodded agreement. "Soon's I pick up my stake," he said. As he reached for the money on the table, he found another hand there first. "Take your hands off my money!" he yelled, and the fight was on. It was a dandy. In a very few minutes the place was a shambles.

Slim and Corks, back to back, edged toward the door, swinging as they went. Slim picked up a man bodily and threw him at the grinning faces of a few men lined up across the table. The two of them hammered their way outside, but not without some evidence of their own to show they had been in a good brawl. At least they were able to walk which was more than a dozen or so of those left inside could do. They went the quarter-mile to Corks' shack. Slim lighted the lamp and fed the stove. Then the two faced one another, and each grinned with swollen cut lips at what he saw through bluish puffed eyes.

Corks held up his two fists bleeding at the knuckles. "Crooks tried to steal my money, but here it is," he said, opening his fists and showing the cash they held.

Slim sat on the edge of the bunk and began dipping his knuckles in a pan of cold water. "Does a fellow good once in a while to get a few o' those barroom punks. Three to one against you was fun, and just about even odds for you, but when the rest of 'em ganged up I thought I ought to help you out a bit. Anyhow, I wanted to see you. I quit pullin' mail an' I'm goin' to locate a trappin' ground. You want to go partners?"

"Sure," Corks nodded. "To save you the trouble o' sayin' good-by I'll go with you. Where you figurin' on goin'?"

"South to the Wrangells. Been wantin' to trap them mountains since I been here, an' up to now I ain't had time. I sure like them mountains."

"Wrangells is all right," Corks agreed, moving alongside Slim to dip his knuckles in the pan of water, "but I know where's a million dollars in silver fox past the Wood River in the Mt. McKinley country. Wrangells is a good three hundred miles. We can get to this other place about half that far."

"All right if you say so, Corks," Slim agreed. "Let's go look it over. I got a outfit and some traps."

"I got fifty dollars." Corks counted it out and handed half to Slim. "Here's yours." Slim took the money without question and stuffed it in his jacket.

Two days later, battle wounds partially healed, the two partners completed their supply purchases and took the trail to the trapping grounds.

At every stop Corks did all he could to make friends with Slim's dogs, and succeeded exceptionally well. The big fellows lying in their harness, resting, submitted dutifully to Corks' overtures. He patted them and told them what good dogs they were. Even though the dogs would far rather eat snow to slake their thirst, they always lapped up a bit of the water that

Corks thoughtfully brought to them. At night he even cut spruce boughs to make beds for them. They didn't know what the boughs were for and didn't sleep on them, but Corks had made his gesture of friendship. Slim loved the dogs too. They knew it, and returned it tenfold with loyalty added. They accepted Corks, but Slim was always the master, strict with discipline, but kind in its administration.

The way turned and twisted through passes and valleys, up, down, and around. Their load was heavy, and for most of the way they took turns in front of the dogs breaking trail. Then Corks called a halt. Slim calculated by the time taken that they had covered nearly two hundred miles. His partner hadn't been far off in his estimate.

"This is it," Corks announced. They were in a sheltered stand of spruce. A perfect place for a trapping camp. It promised to be a rich one, for Slim had seen plenty of tracks.

After a day's rest, and the permanent camp set up, the two went hunting. "We'll get us some sheep for eatin' meat," said Corks.

"I never yet eat sheep," said Slim. "I've eat goat but never sheep. I see 'em but I never eat 'em."

"Better'n goat," said Corks.

"I'm willin'," said Slim.

They came to a clearing which gave a good view of the whole valley. Corks had glasses and halfway up the far slope he spied sheep grazing just above the timber line.

"They're Dalls," he said, pointing, "white ones."

About four miles on snowshoes up the mountainside, then a climb up rocky ridges with the snowshoes left behind, brought them in range. When they were near enough for a shot, Slim downed a nice ram. Then came the harder work of getting the animal down. After an hour or more they finally dragged it back to where they had left their snowshoes. They sat down for a rest, then lashed on their footgear and continued down the slope. It was rocky and hard going. Slim was in the lead, breaking trail, Corks held the ram by the forelegs, towing him along behind.

After two hundred yards, Slim stopped and turned. "Let me take a spell haulin' that chunk o' meat," he called back. Just as he did he saw Corks fall. One of the ram's horns had caught in the *babiche,* the moosehide webbing, of Corks' snowshoe, pinning the shoe down. Corks fell forward directly over a sharp boulder which caught him right at the shin bone. There was a sharp crack, and Corks lay still, face down in the snow. Slim was by him in seconds, turning him over. "Corks, I guess you broke your leg," he announced simply. "I seen it, and it was like bustin' a piece o' kindlin' across your knee."

Corks nodded. He sucked in air sharply between his clenched teeth, and held his breath, staring at Slim. Finally he let it out with a snort.

"Don't stand there starin' at me like a dang fool. Do somethin'! Fix it!"

Slim imagined what pain his friend must be suffering, but he hesitated to move him for fear of causing greater torment. He would have done anything in the world to stop the pain, but he didn't know what to do.

Corks took temporary command. "I ain't no horse, and I ain't no dog, so stop lookin' at me like you was goin' to put me out o' my misery. I got a bust leg, so set the dang thing, an' set it quick and we'll splint it up."

"I don't want to hurt you none," Slim apologized.

"Hurt! I ain't hurtin'." Corks was yelling. "Pull that leg back in place!"

"We need splints and bandages first," said Slim.

"Then get 'em," Corks ordered.

The nearest trees were about sixty yards down the slope. On an improvised litter made of the snowshoes, Slim was able to slide Corks to the trees.

"I'll cut saplin's, and bring 'em to you, an' you split 'em," said Slim after he had made his friend as comfortable as possible, propped against a tree trunk. "That way we'll have some splints. Then I'll cut off your parky tail and mine, and that'll maybe give us wrappin' enough to bandage it up." And he started to work. Corks was kept busy with his knife, splitting and cutting the pieces to the length of his leg.

When they decided they had enough of the makeshift splints, Slim cut the tails from their parkas and stripped them for bandages. When all was ready, Slim cut the mukluk from Cork's foot and slit the pant leg to above the knee, leaving the sock and underwear intact. Then came the moment against which he had steeled himself. He took hold of the leg and felt the sharp ridge of the clean break. He said, "Corks, you dang well better sing, sweat, or swear, because here, by the holy, she goes!" He grabbed the leg, and pulled until he felt the bones slip into place. Corks didn't utter a sound. From then on Slim wasted no time, and in a matter of minutes the leg was encased solidly in splints and bandages from foot to hip. Slim stood up. "There you are," he said.

"Took you long enough," was Corks' only comment, "but for a cheechako I guess you done a pretty good job."

"Good enough to maybe put you on your feet again," Slim countered, "but since I got to nurse you, I'm goin' to camp for the sled and come back and get you. You feelin' all right?"

"I ain't hurtin' a bit," said Corks.

"I know you're lyin', but it's the best I can do for now. I'll be back as soon as I can. It's only about four miles to camp."

Before leaving Corks, Slim built a strong fire of good, heavy logs, which would surely hold until he returned.

He ran most of the way. The trail was clear and most of it downhill, and he made good time. It was near dusk when he reached their clearing.

He was completely unprepared for what he saw. Instead of the neat camp they had left, he looked upon a scene of unbelievable carnage. His first emotions were horror and helpless rage. His nine dogs were dead, their throats ripped and their bodies mercilessly torn. They were literally strewn over the snow in a bloody almost unrecognizable mess. Slim read the sign: wolves! It was pitiful, for the dogs had not had a chance. Some of them had even been pulled out of their collars in the frenzy of the attack. He couldn't guess how many wolves had been in the pack, but he knew they were big. Paw marks in the snow were at least three times the size of the dogs'. He knew that a wolf with a paw that size would weigh at least two hundred pounds. Slim looked almost stupidly at his mittened hands, one of which should have held his gun. He looked around sharply as if expecting the wolves to return, but calmed down when he remembered that wolves do not return to a kill, but rather hunt new quarry. That chilling thought brought him up short. He had left both rifles by the newly killed ram, and Corks, propped up against a tree sixty yards away, would be helpless in case the wolves should scent and be attracted by the invitation of fresh blood.

This was one of Slim's first experiences with wolves and their habits. Predators, vicious killers of wild things and dogs, wolves would not make an unprovoked attack upon a man. [Undoubtedly a wolf, like any other animal, if he were wounded, cornered, or possibly starving, might attack a human being.] But at that time Slim didn't know this and therefore was particularly, although unnecessarily, concerned over Corks' dilemma.

Before he left the camp, he cut the other dogs' bodies free from their collars and disposed of them as well as he could. Then with his necking line he started back up the grade through the quickening dark to help his partner.

He found Corks safe and in good spirits. The fire had been well laid and was still burning with good heat. After Slim retrieved the guns, he sat down and stared at Corks.

"What's the matter, Slim?" Corks asked. "Wake up! You act like you're crazy or seen a ghost."

Slim told him what he had found.

Corks exploded. "Gimme my gun," he yelled, "I'll kill 'em! I'll kill every wolf in Alaska, the murderin', thievin' tramps. There'll never be another team o' dogs like 'em, and them no-good ———. Slim, so help me, I'll kill every wolf in the country."

Slim's reaction was different. He loved his dogs and felt their loss keenly and deeply; it had been such an uneven fight. But after the first shock passed, his feeling was not one of revenge. He somehow couldn't hate an animal for doing what it had been taught to do from puppyhood. Wolves, he knew, spent the first three years of their lives under the strictest discipline, being taught one thing only, to kill. Killing wolves would never bring back his team.

Corks was still voluble and vituperative as Slim put him on the sled and pulled him back to camp. He was glad that he had removed as much evidence as he had, for when Corks saw the camp, he renewed his abuse of the killers.

Slim built a fire and fixed food. After the meal Corks quieted down and became a bit more logical.

"I got to get you back to Fairbanks," Slim told him, "and there's no use losin' all this grub and outfit, so I'll build a cache in the trees, and we'll store it. Then I'll neck you in."

"You can't do it alone," Corks objected. "We'll stay here till my leg gets well and I'll walk in."

Slim paid no attention, but went to work building the cache. First he climbed trees, clearing branches as he went, until he had ladderlike approaches to the upper boughs about twelve feet off the ground. He lashed free lengths of cut saplings to form a platform about ten feet square. To this he carried their full supply of food, several hundred pounds of it, topped it with the dog harness, and covered it with canvas to protect it from animals and birds. It took almost all night to finish this cache and stock it. It was just daylight when he put the coffeepot on the fire for breakfast.

As he worked, he kept an eye on Corks. Corks said he hadn't slept, but Slim knew better. Corks swore he had stayed awake hoping the wolves would return.

After a sturdy breakfast Slim announced he was ready to hit the trail.

"You're crazy, Slim," said Corks. "You ain't slept for twenty-four hours, and God knows when you'll get a chance to rest once we get started back. You lay down and get a sleep."

It was about noon when Slim awoke, partially refreshed but ready, after another good feed, to make a start. He made Corks comfortable on the sled. First canvas, then he wrapped Corks in a wolfskin robe and his own rabbitskin blanket, and backed him up against his snowshoes so he could sit up. "Keep an icicle warm," Slim commented, and finally loaded on their working outfit and food. He tested the heft. The sled was a big one, twelve feet six inches long. In itself, it was heavy, and with Corks and what outfit and food he had he guessed the load about 350 pounds.

Slim never remembered too much about the next fifteen days. The trail was clear, it hadn't blown over, and there had been no snow, but pulling that weight hour after hour, foot by foot, fewer miles each dawn to dusk, became a monotony of effort that almost blotted out reason. There was no place for talk. Corks did from time to time, but Slim either didn't hear or paid no attention. His only thought was whether or not it would be physically possible to complete the task. He did it, but he was bush-bearded, gaunt, and bleary-eyed when he staggered onto the easier trail of the street in Fairbanks. He turned Corks over to the town doctor, and went to bed.

Corks' leg was going to be all right, according to the young doctor's judgment. All he would need would be rest. The doctor even used Slim's splints in rebandaging the leg, saying he could do no better himself.

The next day Slim made a pair of crutches and Corks was up and hobbling about, profanely blaming the Fates for his bad luck. "And we could ha' made a million in furs out there, Slim," he said, "if it hadn't been fer that ram trippin' me up an' bustin' my leg. But we'll try it again one o' these days."

Slim grinned and nodded. "Sure, we will, Corks. You just grow that leg together again and we'll try her once more."

61

A day or two later, as Slim was walking along the street in town, someone tapped him on the shoulder. He turned around and faced "Windy" Smith.

Slim knew three Smiths, "Windy," "Silent," and "Foghorn." Windy talked even less than Slim did; he just didn't talk at all, unless he had to. But if you saw anyone coming along the trail, talking every second as far as you could see him coming and going, that would be Silent Smith. Foghorn sounded exactly like one.

"Hello, Windy," Slim grinned.

Windy nodded, and motioned for Slim to follow him. He led the way to where his dogs were tied, and pointed to two thousand pounds of mail and of freight. He spoke one word, "Nome."

"You ain't goin' to haul that load down the Yukon and across to Nome at this time o' year? You better wait for the boat. It's too late, Windy. Breakup soon, then the Tanana and Yukon'll be clear." Slim turned and started to walk away. He was hungry.

Windy grabbed his arm and pulled him back. "Got to," he said. "Too big a load. I got eighteen dogs, one sled, need you and your sled."

Slim shook his head. "It's near a 750-mile trail to Nome, Windy, an' it's too much of a chance to try to beat breakup. It's mighty near, an' if we didn't make it on the ice, we'd be blowed-up suckers."

Windy nodded emphatically. "Got to," he repeated. "Important. Gave my word."

Slim knew the value of a man's promise in the North. He contemplated his friend, the load, and the prospect of the trip with dim enthusiasm. He slowly shook his head and shrugged. "You're just like everybody else, Windy, get yourself into the gol-hangedest mess an' come to good old Slim to get you out of it." He began to grin. "I can't start till tomorrow, Windy. I got a little more restin' I want to do, an' I got to get me one more feed o' wheat cakes and sirup. Meantime you sit here an' feel sorry for yourself, an' practice talkin' enough so you can say 'no' when somebody asks you to do something."

Windy nodded and smiled at his friend.

Slim went back to the shack and told Corks his plans. Corks nodded. "And when you get back we'll plan some more about trappin', Slim."

Slim agreed, got his things together, built up the fire, then stood and looked down at his friend lying on his bunk. "Take care o' yourself, Corks." He dropped a handful of money on the bunk. "Here," he said, "you'll be needin' this." And he started toward the door.

"Hey, you long galoot, come back here!" Corks yelled.

But Slim went on and closed the door behind him. He found Windy and said he was ready.

Slim and Windy mushed out of Fairbanks at daybreak with nine dogs apiece and a thousand pounds per sled, westward on the Tanana River. The river, so near breakup, was popping air holes and overflowing the ice. Time passed in nightmares of endurance. The sled runners continually clogged with slush and froze to the ice. The eighteen dogs and both men worked to break one sled loose, then the other, only to have the first one refreeze. If they tried leaving the river, they had the heavy shore brush to contend with. There were times when the dogs could not pull at all, and the men packed the loads, piece by piece, over windfalls along the shore, and over ice masses on the river. There were days when with their greatest efforts they were able to make no more than a mile.

After eleven days on this sort of trail they were not even halfway to Nome. They had passed the junction of the Tanana with the Yukon, and this great sprawling river offered no improvement. Both men were almost exhausted. The dogs were able to work only short periods at a time. Then they got their break. One night after a day of brush trail, they made camp alongside the river just at dusk, too dark to see what the river surface was like. They gave the dogs a good feed of fish, thawed themselves out a feed of beans, made a pot of tea, and turned in. That night it turned cold. When spring seems right at hand with daily thaws and warm, soft breezes, it's a trick of the North that the weather may take a dip and harden up for another week or more of a final fling at winter.

Slim thanked his stars when he awoke the next morning and "smelled" the cold. He was out of his rabbit robe in a second, and had Windy on his feet. "It's freezin'," he said, "and look at that river, she's clear ice, an' if the cold holds, we'll make her." Slim leaned his head back and sniffed. "Twenty below," he announced. Slim, like other men of the North, was accustomed to the feel of cold in his nostrils and could tell subzero temperatures almost to the degree by a tentative whiff or two.

The dogs awoke, alert, refreshed, and eager. They too responded to the cold. They wouldn't eat again until nightfall, so they waited in harness while the men had a quick breakfast and broke camp.

The river ice was riffled just enough to give the dogs' feet a good purchase. Slim trotted joyfully along behind his sled listening to the rhythmic chip-chip-chip-chip of the dogs' toe-nails on the ice, and the occasional chucking of the sled runners. Windy with his team was out in front, and before long Slim heard him singing, softly at first, and finally in a full, rich baritone. It was a voice that might at one time have thrilled great audiences. No one knew who Windy was or what he had been. In that country a man's past was his own particular business, and no one asked questions about it. If Windy had been a singer, it was certain that he had never performed in a greater theater than this frozen vastness, nor before a more appreciative listener than Slim. Windy sang "The Old Folks at Home." He sang it all the way through, just once, and that was all.

The cold held. They followed the Yukon until the big river bent south. They pulled off onto the west bank and camped.

"Now we're across and off that danged river," said Windy,

"maybe we can cut this killin' pace we been keepin', an' sort o' take it easy into Nome. I ain't no kid no more, Slim, an' this trip's sure been a heller."

"No time to let down now, Windy," said Slim. "We got four to five days ahead, an' we got to burn the trail before it melts under us. If a quick thaw comes and turns this trail to muskeg, we're just gone, and that's all there is to it. I don't like it no better'n you or the dogs, but we got to make more miles a day from now than we been makin' instead o' slowin' down."

From then on Slim took the lead, and drove the dogs to their full limit. Windy was game but was no match for Slim who ran behind his team with the rhythm of an automaton. It took all that Windy had to hold the gruelling tempo of his long-legged, indefatigable young partner. When he fell hours behind, Slim made camp and waited. By the time Windy caught up, Slim had a fire going, hot food, and a pot of tea ready for the older man.

On the last day, Slim let Windy take the lead going into Nome. Windy at first demurred, but Slim reminded him, "It's your trip, Windy. I just come along."

When they had delivered their cargoes to the mail and freight offices, and taken care of their dogs, they went first to the restaurant, then to bed.

The next day Windy collected his fee, and shared it with Slim. That same day the thaw came and turned their trail into a soggy mass of muskeg. The two stood and looked back over the way they had come, across the flat, treeless marsh of the tundra.

"I guess I'm gettin' too old for this sort o' thing anymore, Slim," said Windy. "Prit near forty I am, an' I been runnin' dogs since '98. Guess I'm like an old dog, Slim, wind an' legs is gone." Windy was quiet a moment, then looked at Slim. "Tell you one thing though, Slim, you're the best man with dogs I ever see. If anybody told me you'd come more'n seven hundred miles from Fairbanks to Nome in eighteen days, nine dogs, an' a thousand-pound load, I'd ha' said they was crazy."

"You done it, too," said Slim.

Windy shook his head. "No, I didn't, Slim. You done it. Without you waitin' for me an' keepin' me goin' them last days, I couldn't ha' kept up with you. Right now I'd be out there somewhere rottin' in that mess o' goo if it hadn't been for you. I'll tell anybody you're the best dog man I ever see."

Slim had been on the trail for about one thousand miles with but the few days' rest in Fairbanks. Such is the uncharted record of courage and stamina of dogs and a man in a country where only the very brave survive, and where a man's generosity is not measured in the gold he tosses away, but in what he gives of himself as a favor to a friend.

·5·

Wild and wide are my borders,
stern as death is my sway;
And I wait for the man who will win me—
and I will not be won in a day.

Slim hadn't liked Nome the first time he saw it. He liked it
no better now as he sat on a pile of driftwood and looked out
over the bleak rotting shore ice of the Bering Sea. Nome had
no harbor, as did Valdez, but was merely a landing place, a
long stretch of beach onto which poured the thousands of
prospectors who had heard rumors that the sands of the shore
were pure gold. The town itself was perched on the edge of
the tundra swamp which rolled treeless out of sight inland.
Shacks of driftwood or lumber whipsawed from beached timber made up the solid structures as well as the streets and sidewalks. Most of the populace were in tents, and very transient.

From October to June the frozen sea sealed Nome from
steamer traffic, and the only contact with the outside world
was by dog team through Fairbanks to Dawson or Valdez.
In summer steamers from Seattle dumped their loads of hundreds of prospectors at every trip. The shore line for miles in
both directions was indented by small streams. The bottom
sands of almost every one of these held the precious metal that
these men starved, fought, and died to get.

There was no beauty to Nome. Its being was solely func-
tional. The country back of the shore was sodden muskeg two

to three feet down to a perpetual frozen base, and it offered no charm to Slim.

When the dog trails to the east thawed, there would be no further use for a mail carrier until freeze-up in the fall. Therefore, Slim sat and evaluated his summer prospects. After Windy had split his meager mail wages with him, Slim invested in food supplies for himself, then turned right around and gave most of what he had left back to Windy for five of the dogs he had just driven. Slim knew that spring was no time to buy dogs. During the summer they were of absolutely no practical value, yet their appetites remained constant. Nevertheless Slim bought them. It was a combination of his fondness for dogs in general, and something to help heal the hurt of the recent loss of his other team that made him do it. So there he sat, with a sled, five dogs to feed, a little money in his pocket, and no place to go.

So far Slim had not succumbed to the love of gold. Even here in Nome, the center of one of the richest, most fabulous placer strikes in history, where millions in dust were being washed out of the sands, Slim's sole interest in life was adventure, to see new and different things. Let others slosh in the creeks and dig in the muskeg for gold, he would even help them; all he wanted was a grubstake and a new trail to follow and he was perfectly happy.

It had never seriously occurred to him to settle down. That would mean having a wife, and a permanent address, and a regular job. He rarely thought of women. Now and then he would take out the memory of the delightful little schoolteacher of Valdez and admire it thoughtfully and reverently, but never with any hope of achievement. Then he'd put it away again. He never daydreamed of anyone else, only Linda. The thought of living in one place he dismissed whenever it came, which was rare. Steady employment was unthinkable. His wealth, his home, and his future, always remained afar.

As usual, when faced with necessity, Slim looked for a job. He staked his dogs near his tent and started the rounds of the gold camps. When there was work to be done, it was his axe that kept him and his dogs in food. And there was always such work in a boom town. Miners who had struck rich gravel, and there were many of them, offered the usual dollar-an-hour wages for men to build sluice boxes and trestles. In some cases water had to be transported for miles to wash the gravel.

At one mine office shack Slim saw something that caught his eye. It was a big chunk of green stone, weighing perhaps fifty pounds, being used as a doorstop. Slim asked, and was told it was jade.

"My grandpa had some jade once," Slim told the mine superintendent. "He was a sailor, from China. I mean my grandpa wasn't from China. He just brought a piece of jade from China. He said it was worth a lot of money. A piece pit' near as big as a marble, and worth a whole lot of money. A thousand dollars, he said, for one little bitty piece."

The super asked Slim if he wanted a job.

"Yeah," Slim, now on his knees examining the chunk of jade, nodded.

"This piece of jade come from China?" he asked, looking up at the super. "A piece this big must be worth a million."

The super shook his head, "It ain't from China, an' I don't know what it's worth. It come from a mountain up north o' the Arctic Circle some place is all I know. I got a job a dollar-an-hour buildin' sluice boxes."

Slim nodded. "You don't know where the mountain is, huh?"

"No, I don't. Do you want the job or don't you?"

Slim rubbed his chin, still staring at the green stone. "Maybe," he said, and walked thoughtfully out of the shack.

Slim had never been north of the Circle and the thought of it intrigued him. Especially if there was a mountain of jade up there, he could possibly make a million. Besides he'd always wanted to see the land of the Eskimos. But to do this he'd need more of a grubstake than he had, or maybe a partner. He hunted down Windy Smith. This wasn't too hard a chore, for Slim knew just about where to find him. The search called only for a round of the joints. Windy, like many another, had faith that his luck would counterbalance house percentages and the skill of professional gamblers. It never did, but he kept trying. Slim found him in the third place he looked. Windy was trying to outfigure a bored, but clever, faro dealer. Windy waved Slim away.

The honky-tonk was a large one. The bar and trimmings, mirrors and wall decorations were finer than anything Slim had ever seen in Fairbanks, Dawson, Valdez or even Seattle, as were the girls. Highly scented, sweet-smelling, extravagantly dressed, all young and beautiful, they attracted Slim only as an excuse to dance. Where Windy's weakness was gambling, Slim's was dancing. He paid willingly for the pleasure. It made little difference to him that he was at least a foot taller than his partners, he just had fun jiggling around the floor to the rhythm, which was noisy if not musical, of the "band" —piano, cornet, fiddle, and drum.

Windy went broke and was willing to listen, after Slim had had about twenty dollars' worth of dancing at the rate of a dollar a minute.

"What do you know about jade?" Slim asked when he'd led his friend outside.

Windy shook his head.

"They's a mountain of it, Windy, up north of the Circle. It's maybe worth a million if we find it. How would you like to go hunt for it?"

"Gold's better'n jade an' you don't have to go haulin' halfway to the Pole to get it. It's right here without huntin' for it. You want north of the Circle, go get yourself a Eskimo." Windy disposed of the topic to his satisfaction, and Slim followed the suggestion to get an Eskimo. This wasn't too difficult. Nome was in Eskimo country, and there was no trouble in finding one. IIe was a friendly old man, obviously eager to please. The difficulty was the language barrier.

As a boy Slim had been able to make himself understood

by the Southwest States Indians by signs and bits of colloquial Spanish. Also, around Valdez, he had been able to make himself understood by the Indians, as well as those near Fairbanks and even the Canadian Indians in the Yukon Territory. A thing he had noticed especially was that the dialects were so completely localized that one Indian band might not have a single word in common with a neighbor band living perhaps not more than fifty miles away. But the Eskimos' talk was completely unlike the Indians', and Slim was to be disappointed in his efforts to penetrate their understanding. However, he gamely tried.

"You sabby jade?" he asked the old man.

The Eskimo grinned and shrugged. Encouraged by the response, he tried again. "Jade all-same green stone in mountain far north." He pointed.

Another grin, but no shrug.

"BIG mountain, plenty green stone, you sabby jade," Slim tried gestures to show a mountain.

This time neither grin nor shrug. The impassive stare told Slim that nothing had got through. The Eskimo had only been trying to be polite.

Slim finally gave up on this one and tried another Eskimo with the same result. This second one, too, was pleasantly agreeable. Before long Slim had himself surrounded by a crowd of grinning Eskimos. One told another, and their curiosity was as deep as Slim's in wanting to know what the other was trying to say.

Slim motioned toward the north. The Eskimos grinned and nodded. Slim made signs describing the height of a mountain. More grins and nods. The Eskimos looked perplexed as Slim repeated, "Jade." This meant nothing. At last he got the thought across to them, of green stones in a mountain by pointing to the color of the sea moss, to a stone, and making the mountain with his fingertips together. One old Eskimo stopped smiling and nodded slowly. "Ai-ee," he said profoundly. Slim knew he had made contact. This Eskimo turned to the others and with a fluid flow of gutturals, and hisses, apparently explained that all Slim wanted to know was where the Jade Mountain was to be found. He knew where the mountain was and would make the white man happy by drawing him a picture. The fellow indicated he wanted to make a sketch. Slim produced a piece of paper and a pencil, and watched fascinated as this old man delineated a perfect map. It showed every topographical detail, and when he made the last mark he pointed with the pencil and said something that sounded like "Kobuk," which Slim liberally interpreted as meaning "jade."

Slim studied the drawing. The Eskimo pressed a dirty forefinger on the spot where he claimed the mountain was, and told Slim, "Fifteen sleep."

That'll be easy, thought Slim, two weeks, and the trails to the north were still good, and there he would have a whole mountain of jade all to himself. Deciding to do the best he could with what he had, he bought food for himself and a good supply of fish for the dogs. Surprisingly this still left him with a bit of cash which he stuffed in his pocket. At the next morning's daylight he and his dogs were away.

The Eskimo's map was perfect in detail, accurate as to the type of terrain and trail. Every stream, the hills, the country he passed through were clearly recognizable. There were only two points to question. One was the distance, the other was the man's conception of a "sleep." Slim went fifteen "sleeps," then fifteen more, following the course of the chart. The trail led straight north past the gold boom camp of Candle, then looped to where the Kobuk River emptied into the sea. By this time the spring thaws were beginning to catch up with him. The snow was gone but there was still ice, and his trail lay upstream. He couldn't count the miles he followed the river, but he hurried to make use of the ice as long as he had it. His days were long and his "sleeps" were short. He was above the Arctic Circle in the Baird Mountains on the southern slopes of the Brooks Range, the northernmost mountains in Alaska, whose northern slopes flatten into the thousands of square miles of the waste tundra bordering the Arctic Ocean, a land of dismal desolation.

He pushed his dogs hard. Each day the terrain became more rugged, rising to the heavy, rocky ridges of the range. The river too narrowed and its shores gave evidence of fast water under the covering of ice.

One day, just as the river ice began to crack, when he was about 150 miles inland, Slim, watching the shore, felt a surge of excitement bounce in his stomach. "Haw!" he yelled to his leader, who turned the team off the ice. The dogs clambered up the bank. When the sled runners hit the rocks, Slim shouted, "Whoa!" In another moment he was on his knees, scratching with his hands. He picked up several pieces of rock and examined them. They were green, and to his memory, were identical with the piece his grandfather had shown him years before. He had found jade. He looked up, and ahead of him was a mountain.

That night Slim camped at the foot of his mountain, secure in the belief that he had his million. That night under the stars, Slim slept in untroubled peace. Let others have their gold. He had found jade, a mountain of it! If Grandpa's marble-size piece had been worth a thousand dollars, what would a mountain of it bring?

For nearly a month Slim and his dogs traveled up and down and around his mountain, which gave every appearance of containing countless tons of jade. When he was satisfied with his data for staking claim, and with his samples for lapidary examination or assay, he started back to Nome with his secret. He figured he was about five hundred trail miles from Nome, figuratively and almost literally on the top of his world. It was early in July and the snow was gone when he decided to go back.

Slim didn't relish the thought of the long walk to the coast. It would be hard travel, but right before him was a river flowing in the direction he wanted to go. In spite of the fact that before, when he had entrusted himself and his outfit to one of his handmade boats, he had met with disaster, he was determined to try again. The Indian phrase, "No walk the way river run," kept going through his mind. He decided to risk it.

His sled was of no further use to him, so he ripped it apart and used the ribs to fashion a boat. His tent canvas became the cover. Game had been no problem, so there was no difficulty in getting bearfat to make the canvas watertight. When all was ready, he loaded in about thirty pounds of his choicest jade samples and started downstream. He turned the dogs loose to run along the shore. Slim guided his craft down the now white-watered Kobuk River in half-hour spurts, pulling ashore after each run to wait for the dogs to catch up.

The third day it happened. Slim ran afoul of a hidden jagged rock which ripped the flimsy boat from bow to stern. He had a hard time getting himself free of the loose canvas and broken ribbing to scramble his way through the rapids and reach shore.

He had done it again! Drowned his outfit. His gun, ammunition, food, his precious samples of jade, were lost. There again he stood on a shore, miserably alone, with nothing. He did, however, have five dogs which needed a daily feeding; his little supply of matches; and the one thing the man on the Copper River had taught him to carry, a piece of fishline and a hook. Because of this, they didn't go hungry. Day after monotonous day he fished his way downstream.

It was slow, tedious going, and called for frequent rests. About noon the fourth day, when he was sitting on the shore looking morosely across a stretch of rushing stream, a bit of white on a submerged rock caught his eye, like a flag of peace waving there underwater. He jumped to his feet and waded out in the icy rapids and retrieved his rabbit robe. It was like meeting an old friend. It had washed loose from the boat's wreckage, and the swift current had carried it down to the place where it had snagged. Slim wrung it out and dried it and slept better nights from then on.

The dogs were having the time of their lives, no work to do, and every night all the fish they could eat. Slim had just about reached the point where he was sure that one more mouthful of fish would turn his stomach inside out. Suddenly he stopped and sniffed the air. There was no mistaking. It was the pungent, aromatic, beautiful odor of cooking. Food! He was weak and tired, but that smell was a stimulant. He started running, following the tantalizing breeze until he came to where Eskimo hunters were camped. Over their fire a pot of stew bubbled and filled the air with smells that set Slim drooling. He joined the men and without ceremony got himself invited to dinner. First, however, he caught some fish and fed his dogs.

Hunger knows no language. One of the Eskimos handed Slim a spoon made of horn. The stewpot was of heavy-weight copper. Slim had noticed many of these copper utensils being used by the Indians, relics of the times when Alaska was owned by Russia. These pots and pans were trade goods from the Russian traders. Slim hunkered down by the stewpot and dipped with the others. From then on the assorted slurps, aahs, grunts, and belches attested appreciation of the feast.

The Eskimos had killed a caribou, and they were enjoying their greatest delicacy of fresh-killed meat, the rich, tangy, vitamin-filled stew of the animal's entrails. Slim had no qualms about the fare, nor was his appetite the least queasy. He had long known of such eating habits, and had shared many a similar meal with Indians. It was, therefore, no great surprise that these Eskimos also, most of whom had never seen or tasted a vegetable, found the balance of their essential diets in the innards of the animals they killed—walrus, seal, or birds. It was the white man of educated tastes who spurned these earthy tidbits and suffered scurvy or other diseases of deficiency. The aborigines ate what nature told them to, and thrived. Slim, therefore, was honored to be a guest at this important meal. The meat of the animal they had killed would be cured and would keep, but the "delicates" must be stewed and eaten at the kill.

Slim stayed at the camp a few days and rested. The Eskimos went about their own affairs but were exaggeratedly hospitable to him, and apparently did not want him to leave until the last drop and morsel of stew was consumed. Slim tried to talk with them by word and gesture, but made little headway. Their dialect still eluded him.

When he left he wanted to give them something for their kindness, but he had nothing to give. He had a little money, but that would have been of no use to them. He had dogs. So did they at home. The best he could do was to shake hands with each of the men and bow. They laughed and bowed and thought this ceremony was great fun. They had probably never shaken hands before with anyone, but it was a pleasant gesture. In parting, they gave Slim some of the caribou meat which helped him on his long trip back to Nome. On this trip he went out of his way to stop at Candle. There he spent some of his remaining money. There was a store where he could buy food. It was run by a young fellow from Texas named Rickard. Then, thus restocked, he continued on the trail.

The first thing he did after reaching Nome and staking his dogs was to go to a restaurant and eat more batter cakes slathered with sirup than it seemed possible for a human being to hold. Like all men coming off the trail he craved sugar, and he spooned up the sirup that was left. After dinner he went down to the shore, fed his dogs, and sat on the same pile of driftwood he had used once before, there to meditate on the state of his fortunes. He had the dogs, but no sled or outfit, he was almost broke, and all around him Nome was dirty, noisy, ugly, and overcrowded. But none of this seemed to bother him any more, for now his star shone brightly. He knew where there was a mountain of jade. He had his million made.

Just at the moment that he was about to become expansive in his reverie, he was jarred out of it by a raucous call. "Hey, there, Slim!" He looked up to see a familiar figure coming toward him. There was just the slightest trace of a limp. Even that might have been because of the uneven footing. It was Corks.

"My leg got well," he said, after he had seated himself alongside Slim, "an' since Alaska ain't so big but what I knew I'd find you sooner or later, I come lookin' for you. Where you been, what you doin', an' where you goin'?"

"Up in Eskimo country, nothin', and nowhere," Slim answered, "and what are you doin' out here in fresh air? Why ain't you in shootin' craps?"

"Broke," Corks announced simply, "but I got a million if you want to go in with me, Slim. Something nobody ever done before, and all I need is you."

"Ungh, ungh," Slim shook his head. "I already got my million, an' I'm plannin' right now how to spend it."

"Where you got a million? Gold?"

Slim shook his head.

"Got a million, huh? You goin' back to the States?"

Slim shook his head. "Nope. First time I saw them Wrangell Mountains I said, sometime I'm goin' to spend all the time I want to just livin' in 'em. I haven't seen anything in Alaska that touches 'em, an' I love 'em, Corks, an' now I've got my million made, that's where I'm goin'."

Corks looked sympathetically at Slim, and shook his head.

"If it ain't gold, what is it?"

Slim squint-eyed his friend, and in a low, confidential voice told him, "I got jade. I got me a whole gol-hanged mountain o' jade." He paused, spit nonchalantly, nodded, "Yeah, Corks, I got me just one whole lot o' jade."

"Eskimo jade?" Corks asked brightly. "That Kobuk River stuff?"

Slim stared at him.

"You better change your mind, Slim. That stuff's no good."

"Jade's jade, an' it's worth a million, an' I got a mountain of it," Slim insisted.

"Listen, Slim, I got real money. I got a million in fur. I got a boat to get it. All I need is a partner like you and a little grubstake."

"Where is it?" Slim asked, but without much interest.

"Siberia," said Corks.

"You're loco," Slim told him, "Siberia's across the ocean."

"Siberia's only about sixty miles of water away from Alaska, and I got a fellow who'll sell his boat, engine and all, for a song an' he'll sing the song. We could go to Siberia, trade with the Eskimos there, and bring back a load of white and silver fox worth a million." Corks studied Slim for a moment, then added, "Besides, give us some new country to see."

That was Slim's weakness, and Corks knew it. "I'd sure like that," said Slim, "and I'm sorry I can't go with you, Corks." He looked at his friend, and grinned. "Tell you what." He dug in his pocket and brought out his remaining cash. "You take this money, I won't need it. I got lots more when I cash in on my jade claim, but you take it an' see what you can do with it. You're itchin' to shoot craps, an' maybe you'll get lucky. Anyway, by tomorrow this time I'll have enough to grubstake you for your boat ride."

Corks grinned back at Slim. He took the money from Slim's hand and ambled toward the nearest gambling joint. "See you tomorrow, Slim, an' we'll talk about this some more."

Slim watched him go, and kept smiling. What difference did a little money make now when he had a mountain of it.

He didn't see Corks until late the next afternoon. In the meantime he had seen three other people, a geologist, an assayer, and the first Eskimo he'd met who could speak a bit of English. All three agreed upon one thing, Corks was right. Slim's jade was commercially worthless.

The young geologist was the first to prick Slim's golden bubble. "There are several sorts of jade, Slim," he said, "and that up there on the Kobuk is what they call 'nephrite.' It's a silicate of calcium and magnesium. It's attractive and Eskimos use it for ornaments, and it's hard enough to make knife blades and so forth. Jewel jade is a silicate of sodium and aluminum. It has a granular structure instead of the fibrous texture of the nephrite. So far as anybody knows, no jewel jade has ever been found in America. As a matter of fact, the best jade doesn't even come from China. It comes from Turkestan, and the finest probably from Burma."

All this technical talk meant nothing to Slim, but he listened politely and patiently, then said, "You mean what I found's no good. I ain't got my million after all."

The geologist shook his head. "Not in money, Slim. That jade's not good for anything. Besides, it's too far away. It's just so much green rock, Slim. I'm sorry."

Slim's next visit was to the Assay Office. There he saw another piece of his jade on the desk being used as a paperweight. The assayer confirmed the geologist's judgment.

An Eskimo had a necklace of jade. He told Slim that his people made hatchets, knives, and ornaments out of it, and offered to direct Slim to a whole mountain of it.

Back on the shore, Slim sat again on the pile of driftwood, and turned when his disconsolate partner sat down beside him and joined him in voiceless staring across the water.

"Broke?" Slim finally asked.

Corks nodded.

"My million's gone too," Slim said sadly. "You were right about that jade, Corks. Guess we'd better go to swingin' axes an' get ourselves a grubstake and buy your friend's boat and start for Siberia."

Corks nodded.

"Come on, then." Slim got up. "I know where there's a fellow'll pay a dollar an hour for a couple o' good hands."

Slim led the way toward the mine superintendent's office where he had first seen the chunk of jade.

"That boat your friend's goin' to sell us better be awful cheap," he said, "an' he better sing a purty song."

· 6 ·

. . . . 'Could I find my proper groove,
What a deep mark I would make!'
So they chop and change, and each fresh move
Is only a fresh mistake.

The two went to work. By day they worked hard, and Corks
did his best to be lucky by night. Slim dolefully donated his
daily portion with no faith whatever in the mystic mumbo
of the crapshooters' liturgy. Therefore he was more than surprised to be yanked out of a sound sleep by Corks yelling at
him. "I made it, Slim, three passes straight and we got our
grubstake, and I got out without a fight."

Half-asleep, Slim looked at his friend and said, "Good,
give it to me," and took the money from Corks' outstretched
hands. "I'll keep it for you. I'm going back to sleep."

The next day their plans took shape. First they went to
see the man about the boat. It was a decrepit homemade river
boat which had seen hard service on the Yukon. It was scow
bowed, nearly flat bottomed, about thirty-five feet long with an
eight-foot beam. It boasted a small cabin, plenty of storage
space, a balky, wheezy gasoline engine. Slim looked at the
boat and then out at the slow rolling Bering Sea. "I'd hate to
be out there in this thing with a storm blowin'," he said.
"Maybe you better throw in that dinghy for good measure so's
we'll have somethin' that'll float us to shore. The owner added
a five-foot rowboat to the deal.

They caulked and worked over the hull until the leakage was not too serious, and then set about loading the trade goods—flour, sugar, tea, tobacco, a dozen pairs of overalls, a dozen shirts, pots, pans, and a generous assortment of miscellany. When they were ready to leave, Slim had one final chore. He reluctantly sold his dogs.

Neither Slim nor Corks knew a thing about a gasoline engine or the science of navigation. It took all of Slim's ingenuity and his great patience to keep the engine running. Their course was pure guesswork. They followed the shore line from Nome westward and north, holding the coast of the Seward Peninsula in sight until they reached the western tip at Cape Prince of Wales. By dead-reckoning westward they sighted the Diomcdc Islands and headed toward them. From there they picked up the coast of Siberia beyond.

They talked but little on the way. Once Slim asked Corks where he had learned about this great wealth in Siberia.

"Heard some fellows talking about it in a saloon in Fairbanks. That's when I started huntin' for you, knowin' you're always wantin' to go some place you ain't never been before. Then when I got to Nome, I got to talkin' with a Eskimo. Said he'd been to Siberia lots o' times and they got plenty of fur and gold if anybody wants it. I tell you, we'll make our million this time, Slim."

Slim puttered with the engine and somehow kept it running. From time to time he judged the prodigious amount of fuel it was consuming, and hoped they had not been too conservative in the reserve they had so dearly bought. They had stinted on their own supplies and equipment in order to carry as much trade goods as possible.

The Bering Sea was kind to them, and offered only the long, rolling swells.

"Hate to have a wind come up sudden," Slim observed. "A storm could sink us or blow this tub clear to the North Pole."

"Good thing it ain't far across, either." Corks pointed toward the hazy outline of the shore of northeastern Siberia.

A few hours more and they entered a protected inlet, and ran their boat onto the beach. The country was ruggedly mountainous practically to the shore, leaving only a bare thirty-foot strip of muddy beach. There was very little vegetation, and the whole scene contrasted strongly with the flat tundra of the Alaskan peninsula directly across the straits. But the shores of the two countries had one thing in common, they were equally bleak and barren.

Slim quickly took a practical view. "First thing we fix a place to stay. There's driftwood, and plenty of mud."

An outjutting rock formation from a sheer cliff offered a combination back wall and partial roof. With this as a beginning it was no great chore for these two bushmen to erect a serviceable dwelling. There was a good supply of driftwood along the shore, even some sizable cottonwood logs. These became the three faces of the hut, chinked and mortared with the gummy shore mud.

"I hope the next partner I get'll be a midget," Corks complained as Slim insisted upon extra height for the roof. "You bein' so doggone stretched out makes a lot o' extra work. You don't have to stand up straight in there, do you?"

In spite of Corks' grumbling, Slim built the ceiling to a six-and-a-half-foot clearance inside. They lashed pieces of driftwood together to make a door and hung it with leather hinges, then went inside to test the dwelling. They had made one miscalculation: they had built an airtight structure. When they lighted their little Yukon stove, they had to cut a hole in the roof to let out some of the insufferable heat. With ventilation solved, they were well satisfied. They left their trade goods in the boat, which served as a warehouse.

For the next several days they prospected the country. They ranged inland into the mountains, and in both directions along the shore. They found signs of neither animals nor humans. Slim sampled sand in some of the creeks, and found a spare showing of "color," but hardly enough gold to make panning overly profitable.

One evening before their campfire, Corks asked quietly, "Slim, you sure this is Siberia?"

"Ain't no place else to land goin' west from Cape Wales. It's gotta be Sibera."

"Well, it was sure Siberia them fellows was talkin' about which said there was nothin' but a million in fur and gold when we'd get there."

"Siberia's a awful big place," said Slim, "and maybe we just pulled ashore at the wrong spot. Now maybe tomorrow we ought to pull out and try up and down the shore in the boat and see what we can find. Must be somebody livin' in Siberia."

Corks nodded. "Must be. Them fellows was awful sure."

Just after daybreak next morning Slim came out of the shack and faced a surprise. There were fourteen Eskimos staring at him, all men, standing in a semicircle about fifteen feet away. They were little men, much shorter than Alaskan Eskimos; otherwise they looked exactly the same.

Slim's face broke into its big grin, and he stretched out his arms. "Hello, there," his voice boomed, and he stepped toward the visitors. In like movement the Eskimos moved backward step for step. When Slim stopped, so did they. There was no change of expression on their round brown faces. Their sloe-eyed squints never wavered.

"I didn't mean to scare you, little fellows," Slim lowered his voice, "it's only that I'm awful glad to see you." There was no response. Slim turned toward the shack and called, "Corks, come on out here, we got company!"

When he arrived, the Eskimos transferred their stares to Corks for a moment, then back to Slim. They seemed fascinated by this big, smiling man.

"Where'd you come from?" Slim asked them. "Where's your village? We looked all over for you, and we couldn't find you."

The Eskimos continued to stare. Slim and Corks tried every form of language and sound they knew. They made motions, gestures, and not a glimmer of response did they get.

"Maybe if we give them something," Slim suggested to Corks, "then they'll get the idea." He looked at each one of them. "I wonder which one's the head man? They're all dressed alike, same kind of skin parky an' mukluks. Cute little fellows, ain't they?"

The Eskimos seemed to enjoy listening to Slim talk. His voice was big, and full, and rumbled deep. It probably sounded like a sort of melody to them.

"Look at that little fellow on the end," Slim pointed out. "Seems like one leg's shorter'n the other, lame kinda when he walks. You see him?"

Corks nodded.

"Funny, ain't it," Slim went on, "to be talkin' about people like this, an' they can't understand what you're saying about 'em?" As he talked he went to the boat and brought back some tea and passed it to the men. Corks singled out the little lame man and gave him a plug of tobacco. "Sorta extra," he explained to Slim.

"Now let's go back in the shack and see if they'll go, then we'll see what happens next," Slim suggested. After a few minutes' wait, they came out again. The Eskimos were no longer there.

"Where do you suppose they come from?" Slim asked. "We didn't see a village or smoke, or anything."

Corks shook his head. "Poor little guy with the bum leg."

The next day the Eskimos were back again. They brought armloads of fur, and pieces of ivory and put them on the ground and backed up a few paces and stared at Slim and Corks.

"They caught on fast, didn't they?" said Slim.

"All but the little fellow, Slim, the one with the bad leg. You notice he didn't bring anything," said Corks.

"Maybe he hasn't got anything to give."

Again they gave the Eskimos more trade goods, the little lame man included.

Later that same day the lame man came back. He brought

a young girl with him. She was dressed in her undoubted best, fur-trimmed parka and decorated walrus-hide boots.

Slim looked at the pair and said softly to his partner, "Look at that, Corks, the little fellow brought the only thing he has, must be his daughter. Couldn't be over thirteen, fourteen years old, and ain't she a purty little thing."

The little Eskimo girl's moon-shaped face shone with delight at being noticed. Her father, as apparently he was, looked from Slim to Corks and back again.

"Tryin' to make up his mind," said Slim. "You're the one who gave him the tobacco, so he'll probably give her to you."

"I don't want nothin' to do with no women!" Corks was vehement.

Slim shook his head. "I guess you don't know Indians and Eskimos, Corks. This ain't no casual affair with that fellow. These girls don't go in for flirtations. If he gives you the girl, he's givin' her to you for keeps. This is a marriage he's figurin' on."

"But I ain't goin to marry no fourteen-year-old Siberian Eskimo girl I can't even talk to." Corks was getting excited. "I ain't plannin' to get married."

"Purty little thing, ain't she," Slim continued his teasing, "look at how her eyes shine, an' the way she's smilin'. I bet she's happy her poppa picked out a nice husband like you for her."

Just then the Eskimo limped toward Corks with the girl before him. She needed no urging, and looked anxiously up into Corks' face, obviously willing to place herself and her future in his keeping. Corks took hold of her shoulders, turned her around, and pushed her gently back toward her father. This went on for four or five exchanges, the little girl giggling her enjoyment, the father undisturbed and insistent. Corks was becoming worried. "What'll I do, Slim? I don't want her."

"Go in the shack, Corks," he said, coming to the rescue, "and I'll see what I can do. I don't want to hurt her poppa's feelin's."

When Corks was out of sight, Slim very gently put the little girl's hand in her father's and without hurry, urged them both away from the camp.

The next day the lame man came back, alone, and brought the tobacco and tea he had been given. A little of the tobacco plug had been cut away, some of the tea had been used. He set them down before Corks and walked dejectedly away.

"Almost a little bit sad, ain't it, Corks?" said Slim seriously. "He didn't have no furs and no ivory to give you for the tobacco and the tea, so he tried to give you the only thing he had, his girl, and you didn't want her, so it wouldn't be honest for him to keep the things you give him if he couldn't pay you for them. An' she was a purty little thing, all dressed up in the best she had."

After that the trading with the Eskimos was brisk, all excepting the little lame man. Both Slim and Corks tried to give him presents, but he would either not accept them, or, if he did take them, he would immediately give them to someone else.

Their store of furs, sable and white fox, and ivory grew. They were also welcome visitors at the Eskimos' village about ten miles down the shore in another inlet. The village contained about forty men. Slim never got a full count of the women, who kept out of sight. Like those of the Alaskan Eskimos, the igloos were of driftwood and mud. Their boats were also the same, walrus hide over whalebone and driftwood frames. But what interested Slim most were the dogs. These were the true Siberians, about sixty pounds, small for heavy sled work, friendly and brightly blue-eyed.

It wasn't too long before Slim and Corks found themselves almost without trade goods. "You know," Slim suggested one morning, "maybe we better go back to Alaska with our fur and ivory and get ourselves a bigger boat and more trade goods and come back and go into real tradin' business. We've done all this with just one village, and there must be more Eskimos in Siberia. Maybe those fellows you heard talkin' were right, an' we got our million made. And you know something funny, Corks?" he concluded, "we did all this trading without anybody saying a word."

So it was decided to go back to Alaska, re-outfit and return for business on a larger scale.

This was the inopportune time for the arrival in the cove of a potbellied little steamboat carrying about fifteen Russians, armed with rifles.

"Who are them fellows?" Corks asked his partner.

"Russian traders, likely," said Slim, watching as the boat slid onto the mud and the men jumped ashore. "These fellows trade with their Eskimos here like we do with ours over on our side, and they either learned somehow that we were here, or it's just our hard luck they come in here."

"What d' you s'pose they'll do?" said Corks.

There was no doubt what the Russians had in mind. They set methodically to work transferring the bales of fur from Slim's and Cork's boat to their own. The Russians shouted, shook their fists, and brandished rifles, but that did not stop them from being fast and thorough. Slim and Corks could do nothing but stand and watch the sorry end of their project. A few Eskimos also stood off watching in emotionless silence.

Slim and Corks watched until the Russian boat had puffed out of the cove. Corks turned to his partner. "Now what do we do?"

"We don't do nothin' except to be mighty glad they didn't get an idea it'd be fun to pop at us with their guns. We're not on United States land now, Corks, we're on Russian land, and them fellows know how to use them guns."

"Anyway," said Corks, "they left us our boat."

Slim pointed. The Russian boat was chuffing back into the inlet. The crew went silently to work. In a few moments they steamed once more out of sight, this time towing Slim and Cork's boat, leaving only the little dinghy. The Russians probably thought this tiny five-foot rowboat would give them little comfort.

"Now what do we do, Slim?" said Corks.

Slim, still staring at the point around which their boat had gone out of sight, shook his head. He walked slowly to the shack, entered it, and in a moment rejoined Corks at the shore. "We were all packed and loaded and ready to leave, and now all we got is this dinghy and our .22 rifle, no food, no fur, no nothin'." He sat down on the end of a cottonwood log. "You know, Corks, seems lately like I'm always sittin' on some driftwood somewhere, broke, and no place to go. Only difference this time is I got no way to get where I ain't goin'. Looks like we're really blowed-up suckers this time. But maybe the One that keeps lookin' after crazy people like us will take a hand somehow. Anyway, I still got my rabbit robe in the shack."

"Wonder if we'll ever get home," Corks said quietly after a while.

"I don't know," said Slim, "but I ain't goin' to worry about it, and I ain't scared. Like an old Indian once told me, 'My poppa say, you worry, bad come; you no worry, it go 'way; my poppa say, worry no good.' I guess I'm like an Indian that way, Corks, I just don't get scared until after what I'm supposed to be scared of is all over. Then it's too late."

The two friends sat side by side on the log, each occupied with his own sorry version of what could well be a most serious situation.

Some time later they heard sounds behind them. Some of the Eskimos had come, probably, Slim thought, to sympathize. Instead he was surprised to see them with meat, and tea, and tobacco, and a pan to cook in. These people did all they could to prove their friendship, and to show their displeasure over the treatment passed out by the Russian traders.

By sign and action these Eskimos showed Slim that they would make a further trade. They would give one of their seaworthy walrus-hide fishing boats in exchange for the dinghy and the .22 rifle and shells. They did this by showing great affection for the dinghy, touching it, and handling and laughing over the small oars. They pantomimed a successful hunt with a pretended rifle. Finally they brought one of their hide boats, a splendid example of their craft, about fifteen feet long with a five-foot beam. In it was enough food and fresh water for the crossing. The partners greatfully made the trade. As a final gesture of good will, the Eskimos collected three or four hundred pounds of rock which they loaded in the boat for ballast. Then began the long paddle eastward. The little crowd of their friends stood immobile on the shore as long as the canoe was in sight.

"I'm sure goin' to miss them," Slim said. "I never see nicer people."

"Sure were friendly," Corks agreed. "You know, Slim," he added after a long pause, "I feel sort o' sorry for that little fellow with the bad leg."

Slim agreed. "Anyway, Corks," he said, "you almost got yourself a wife," and then he softly mused, "She sure was a purty little thing—just a kid, all dressed up playin' she was a bride."

The One-who-looks-after-crazy-people-like-Slim must have smiled benignly, for the water of the treacherous Bering Strait rolled smoothly in long, easy, steely gray swells. When darkness settled tight about them, Slim put his paddle in the boat. "We stop paddlin' now," he told Corks. "With no wind like it is, we won't drift out of sight of land by the time light comes. If we go paddlin', we'll pull around in circles and end up anywhere."

They slept for a while, and took up their paddles at the first sign of dawn. The shadowy substance of the Alaska shore line in the east gave strength to tired muscles. Several days later it was an exhausted pair who skidded their boat onto the sand beach at Nome.

Slim's first contact with foreign trade had been a very costly one, except in experience, and in this he was building a very rich store.

·7·

There's a land where the mountains are nameless,
And the rivers all run God knows where;
There are lives that are erring and aimless,
And deaths that just hang by a hair.

After his foreign invasion Slim felt the urge to go back east and trap and possibly explore for a while. Corks decided to stay in Nome and take his chances there.

Slim, as usual, chopped his way into a grubstake. He borrowed an axe, then with it he paid for it, and day after day added to his store until by the time the Yukon trail was frozen, he was ready and willing to take a load to Fairbanks. He had bought five good dogs.

In Fairbanks he hired out for a haul to Fortymile, a former gold boom town, on the Yukon River just across the Canadian boundary in the Yukon Territory. This had been one of the great gold towns of the early nineties. It was the westernmost outpost of the mounted police and Canadian law until the take from the diggings dwindled and the fabulous '96 strike on Bonanza Creek pulled prospectors from as far away as Texas, and Dawson became the gold headquarters of the world. And now, in the late fall of 1905, the Klondike region was still producing into the millions of dollars in gold, and Dawson was at full boom.

When Slim arrived in Fortymile, he heard that a big dance was to be held the next night in Dawson. Some of the

Fortymile sourdoughs were even taking their wives to the party, so it must be a good one, Slim thought. Slim's feet itched. He hadn't danced since before he and Corks had left for Siberia. He had just finished nearly a thousand miles of trail, but the added forty-seven miles of Yukon trail to Dawson at forty below couldn't even cool his dancing ardor. He was on the trail at daybreak. His dogs had had little rest, but then he had had no more, so he drove himself hard as well as his dogs. He didn't want to miss the first dance.

Moonlight silvered the town when he braked his sled to a snow-swirling stop by the log shack where the dance was just starting. The music, a piano and fiddle, was testing a rhythm or two, and the burly rumble of the men's voices was a background for the excited high pitched laughter of the women. Slim was anxious to join them, but first he took care of his dogs, staking them a safe distance from other teams, so volatile dispositions would not start a fight. He fed them extra rations. They were contentedly crunching the fish as he started for the party.

The shack about thirty by forty feet and was cleared of everything except a rim of benches along the walls. It was comfortably crowded, yet couples had a chance for a whirly dance, if they liked, without too many collisions.

As Slim reached the door, he stopped, shocked. Everybody was dressed up, not in trail outfits or fur-trimmed clothes of the North, but in city clothes; and the men and women alike wore masks. The dance was a masquerade!

For a moment he almost turned and fled into the darkness, but just then the music started, laughter rose, and the wafted smell of perfume overcame his embarrassment, and he went in. There to his happy surprise were a few others who, like himself, had also been ignorant of the masquerade, or had come in their regular dress in spite of it. Such a one was a very pretty figure of a girl, dressed in a blue dress. She was unmasked, and stood quietly apart, as if she too were a stranger. She had fair skin and large luminous eyes. In Slim's imagination she became the transfiguration of his lovely Linda. He hurried, lest someone should reach her first, and asked her to dance. She demurely bowed her head and closed her eyes. She raised her arms toward him and he folded her supple body to him. She felt as light as a feather, and looked as pretty **as a doll.**

"I'm sorry, miss," he leaned his head down to mumble a self-conscious apology, "I didn't know it was a dress-up-special dance, an' if I did know it, I couldn't of done it because these trail clothes is all I got. I just come off the trail from Nome to Fairbanks to Fortymile, and I heard about this dance yesterday and come on today just for it. My name's Williams, Slim Williams."

She looked up at him and smiled. She didn't answer, but gave herself fully to the dance. When the round was over, she made no effort or excuse to leave Slim's eager company. He talked and talked, and she coyly smiled approval and encouragement of the tales of his adventures.

Dance followed delightful dance. The weeks of endless miles on frozen trails had no effect upon his effortless dancing. He held his partner in a sort of delirium. He pressed the small hand and was certain he felt the answering pressure in reply. The slight body he held was close and warm against him. Her cheek was on his chest, and the smell of her hair stirred in him new strange thoughts.

The dance ended at dawn. No amount of applause, shouts, or offers of money could wangle another note from the exhausted musicians. It was time to break up, and time for the masqueraders to unmask. Suddenly there was quiet. Slim looked around and found that the dancers had all left the floor except his partner and himself. They stood expectantly along the wall, staring at the lone pair in the center of the floor. He flustered a moment, then offered his arm, and said, "I . . . I guess that's goin' to be all, and we better go, so I'll walk you home. And you still ain't told me your name."

His partner looked up at him from eyes that sparkled and

smiled a broad, friendly smile. "You're a great guy, Slim," said a sturdy, solid bass and thoroughly masculine voice. Slim watched in amazement as off came the delicately scented hair, a wig, showing underneath the well-trimmed poll of a good-looking young man. "And sure I'll tell you my name," and he put out his hand, which Slim took and now felt the pressure of a man's grip. "I work over at the bank here in Dawson. My name's Service, Robert W. Service."

Slim, standing tall in his moccasins, looked around the room. Some of the people smiled, a few laughed, others waited to see how this young Alaskan giant would react.

He'd been made a fool of! At first his embarrassment was a flame of fighting rage, rushing to his head. He balled his fists and looked at the men for the first sign of ridicule which would have certainly started a fight that would have rocked the North.

"It was all in fun, Slim, take it easy. After all it *was* a masquerade." Young Service's voice brought a rational thought that cooled Slim off a bit. He looked again at the smiling young fellow beside him, and the others around the walls. "What did I come for?" he thought. "I come to dance. I didn't come to see a girl or to fall in love." And he had danced, and enjoyed it, and quite suddenly there was nothing to fight about, so the low rumble of anger that had started in his throat softened and ended in an explosive laugh. He shook Service's hand with sincere warmth. "You're all right," he said, "a dance is a dance and I had the fun I come for."

"Stop in any time, Slim, and we'll crack a crock or tip a pot, whatever you say. Anyway, you're a good sport, and I hope you had as much fun tonight as I did. I'm sorry, though," Service apologized "that I had to lean all over you most of the time, and hang on the way I did. It was hard standing up, and my feet were hurting from these shoes! I'll be seeing you again, Slim."

So the dance was over. Slim stayed in Dawson for a few days for a rest. Before he left he was laughing with the others at himself. It was this wonderful warmth of his nature that caused Slim to make friends along every trail he traveled, and to keep them.

There was another fellow around Dawson he got to know, a brawny young bruiser named Jack London. He wrote stories about the gold camps and their characters and sent the pieces to newspapers back in the States. "You know, Slim," he said, "you're a crazy galoot, and you're the greatest dog musher I know. No trail is too long or too tough for you, and I've never seen a man burn daylight the way you do. I'm going to write a book about you some day."

It was true that he usually performed the almost impossible, and regularly the improbable, with his team of dogs.

Rest and idleness never fitted into Slim's scheme of things. With him there was always something to be done, and an immediate need for doing it. Since he had come east from Nome to trap it was obvious that he was wasting time in Dawson. To pay his way back, he picked up a load of freight and took the westward trail through Fairbanks. He was headed for the Wrangell Mountains and the Chitina River Valley. Stopping in Fairbanks to buy more supplies, he ran into a young friend of his called "Swede" who temporarily changed his plans.

Swede grabbed him. "You yoost d' feller I lookin' for," he enthused. "Ay got good shance to make some qvick money, Sleem, an' it take d' two of us yoost two, t'ree days. Dese fallers diggin' gold in vinter-time ain't got time to hunt, an' dey pay good money for meat. And you good shot, and ve two ve go get mooses and make good money qvick. Vot you say?"

Slim shut one eye and squinted at Swede with the other. As if to air a decision, he rubbed the back of his neck. He figured that a few more days' or even a week's delay in starting for his trapping grounds wouldn't make too much difference, and besides a little extra backlog of cash would come in handy on a deal of his own he had in mind. He'd worked with Swede before and knew he was a good man. He nodded.

"Good!" said Swede, "ve take bote dog teams and ve bring back maybe a t'ousand pounds moose's meat. Dese fallers diggin' good gold, pay a dollar in gold for pound o' meat."

"So we ought to make about five hundred apiece," said Slim. "I could use it all right, Swede. Let's go make ourselves a stake."

Swede had his own ideas about where to hunt, and led the way, breaking trail on snowshoes for the dogs. Once he stopped and called back to Slim, "Ve go out of our vay yoost a leetle bit, about ten, fifteen mile maybe. Ay got friend name Yorgensen who trapping dis vay. Ve yoost stop and say 'hallo.' Dis Yorgy, he ban purty good faller."

Jorgensen, like most Scandinavians in the North, had found it easier, and far more comfortable living, to put up a log shack than to camp in the lee of a canvas windbreak or in a tent. It was no surprise to Slim, therefore, to find a fine, snug cabin, well located near the shore of a tumbling cataract, white water so fast it didn't freeze. They stayed an hour or so, had a good visit and plenty of hot coffee. During a break in the constant flow of Swedish Slim commented, "You can just about nearly always tell you Swedes by the smell of what you're cookin'. If it's coffee, it's Swedes; if it's tea, it ain't."

Jorgensen was a husky, rawboned, towhead nearly Slim's age. He brought out and showed some of the fine fur he had trapped. Slim commented on the perfection of the skinning and care of the pelts, and decided that Jorgensen was a pretty smart trapper, and a fellow well worth knowing.

"I been trappin' since I was a kid," said Slim, examining a near-perfect prime silver fox. "I learned my trappin' from Indians down in the States, but I never seen as good a job of skinnin' and stretchin' as this. This is worth five hundred dollars anyway. You know, a fellow can trap all his life an' still not know all they is to know about it. I guess maybe it's because you never know what a marten, or a mink, or a fox is thinkin' about, or what he's goin' to do next."

Before Slim and Swede left, Jorgensen made them promise to stop on their way out.

Hunting was poor. There was lots of wind, snow was heavy, and temperatures low. From the signs no game was moving. They hunted far and long. They worked up a river course which showed no tracks, then left it again for the higher timbered ridges. They had been out several days when Slim called a halt.

"We'll make us a camp here, Swede," he said.

As they worked, caring for the dogs, putting up their windbreaks, and setting a fire, Slim explained, "It's no use in walkin' these dogs all over Alaska while we're lookin' for game. One thing I learned a long time ago from the Indians down in the States when I was a kid was about huntin.' They used to say, 'You no find game, game find you.' An' they got it about right. Pit' near every time you can't find game, you stay still long enough, game'll find you. We ain't huntin' now, we're just gettin' tired."

They stayed in camp for two days. About noon the third day Slim looked up sharply when he heard noise back in the bush. He reached for his rifle, and slowly lowered it when a man came out of the underbrush into their camp clearing. He was a little fellow, not more than five foot, six or seven inches. He had no dogs, and was carrying a light pack on his back to which were tied a few scraggly pelts. He was trail weary and his eyes were stary. After he had gratefully absorbed the good hot feed Slim set out for him, he said, "I'm sure glad I stumbled across your trail. I been trappin' about twenty miles over the ridge, and I decided I wasn't doin' no good, I only got a few skins, and I quit and started to go out, and I been lost for a couple o' days till I run across your trail out there."

"Well, you ain't lost now," Slim assured him, "and you can camp here with us if you want."

"No, thanks," the man insisted. "Only thing I want is to get out o' this freezin', lonesome country. I'm goin' home."

"He could follow our trail back, Sleem," Swede suggested, "ve leave good trail."

"I ain't goin' to stay here no longer'n I have to, an' I'm much obliged to you for helpin' me. I'll get out o' this country if it's my last act, believe me!"

Slim saw to it that the stranger had food and things he'd need and started him on their back trail. "When you get to the river, keep on followin' our trail downstream."

Slim watched the stranger out of sight, and said softly to himself, "Poor fella, he's broke up, and he's scared."

Slim's judgment about hunting was sound. The following day Swede saw a big bull. It was a long shot, and he saw the animal fall.

"Ay, golly, Sleem, I got vun!" he shouted, and started on snowshoes toward the wounded moose.

Slim was close behind with a dog team. They butchered and took the hide and about eight hundred pounds of meat back to camp.

The next morning Slim awoke to hear Swede yelling for him in English and swearing in Swedish. "Sleem!" he shouted, "Get me out!"

Slim climbed out of his bedroll and hurried to where Swede had bedded down on the other side of the fire. One look at his partner and he started to laugh.

"Ay tal you, you damfool, you stop dat laffing an' get me d'hal out o' here before I die!"

Slim was still laughing hard as he cut his friend from a cocoon of frozen moose hide. "How in the name o' all that's unholy did you get yourself into it?" he asked. "You ain't got a lick o' sense."

"In de night ay get cold. I vake op an' look around what I can find to keep varm. Here d' moose's skin. It all soft and varm an' ay yoost roll op in it an' ay go to sleep."

"An' you'd be sleepin' in it till kingdom come if I wasn't here to chop you out. Sure that fresh skin was soft and warm, it was a wet skin an' hadn't froze yet. An' after you rolled up in it, and it froze, that moose hide'd hold you like you was rolled up in steel. Don't never wrap yourself up in a soft, wet hide. In summer you cook. In winter you'll freeze to death." He began to laugh again.

"Ay tal you, it ain't so funny inside dat t'ing ven you can't move. Ay von't do dat again in a long time, ay bet you my life."

Two more days resulted in another moose, about the same size. This was about all the meat they could transport, so they loaded their sleds and started for town.

The trail was a mean one. Wind and more snow had almost filled it, and it called for snowshoe trail breaking for the dogs to follow. They could see where the stranger had found the way to the river. But when they reached its open stretches, they saw the diagram of tragedy.

Their old trail had been filled and blown over, but there were new trails that told a story of frustration, fear, and panic. Slim put them into words.

"The poor fella," he said sadly, "he didn't know which way was upstream, or down. See, Swede? See what he did? Our trail through the bush was good enough so's he could follow it. But the wind and fresh snow wiped out our trail on the river, so's when he got here he didn't know which way to go. Then he did what all cheechakos do. He got scared and started to run. See where he ran up that way? And he stopped and ran the other way. He ran until he got tired. The trails don't go anywhere, Swede. Except that last one he made. That's when he got tired and laid down for a rest. You stay here with the dogs, Swede, I'll go find him."

Slim followed the short loops of the frenzied trails until he found the body. It lay face down, arms out, as the man had fallen from exhaustion. Slim looked down. "Poor fella," he said, "he finally got home. He was just too scared to live."

They agreed, since Swede had the lighter sled and could make better time with a lighter load, that he take the dead man's body and only what meat he could, and go straight to town. Slim, with his larger sled and stronger dogs, would take the greater weight of meat and go the long way past Jorgensen's as they had promised.

It was cold, at least thirty below. Slim broke trail every step of the way for the dogs. They leaned into their collars, heads down, and strained with all their strength to pull the heavy load over the soft packless snow.

At the end of the third day the cabin was in sight. When Slim reached it, he tied and fed his dogs, and then looked closer to see what was wrong. The cabin didn't look right. Bucket after bucket of water had been carried from the stream and thrown on the cabin until it was almost covered with ice, yet smoke was coming out of the smoke pipe. Slim yelled to make his presence known. He knocked on the door. Finally he lifted the latch and went in.

The cabin was neat and tidy, a good fire was in the stove, and Jorgensen lay fully dressed on his bunk. A candle burned at the head of the bunk, and another at the foot. He didn't look up, nor pay any attention to Slim, but kept frantically thumbing the pages of a magazine he held in his hands, eight and ten pages at a time. When he reached the end, he turned the magazine over and went through it again as fast as he could. Slim walked over and spoke to him, but Jorgensen didn't look up nor speak. Slim knew what had happened. The solitude of the North had claimed another victim. Jorgensen had lost his mind. Slim cooked and ate his supper, and even with food could get no interest from the trapper.

Slim was tired, but it was impossible to travel at night; so there was no alternative, he would have to stay where he was. But before he decided to spend the night in the cabin, he looked around for Jorgensen's gun. He had no wish to sleep in a cabin with a crazy man in possession of a gun. No rifle was in sight. There were no wall pegs, nor was it standing in a corner. Slim couldn't believe that Jorgensen had no rifle, but at least it was sufficient assurance that he couldn't find one. He didn't welcome the prospect of building a fire and making a camp outside, so he got his bedroll and brought it in and unrolled it on the floor across the room from Jorgensen's bunk. All this time Jorgensen continued to turn the pages of the magazine as fast as he could flip them.

When Slim was about ready to slip into his sleeping bag, Jorgensen put the magazine aside, turned and blew out the candle at the head of the bunk. Then he reached down between the bunk and the cabin wall and pulled out a brand new .30-30 rifle. Slim was stunned for a second and watched mesmerized as Jorgensen raised the rifle, aimed it, and pulled the trigger. The tiny cabin was filled with the roar of the shot, and it was suddenly dark. Jorgensen had shot out the candle at the foot of the bed.

Slim hit the floor and rolled. When he stopped, he was right against the door. The faint eerie bluish glow coming through the window and the rosy flickering from the stove's draft door gave light enough to show a moving shadow. Slim had no intention of becoming a moving shadow for Jorgensen to shoot at. The last thing he wanted to do was to startle Jorgensen, for there was no telling what the man with the gun might do. Slim stayed where he was, as quiet as possible. He heard Jorgensen putting the rifle back in its hiding place beside the bunk, but that was no proof he would leave it there. From then on Slim concentrated on keeping quiet. He knew that his life might depend upon his ability to stay awake. He shook his head, and bit his lips. Finally, when he could hardly hold his eyes open, he heard Jorgensen's breathing settle into the smooth, deep, even pattern of sleep.

Inch by cautious inch Slim slid along the floor toward the bunk. He reached beside the bunk and felt the barrel of the gun, and ever so carefully pulled it from its hiding place. With it he crawled silently back to where his sleeping bag lay across the room. Jorgensen's breathing continued to be that of untroubled sleep.

Slim put the gun into the sleeping bag, and muffled the metallic clip-chunk as he pumped the shells out and unloaded it. Then he crawled into the bag beside the gun and went to sleep.

He was awake at daybreak, and was relieved to hear that Jorgensen was still asleep. He quickly rolled his sleeping bag with the rifle inside, and put it by the door. Then he went about getting breakfast. Jorgensen awoke, but there was no resumption of the magazine-page-turning episode of the night before. He looked once at Slim, then turned his face toward the wall. Slim talked to him, offered him breakfast and coffee, but there was no response.

Before he left he saw that the fire was fixed, plenty of wood in the box, fresh water in the pails, and all the man's needs cared for. He fixed the pillow under the man's head, covered him with his blanket, and stood for a moment looking down at him, his thoughtful eyes troubled and sad. "Poor fella," he said softly. He shrugged into his parka and soon, head down into the wind, he was again on the trail.

Slim's first stop on reaching town was the sheriff's office. He reported what he had found and turned in Jorgensen's rifle. Then he looked up Swede, and told him about his friend Jorgensen.

Swede shook his head. "Ay golly, it's too bad. Yorgy vas good friend an' good man. But ven d'Nort' get a man—like dat leetle feller ve find froze dere on d'creek—ven somet'ing goes wrong up here," he tapped his forehead with a finger, "is not'ing ve can do. Ay vant to t'ank you too, Sleem, for take care o' him. Yorgy vas good friend." Swede sighed deeply, shook his head again, then as though dismissing the incident, said brightly, "Now ve better gat beesy vit gettin' rid o' dis meat."

The sale of the meat resulted in the division of nearly $1,500. Swede was all in favor of going back for more, but Slim could not be enthused.

"No, Swede," he said, "I got some ideas about somethin' I want to do. You'll find yourself another partner. I'm goin' trappin' on my own, and work out somethin' I got in mind."

They brought Jorgensen out, and so far as anyone knows, the visit Slim and Swede had with him that day in his cabin were the last words he ever said. He was sent outside, back to the States, where he spent the rest of his life in an institution for the insane. No one knew who the stranger was who had died on the river trail.

Slim revised his outfit and went on with his plans to trap the Chitina Valley. Going south from Fairbanks he hit weather. There were blistering blizzards and night temperatures that broke to sixty and seventy below. There were days when five miles were counted as headway. There were nights when he wondered how man could endure. But he kept on.

Late one day, fumbling sightless in a blizzard, he mercifully came across a log-canvas shack some prospector had abandoned. An eight-by-ten base of logs built up about three feet supported a canvas tent topping with three-foot walls. Inside was a stove and some wood. His dogs bedded down in the snow with their noses in their tails and went blissfully to sleep.

Slim had hoped this makeshift would present protection for him, but the wind whistled between the logs where chinking had long since been blown away. A sleeping bag on the floor would be like bedding down in the middle of a gale. The only protection was the windproof canvas. Slim first fed the stove to a red glow. It did not push the cold back through the logs, but it did fill the canvas topping with heat, like a balloon. The prospector had built a framework above the stove, probably for drying sweat-soaked socks and underwear. It was only a small rack, about three by five, but it was strong and sturdy enough to hold his weight. Slim spent the night alternately stuffing wood into the stove and climbing onto the drying rack to absorb as much of the heat as he could. He had never suffered more nor considered himself luckier than he did that night.

Dawn saw the death of the storm. Slim hurt. His chest hurt, his throat burned, and when he tried to mush his dogs the only sound was a raspy croak. He tried again, but his voice was completely gone. He set out on snowshoes and the dogs followed.

He made the Chitina Valley. About a day's trip up the Chitina River from the Copper River he selected a spot where he decided to establish a permanent camp. He cleared a space and built himself a cabin. He set out his traps and did well with his fur. But, for the balance of the winter his chest hurt, his throat never stopped burning. It wasn't sore or raw, it just hurt. Gradually a voice returned. It took on the peculiar quality of bass tones being dragged slowly over coarse, rough gravel. He took his fur out to trade in Copper Center just before breakup, and found a doctor in the settlement. He wasn't really a doctor, he was a veterinarian, but he had served once in a hospital, and he was all that Slim could find. He examined Slim, and put him off for a couple of days before making his diagnosis and offering advice.

"Slim," he said very seriously, he was gruff but not an unkindly person, "you frosted your lungs. Now when a dog freezes his lungs, he dies right away. When a horse freezes his lungs, he dies next spring. I don't know when you're going to die, Slim, but if you've got any near relatives, I'd suggest you go see 'em and spend as much time with 'em as you can."

Slim walked slowly down to the river bank where he'd made his camp. He had just been told he was going to die. Dying was something that had never occurred to him, not as applying to himself. He had seen death many times, but always it was a detached and impersonal thing. Now the bony finger had touched him and he didn't like the way it felt.

When he reached his camp he sat and leaned against a tree and looked toward the Wrangell Mountains. He reached out and laid a hand on the head of his big leader.

The dog turned his huge head and leveled a blue-eyed stare directly at Slim's friendly smile. The dog's tail thumped, then the head went down across Slim's lap.

"Them mountains sure is purty," Slim mused, then he sighed.

· 8 ·

There's nothing gained by whining, and
you're not that kind of stuff;
You're a fighter from away back, and you
won't take a rebuff.

The doctor had drawn an indistinct but nevertheless recognizable picture of death. Slim held it before him and didn't at all like what he saw. He stroked the dog's head that lay across his lap. "You know, Blizzard," he said, "I ain't ready to die."

Slim spoke aloud in the general habit of men of the North who live alone. He talked to his dogs, his canoe, animals, to trees, the sky, the weather, even to himself. These bits of monologue were generally philosophical, always introspective. Although men of the bush were recklessly personal in this type of conversation, they rarely talked about themselves, their past, or their deeds, with other humans. Those babblers who did talk were pop-off braggarts with little other than their voices to back them up; the failures moaned over their discouragements; and the out-and-out liars spoke of things they'd never done and lived their vicarious glory by filling gaps in the barrroom talk. But the men of Alaska who blazed its trails and wrote its history in hardships and hunger were the silent men of the silent North.

In these little private visits, Slim was sure of a receptive audience with rarely a contradiction. The exception was when he addressed himself; then he was in for some active argument. But Blizzard was always understanding and sympathetic.

"Maybe I am goin' to die like the doc said," he went on, "but I got just a whole lot o' things I want to do and places I want to see in Alaska before I do. Besides, a fellow's got to die inside, in his mind, before they can put him away, and I'm not goin' to waste any time thinkin' about it. Maybe that fellow knows about horses an' dogs an' things, but he could be wrong. I'm feelin' all right."

For a long time Slim had played around with some theories of his own about dogs. He had driven practically every strain and breed in the North, and he had dreams of a perfect sled dog. His knowledge of dogs had come solely from his own experience with them, and from his keen observation and his natural understanding of them. It was his ambition at some time to own and drive the finest team of dogs in Alaska. Several times he thought he had, only to learn later that other teams, more powerful and better bred, had bested his claims for speed and endurance.

When he was in Dawson, he studied the different teams of Canadian dogs. Most of them were larger dogs than his, and he remarked about this to one of the drivers. "Everywhere I go dogs seem to be different," he had said. "Same strain of dog, all look pretty much alike, but some are li'l bitty fellows, like in Siberia and Arctic Alaska, with blue eyes. Eskimos all drive those little fellows, about fifty-pound dogs. Southeastern Alaska the Indians have rangier dogs, smaller feet, shoulders not so big, but heavier, go maybe ninety pounds. And here in the Yukon you got the Mackenzie Husky, same strain o' dogs, but big. Your dogs must weight 110, 115 pounds apiece. Big brown-eyed fellows. Now why do you suppose the same dog will be different like that?"

"May be d' dog she grow like d' kind o' country, no?" the driver said. "T'ousand years dese dogs be here—dey be like country, beeg. O'er een h'Alaska maybe not so beeg. *Je ne sais pas.* H'all I know ees dey bes' dam' dogs in d' whole worl'."

Slim talked to other men who had learned what they knew the same as he had. Some of the dog owners talked about crossbreeding with other strains, collies and such, to produce individual characteristics of size and strength. He listened and observed, until little by little he formed a theory of his own about dogs that he now decided to try. He knew nothing at all of the science of genetics, had never even heard the word, but a practical sense told him that what he had in mind was reasonable and would succeed in producing a dog of greater pound-for-pound power, stamina, courage, and speed than the North had ever seen.

The dogs in his present team were five-year-olds, almost too old for what he planned, so he hunted up dog owners who were in from their trapping grounds. Finally he found just what he wanted, five beautiful puppies, about three months old. The owner made no bones about his feelings.

"You're crazy, Slim, buyin' young pups in the spring to feed all summer an' even then they won't be big enough to do heavy haulin' next winter. What d' you want 'em for?"

"I just like dogs," said Slim, "an' these are cute little fellows, and if you don't want to feed 'em, I'll take 'em off your hands."

The dicker was as short as the price, and Slim led the playful youngsters back to where his big team was tied. Blizzard examined each pup with calculated sniffs, passed quick judgment, and dropped his head on his paws.

"So they're all right, are they?" Slim asked. "I want you to take a hand in trainin' 'em, cause I figure it's goin' to take about three years at least for me to work out my plan. So, since spring's comin' on, let's us go visitin'."

Slim's "plan" was still nebulous, but he reasoned that over a period of years by crossbreeding wolves and dogs, he could produce a superlative sled dog exhibiting the best characteristics of each parent line. He had taken the first step in the process.

Slim's friends were milestones of welcome along every trail

he traveled. Indians, Eskimos, whites. They were much the same to him, they were people, and they were friends.

Ice was still on the Chitina when he started upstream from his camp. The weather was mild. The warmth of the sun penetrated air that was just above zero, and Slim let the dogs have their way. Spring was in the air. The little dogs took turns running along behind and riding on the sled when they got tired. Three days and a hundred miles east Slim geed his dogs to a stop at a village of about thirty Indians.

Slim knew these Indians and had befriended them many times, helping them out with gifts of meat. He was heartily welcomed until he spoke. It took his some time to convince them that no evil spirit had stolen his voice. Then he set up his tent.

Like all small bands, this little group would live and die within the limits of their valley. They would know nothing of the outside world except as that world was brought to them. They had contact with white traders for their fur, perhaps once or twice a year. Some of them even spoke English. Slim had already learned that in these small Indian settlements members of villages from another valley as close as fifty miles could not understand the dialect of their neighbors. In his travels Slim had managed to pick up a few words, but he generally relied upon signs and felt fortunate when he came across English-speakers.

Like all Indians and Eskimos these were strongly super-stitious. Living as they did in the shadow of Mt. Wrangell, a live volcano, they had great awe and reverence for this moun-tain which they believed gave forth spiritual smoke. They were continually waiting for a 'sign.'

Their old chief, Hanagita, had died. There had been a great funeral potlatch and ceremony, then his spirit had gone to the Smoking Mountain to become very wise. Until he should return as a bird or an animal or give some sign or portent, no member of his band could speak his name. The sign might come when, by reason known only to herself, some squaw should decide that her new baby was the chosen one. Then there would be great rejoicing and another Hanagita would replace the old one in their respect. But until then, even though the valley in which they lived bore his name, it could not be voiced under penalty of some fantastic punishment based upon their superstition.

One day, sitting in front of his tent, Slim was watching a great white wild goat feeding down a mountain trail across the valley. A young Indian came quietly up to him, pointed and whispered, "Don't shoot goat." Soon another Indian came with the same warning. Each one had hurried back to his hut after delivering the warning. These two men had been very sick when Slim arrived and apparently were expected to die. But they showed themselves when this goat appeared on the mountain trail.

In a short while the two men came out of their huts again, this time dressed in their best leather, carrying neither gun nor knife. Slim asked where they were going.

"Go see goat," they answered, and trotted off along the valley trail toward the mountain.

Slim watched the goat. It browsed unconcerned, and finally sauntered off up and over a ridge. He didn't even catch a glimpse of the two Indians, but after about an hour they came trotting back. Slim called them over. "Did you talk with goat?" he asked.

The men nodded.

"What did goat say?" he asked one of them.

"Five day no eat," he answered and went on to his hut.

Slim asked the second one, who said, "Seven day no eat."

"Is goat Hanagita?" Slim asked.

The Indian glared at him and said ominously, "No say name!" and ran to his hut.

There was suspense in the village, but it had nothing to do with the young men. The village was waiting for breakup. The day the ice went out of the river and the salmon began to run, excitement burst loose. It meant new food, fresh fish, and a great celebration over the first fish caught. He joined in the fishing with long-handled, netlike scoops. Men, squaws, and children, and Slim, too, flailed the water and tossed their catch on the shore. Then came the great feast of fresh salmon.

This was topped off with tidbits of their favorite delicacy called "sand salmon." This consisted of heads and other portions of salmon that had been buried deep in sand and left to rot since their feast a year ago. When it was dug up, it turned out to be a sticky stinking gelatinous mass which shamed the ripest limburger for smell. The Indians dipped their fingers in it, stuck them in their mouths and smacked their lips over it. This was one treat that even Slim's well disciplined stomach found difficulty in handling. But so as not to offend his hosts, he ate some, and it took all his will power to keep it down.

Slim kept close watch for the two 'sick' men. Neither left his hut, nor, as far as he could tell, did either of them eat. At the end of the fifth day one of them showed, and two days later the other. They were both obviously very weak, but each did the same thing. They went fishing and gorged on the rich, greasy fish meat. This literally half-killed them, but they survived and in a few days were whole, hearty, and fishing again.

Gud-le-ta was head of the band. He was a good Indian and Slim was very fond of him and his squaw and his two children, a boy and a girl about eight or nine years old. It was from Gud-le-ta that Slim heard many of the my-poppa-say stories of the Indians. These were the legends passed down through generations. "My poppa say" was as the white man's "once upon a time." From descriptions in these stories Indians and Eskimos carved likenesses of snakes, great boa constrictors, even dinosaurs. My-poppa-say stories told of the rich, lush vegetation of times when Alaska was tropical. They told stories about a fabulous itinerant spirit they called the Little Man, a roving somewhat belligerent spirit who spent much time about the Wrangells, but whose home was the "big flat country" beyond the mountains. This country was conceivably the plains of Canada which these Indians had never actually seen, yet they spoke of it with apparent familiarity. The Little Man was a spirit of severe and sudden retribution to transgressors, and he commanded great respect.

One day when Slim and the old man were visiting, Slim asked about the volcano. "Forked-tail Indians," Gud-le-ta replied, nodding sagely.

He hunkered down comfortably on his heels by the fire and motioned for Slim to join him. Then he went on to tell one of the strangest of the legends Slim had ever heard.

"My poppa say," Gud-le-ta recounted, "times were hard, dogs starve, Indians starve. Indian almost all die before one man kill moose. All Indian eat, then starve some more. Next time no moose. One day dog run away, gone two days, come back fat and feel good. Chief say to man, 'Next time dog go away, you trail, find food.' Dog go, two Indian follow. Dog come back fat and feel good. Indians no come back. Chief tell best tracker, 'You trail dog, find food.' Dog go. Tracker trail him. Dog go through high grass, around deadfalls, by snares, past traps. Dog no get caught. At last come where naked Indians camp. Indians have forked tails. Have lots meat. Dog eat. Indians play game of ball. No ball. They play with heads of two Indian trackers that no come back. Then it start to rain. All naked forked-tail Indians run into holes in ground.

"Indian go back to village, tell Chief about dog eat meat and forked-tail Indian. Tell about forked-tail Indians play ball with tracker Indians' heads. Chief say forked-tail Indians bad, kill our people. We fight. Kill all forked-tail Indian.

"So Chief wait for rain. Then all go to place where forked-tail Indians run into holes, and pound on ground with war clubs.

"Forked-tail Indians come out to fight. Indian chief kill forked-tail chief and go to help his people. Forked-tail chief get up and fight some more. Chief kill forked-tail again, cut in two with knife. Again forked-tail not die. Next time chief kill forked-tail chief. This is three time he kill him. This time he chop him to little pieces. Build fire and burn him. One little piece of forked-tail start to crawl away. Chief catch tail and put on fire. Fire begin to crackle and chief say, 'No come back, no come back, no come back . . . .' Chief keep fire going. Ashes pile higher and higher. Always forever keep fire going. Ashes make mountain. Smoke come out of mountain. Spirit of good Indian keep fire burning so evil forked-tail Indians never come back.

"Then two big birds come to high cliff on mountain. Birds take Indian babies away. Brave Indian climb cliff and find boy bird and girl bird in nest. He kill boy bird, and then kill girl bird, and mamma bird come and he kill mamma bird. Then Indian lose his spear. Poppa bird come. Indian fight with club and kill poppa bird.

"Indian chief glad birds are dead. Give brave Indian half his tribe. My poppa say that way all Indian in world start from one tribe. Big Chief always give brave Indian part of tribe. Brave Indian go away start new tribe."

Gud-le-ta poked the fire with a stick and watched until the burst of sparks died. Then without another word got up and went to his hut. Slim looked past the old man to the smoking top of the mountain and thought how long those Indians must have been stoking that fire to build a 14,000-foot pile of ashes that became Mt. Wrangell. He figured it was probably about as long as it had taken the old chief to populate the world with Indians by parceling out gifts of his own progeny. Slim didn't rule this out entirely. Every Indian he had ever seen looked as though he had a common racial background with every other Indian. Same as sled dogs, he thought, the same breed, apparently producing a different dog depending upon where it lived. There his ethnological thinking stopped, the how or why of it neither worried nor interested him too deeply. It was easier for Slim to think about practical things.

Now that there were ten dogs to feed, he had a store of fish to catch for the winter. As he watched the Indians standing on platforms along the shore slapping at the water with their eighteen-inch scoops at the end of fourteen-foot poles, getting a fish at about every fifth slap, he foresaw a summer of hard work for himself.

Then Slim hit upon making a fish wheel. He had never seen one, but he had heard of them, so he decided if someone else could make one, he could too. As a boy, Slim had seen a water wheel at a grist mill in California, and knew that he could depend upon the current of the river to turn his wheel. With this picture in mind he set to work with his axe.

When he started work on his mechanical fish-catcher, the Indians gathered in groups and stared in silent, skeptical curiosity. They even sort of sniggered at the idea. Slim knew that once having begun he would have to finish. The Indians expected great things of the white man and especially of him, because he was their friend. He would lose their respect if he failed—and be like a god if he succeeded.

First he cut two sixteen-foot logs. These he laid on the shore, parallel, about four feet apart. To hold them thus he bound two lighter crosspieces at the ends, thereby forming a frame sixteen by four feet. The heavy logs served as pontoons. At the middle of each log he erected a four-foot pole, well braced. These became the supports for the wheel's axle.

With the frame structure complete, Slim sat on a log and stared at the result. The Indians stared at Slim. They probably thought he had failed and was feeling very sorry for himself. They were thoroughly unfamiliar with the process of thinking and planning, so had no way of knowing just what he was doing. Slim visualized the water wheel of long ago, and coupled it with the descriptions he had heard of fish wheels, and added his facile imagination to the picture. He decided that he would use the paddles of the water wheel, but for some he would substitute willow-basket-like scoops; two paddles alternating with two scoops should do it. Then he set to work again. The Indians shrugged at the strange ways of the white man.

Slim cut shore willows, about as thick as his wrist, and bent them to form the frames of his two scoops. These he made fanlike, with the point attached to the axle and broadening to a three-foot span at their dipping end. They were not rounded at this end, but straight across. Then he cut a good supply of willows about the width of his thumb and by weaving, filled in the frame to form the scoop basket, cupped toward the outer end. Across the middle of the scoop he fastened a board as a baffle to prevent the fish from slipping out the top.

The paddles were easily made. Two flat boards three feet long by about two feet wide fastened to poles. The paddles and scoops were of equal length, about six feet from axle to tip. He mounted them crosswise on the axle. When they revolved, they would have plenty of clearance in the open water between the pontoons, and would dip under water to the proper depth.

Next he built a catch box and attached it across the upstream end of the center frame, just close enough that the scoops would clear as they passed. As the wheel turned, the scoops would pick the fish from the river, turn with them cupped in the woven scoop and held against the baffle-board. On the downstream turn the silvery salmon would drop into the catch box, thus the scoop would empty itself ready for its next productive dip.

When the axle had been attached to its uprights, the next thing was to try the contraption out. The Indians stood in wonder at what Slim had put together.

Like any fisherman, Slim knew that the place to go was where the fish were. He knew that in the spring runs, about ninety percent of the millions of salmon going upstream to spawn, moved from one side of a river to the other. They preferred rocky bottoms, so for some miles the hordes of fish would hug one shore, then as the river bottom changed, the fish crossed over to hug the pebbly bottom on the other side. Then too, Slim watched these spring runs and knew that the majority of the fish swam from three to ten feet from shore, in about three feet of water and not over four or five inches from the bottom.

Therefore, with this knowledge and experience, he knew where to place his wheel. He carefully chose his spot, and launched the pontoons, securing them to land by ropes and held off the the shore by lengths of logs. This done he fastened one end of a log to shore with the other end extending past the wheel, upstream of the wheel. This was a sheer boom to ward off floating logs and driftwood and prevent them from jamming the wheel. On the downstream end, he built in the water a fence between the inner pontoon and the shore to keep the fish from swimming past the wheel on the inside. Finally he built a walkway for the few feet from shore to the catch box for the easy gathering of the fish.

When all was ready he pulled out the pole he had stuck across the uprights, releasing the wheel, and let the current go to work. He was sure that if the wheel turned it would catch fish, the stream was alive with them.

The Indians had gathered along the shore to watch the performance. Slowly the wheel began to move. As the current caught each paddle its force resulted in an even turning. *Splat—swish—splat—swish!* Paddle and scoop alternately smacked the water, and at almost every turn a scoop came up with a flapping salmon or two which slithered exactly into the box. Although the scoops did not dip deeply enough to reach the heaviest run of fish, there were just so many fish that they couldn't help but produce. Slim was nearly as surprised as he was delighted.

At first the Indians stared in amazement. Then, as though this was a signal, bedlam broke loose. They howled and danced, pointing at the miracle their good friend Slim had performed right before their eyes. He was a hero.

The fish wheel an established practicing fact, a dance and feast was held in celebration, with Slim the honored guest. There was considerable hubbub and excitement during the preparation. They all gathered noisily around the fire over which the stewpot was simmering to prepare the salmon. The gathering quietened respectfully at the appearance of the tribe's medicine man. He stalked in with dignified silence to the place prepared for him by the fire, and sat cross-legged on the ground. Over his head and shoulders was his grotesque ceremonial mask, the mark of his calling. It was made of hide drawn over a sapling framework, cunningly fashioned in the form of a fox's head, garish in color, and bedecked with bits of fur and some feathers. Softly at first, then rising in tempo, pitch, and volume, he began an interminable chant, waving his arms, pointing as if angrily at times, then again motioning in a friendly beckoning motion.

When the medicine man's activity was well established, a young Indian whispered to Slim, "Medicine Man tell all bad spirit go 'way. All good spirit come. Spirit no know Medicine Man when he got on mask. Bad spirit afraid Medicine Man eat 'em up. Good spirit like Medicine Man, come and stay like good friend. Medicine Man tell all spirit you great man. Tell spirit bring lots fish. Keep away high water. Keep away storm. Bring lots food. Pretty soon you sing too."

Slim realized that this ceremony was more than a joyous celebration, the central theme was religious. He had heard of these meetings, but this was the first time he had been an active member. And this was unusual, since only Indians, and especially tribal members, were permitted to participate. But Slim had accomplished a great thing, and had proved himself wiser than even the oldest member of the band.

His young friend nudged him. "Now you sing," he whispered.

Slim had no idea of singing, and said so.

The Indian was positive. "You sing, you great man. Make fish wheel. Catch lots fish. E'rybody have lots food. All because you. You sing."

It was up to Slim to offer a lyric solo to his own cleverness and achievement in building the fish wheel. He knew a little of the Indian language, enough for casual conversation, but his vocabulary wasn't equal to this need. When he stepped forward he used English. Nor did he actually sing, but from somewhere deep inside he dredged forth a husky rumble and told his story in a monotone cadence that seemed to satisfy his audience.

When he finished his friend stepped out and interpreted in a more professional singsong whinelike tenor the story of Slim's great prowess.

The Indians sat in rapt attention, grunting and nodding approval. This, Slim knew, was generous applause. Then there were gifts. Slim received beaded moccasins, a belt, a jacket, all beautifully made and artistically decorated.

During all this the medicine man maintained his monotonous intonings. Slim suddenly realized that the man was praying, a continuous running prayer of deep and sincere gratitude for good received, and hope for fulfillment to come. The medicine man, Slim now understood, was actually "talking" with the spirits, bidding the evil spirits of want and famine and sickness to stay away, and inviting the good spirits of health, well-being, and plenty to abound.

At first Slim had doubted, then he wondered, and finally, in full respect, decided he just did not know. Perhaps it was all superstition, but he certainly could not deny the proofs of the faith of these Indians in their tribal religions that he had actually seen.

After the singing and the banquet came the dance. This broke up at daybreak when the whole village gathered by the river to watch the wheel again perform its magic. Squaws scurried out on the runway to collect the fish and bring them ashore for cleaning and drying. Then they gathered to watch some more. The excitement lasted for a whole week before the Indians finally accepted the wheel as a part of their future.

From then on the wheel turned and produced fish. The village had more fish than the river had ever given them before, and wonder of wonders to the men, they didn't have to work to get them. This left the men with nothing to do during the spring salmon run but to sit and meditate. It left the squaws with nothing to do but to tend the fish wheel and clean and cure fish.

As if this accomplishment weren't enough, Slim grew greater in stature when he explained the operation of the solar system to one of the Indians. They were sitting, he and the young Indian, along the river bank watching the night run of salmon at its height. The salmon ran mostly at darkest night with the greatest catches taking place between one and three o'clock in the morning.

The Indian pointed toward the east. "Bimeby come light. When sun come fish go 'way. More better when sun turn around."

Slim told him that the sun stood still and the earth turned. The Indian stared, unbelieving, as Slim illustrated with the use of two round stones. He held one for the sun and slowly turned the other, telling his friend of the earth's movement. The Indian shook his head, "Nighttime come e'rybody fall off. No good."

Slim dared not smile. He wouldn't offend his friend. Very seriously he reached in his pocket for his prospector's magnet and indicated that inside the earth was great power like the magnet. The Indian nodded his head sagely. His eyes squinted slightly as he slowly assimilated this almost unbelievable fact. But Slim had said so, and Slim knew, and always told the truth. Thereafter for several days, the Indian came to Slim to borrow his magnet, and Slim watched as the Indian explained to others the new miracle that their good friend had explained.

It was such things as these that not only endeared Slim to the Indians but placed him almost on the pedestal of an oracle. To the Indians Slim knew all and could do all.

It wasn't long before Slim had cured down all the fish he would need, and he decided to move on to his own camp. He wanted to start breaking his young pups into harness. He said good-by to his friends, and Gud-le-ta bade him farewell with, "You come any time. Stay all time you want. May be more better you come live here. You good man, Slim. You be good Injun."

"I'll be by to see you again, Gud-le-ta," Slim promised. "I leave sled. No need sled till winter." He waved to the other Indians who paid no attention to his departure, although he knew that they were as sincere friends as the old man.

For the trail he put his supplies in back packs for the dogs, and carried a heavy pack himself. The little dogs followed free of weight. "You're too little now," Slim told them, "but next winter you'll be ready to pull and carry. But right now you run and play if you want to."

Two days on the trail took him to his camp. He had left a cache of food suspended in trees and was thankful that it had not been molested by wolverines. These fellows are the tough ones of the North. Relatively small, rarely reaching fifty pounds in weight, the wolverine is dreaded by every trapper, not because the trapper is afraid of it physically, but because of the animal's demoniac habits. The wolverine, like other members of his weasel clan, is bloodthirsty, mean, and vicious, and he isn't afraid of a thing. On a trap line he ruins pelts, even steals traps. In a camp or cache he eats what he wants; smashes, tears, and scatters all else, then fouls this complete destruction with a fetid reminder of his cussedness. He has no home, no range, but roams indiscriminately wherever his hatred guides. Wolves, running to two hundred pounds, and the North's most relentless predator, will leave a fresh kill at the approach of one of these undersized fireballs.

Strangely enough, the wolverine was not hard to trap, not for one of Slim's patience and skill. He let the animal's own gluttony be its downfall. At the first sign of one, Slim downed a tree, a small one perhaps four or five inches through, cut about three feet from the ground; he trimmed the tree and propped and fastened it on the stump with the up end extending four or five feet beyond the stump with the tip about four feet above the ground. He set a bare, unbaited trap in plain sight about two or three feet from the top end; then he secured a caribou head or some other tempting piece of bloody, freshly killed meat to the tip end of the log. The process never failed. The wolverine wanted the meat. It was too high to jump for. The sloping approach was cleared and handy. The trap offered no obstacle, he merely stepped over it with arrogant contempt and fastened his bearlike claws and his jaws into the feast. In the uncontrolled rage of frustration in not being able to free the meat from the log, the hind legs invariably stepped into the trap. Slim found many a wolverine hanging from his setup with teeth and claws clamped into the lure and both hind legs secured by the steel trap. He often thought that this was an example of greed so great it actually destroyed itself.

The wolverine's fur brought a good price. The fur is heavy and thick, dark brown to black with light yellowish stripes on its sides from shoulder to rump. Slim had early learned the practical use of this fur: it is the one fur that does not frost. Therefore, its desirability for parka-hood trim where, although it does not keep the face from freezing, it does prevent the formation of icicles of frozen breath.

Slim had seen one other method of besting the wolverine. The winter before he came across an Indian friend of his whose trap line joined his some forty miles to the north. His name was Sam, and his home was in the Indian village of Mentasta. Slim reached Sam's camp late one afternoon. Sam was furious and poured out the story of his anger. It seemed he had killed two caribou, butchered and cached the meat, giving him and his squaw security for months to come. A wolverine had found the cache and ruined the meat. Sam had taken violent measures. He set traps and caught the animal. Instead of killing it, he secured the jaws and lashed the feet together. Thus disarmed, the wolverine could only glare his promise of vengeance.

As Slim had approached the camp he noticed the smell of burning fur, and when he arrived it was upon a scene of aboriginal retribution. Sam and his squaw were hunched down with the campfire between them. They held the snarling, snorting wolverine, passing it back and forth over the flames, singeing and burning the fur from the writhing body. Slim tried to stop this inhumanity.

Mentasta Sam glared at him, "Dis 'borene he take my caribou. We got no meat."

Same had difficulty with his English, and Slim knew that "borene" was the best the Indian could do with wolverine. "Why don't you kill him?" Slim suggested. "It won't do any good to torture him that way."

Sam looked up slyly at his friend. "You wait, Slim. You wait. I burn all fur off dis 'borene. Den I cut him loose. He go all o'er country," Sam gestured with a wide sweep of his arm, "he go aryw'ere, an' he tell all udder 'borene, he say, 'You stay 'way from Mentastas Sam! Stay 'way! Mentastas Sam, he sonomagun!'"

Slim never learned the outcome of this experiment, but he doubted its efficiency.

Slim's camp on the Chitina River was laid out with the skill of an expert, well back on the rise from the river's edge in the protection of spruce. His trails to his fur trap lines were well marked on land, and in winter the frozen river served as the main thoroughfare. He had a good tight cabin, and had cleared a sizable space for his dogs so each one had room to walk and exercise at the length of his chain. The five big dogs were staked in line, and opposite them the little fellows, with an open aisle between.

Slim felt that his world was secure, but again he reckoned without the Spirit of the North. The first sign that evil was on his trail was when the dogs saw the ghost.

·9·

Half dazed, half crazed in the winter wild,
with its grim heart-breaking woes,
And the ruthless strife for a grip on life
that only the sourdough knows!

Slim looked forward to a soft, easy summer. He had a good camp, a good grubstake, and could spend his time in teaching his new pups. By freeze-up the puppies would be about eight months old and could begin to pull a light sled. At a year old they would be grown dogs and ready to pull full loads.

Slim loved his dogs, but his love took the form of good treatment rather than demonstrated affection. His emotions never crossed the line whereby the dogs were given the opportunity to become pets. He never beat nor mistreated his dogs, but nevertheless maintained stern uncompromising discipline.

Sled dogs, the draft animals of the North, require very special handling. Exceptional kindness or special favoritism might very quickly turn a dependable work dog into a lazy sluggard that could never again be counted on at moments when strict obedience might mean the difference between life and death. Unfortunately, sled dogs shown undue affection quickly take advantage of the situation to goldbrick their way until the only solution is to cut them out of the team. There being no use for nonworkers, they would be destroyed. The paradox, therefore, was that the kindest way to treat the dogs was not with kindness, but with understanding.

Work dogs were bred for size, strength, heavy shoulders, broad chest, and handled for the conservation of their pulling power rather than to burn it up in speed.

Slim had seen Huskies trained for racing, but he had never cared for the sport. That training was simple compared with the exacting schedule for working dogs. Dogs naturally love to run, and once accustomed to harness, racers could easily be urged to run until they'd drop from exhaustion. These dogs could become pets and still perform, for they run mainly for the sheer joy of running.

Slim was a master with dogs. He knew and understood them. First he made friends with his puppies; they were loving little fellows and, like children, were at first too young to know rigid discipline. When he felt that he had their full trust and confidence, he started breaking them for work. He made a tiny harness for each puppy and a puppy-sized sled. He drove a peg into the ground, and with one end of a ten-foot rope fastened to it, he marked off a training circle. Each pup was worked singly at first. Harnessed, and hitched to the small sled, the dog was trained to walk the circle at the end of the rope. Around and around he went with Slim's gentle urging. Little by little the weight of the sled was increased, which gave them the feel of a load and their shoulders against the collars. Slim taught them to "stand," to "lie down," to stop at the call of "whoa," and to go at the command of "mush!" They learned to "gee" and "haw." The puppies looked forward to their daily stint in the harness. They seemed to love nothing better. They were certainly eager to please Slim, who praised them generously for their efforts.

The training period was lengthened a few minutes each day, and never a day missed, regardless of weather. Then gradually came the discipline—slowly, yet sharply and with understanding, but never with a whip or a club. In his work of training Slim demonstrated limitless patience and never once compromised until he had perfection. The result would be a perfectly trained team with absolute trust in their master.

All during the training big Blizzard and the other dogs watched condescendingly from where they were chained.

With these youngsters Slim had the first element for his experiment. One important ingredient was yet needed; therefore, during the time away from the training, he hunted for what he wanted. He found it. It had taken all his knowledge of the bush to find the three very young wolf cubs that he chained alongside the dogs.

Slim knew wolves. Notwithstanding the brutality and ruthlessness of the predators, they fascinated him. He trapped or killed every one he could for the bounty, and every hunt increased his respect for their cleverness. Wolves, he had learned, were smart, probably smarter than any other animal in the bush; they were practically tireless; they were unbelievably strong. His interest in them began when, as a kid in the Southwest States, Indians gave him his first lessons in trapping. He had been learning ever since. He'd never read a word about wolves, and most of the stories he heard he didn't believe. His knowledge came from his own observation and experience.

What he wanted most was to cross wolf with dog. In the right proportion, which he could gain only by years of trial, he hoped to find the perfect sled animal. There were, however, certain biological factors that might cause him difficulty, but since he was totally ignorant of the science of genetics or animal husbandry, any such problems were no deterrent. He had an idea and was determined to try until he proved or disproved his point.

Dogs, he knew, are polygamous; wolves, monogamous, mating once and for life. His first hurdle, after getting his experimental wolves, therefore, was to hope that one would be satisfied to mate with one of his dogs. It would have to be a male wolf. Slim had seen the courtship of wolves. The male made his choice, the she-wolf accepted her mate only when he had accountably disposed of other suitors, and many a scar attested the ferocity with which she protected her virginity.

She would kill any philandering male dog with ease and contempt before she would submit to his attentions. Time was another consideration. The dog matures for mating at approximately nine months of age, the wolf comes to adulthood at three years. Slim recognized that he had a lengthy project on his hands, but he had no other plans and a very strong determination.

When the wolf pack breaks up in the spring, the couples mate and the she-wolf picks her spot to have her cubs. It would be a den of some sort. Even if she had to start with no more than a squirrelhole, she would dig down as much as six or seven feet and make it large enough for a man to crawl in, and there she would retire. The male dared not enter the cave. While the cubs were tiny, and after weaning, he would dutifully hunt food and carry it to the mouth of the cave. She would take it inside, but if he so much as took a step inside, her teeth would rake him mercilessly.

Slim was lucky. One day not more than a mile up the trail in back of his camp he saw a she-wolf come out of her den. She was away into the brush before he could shoot, but he hurried to the den opening. Convinced that there was no adult wolf there, he crawled in, and brought out three snarling, spitting bits of young wolfhood. With only a few nicks and scratches he got them back to his camp and chained them. They were males.

He thought it strange that the mother had left them. He figured her mate had either fallen down on his job of supplying food, or she had become careless. Whatever had happened, he knew that she would not easily give up her cubs. At dusk he built a not-too-large fire, but big enough to illumine the clearing before his cabin, and sat in the doorway. He leaned his rifle against the jamb. He had no hope that the she-wolf would show herself, but he was certain she would come. The dogs were quiet. They had overcome their earlier uneasiness at the arrival of the wolf smell.

The cubs were chained near the end of the open aisle between the dogs. Slim selected this spot first to accustom both dogs and wolves to each others' presence, second to place the cubs where the mother would make no effort to reach them for fear of her own safety, and third because they would be handy for him to watch. After the first few frantic moments at finding themselves chained up, they apparently took their captivity philosophically. They had curled up, the three of them in a tight ball, and gone to sleep.

Slim noticed the first evidence that the she-wolf had arrived as darkness overtook the twilight. There was no unusual sound that he could distinguish, but the cubs heard something. Three black heads came erect from the bundle of fur where they lay. The firelight reflected silver sparks from six sloe eyes all staring at one spot back among the trees somewhere in the black shadows. Up to then the dogs hadn't moved. Blizzard finally became restless, raised his head and sampled the air, then gave low throaty resentment over what he smelled.

Slim, used as he was to sounds of the wilderness, had difficulty in picking out the voice of the wolf mother. She had undoubtedly weighed the chances of reaching her babies, and decided it would be unwise and probably dangerous for them as well as for herself. She knew well the law of the wild. She reached them with her voice.

"Listen to her," Slim whispered to himself, "she's tellin' them cubs what to do. An' just look at them little fellows, hearin' everything she says. Difference between a puppy dog and a wild thing. Dog pup'd break his neck tryin' to get loose to get to his momma if he heard her like that. The wild young'll stay where they are until their momma tells 'em what to do. An' right now she's tryin' to figure it out, and tellin' 'em to be quiet until she does. She knows she done wrong in leavin' 'em in that den, and this is all her own fault. But she won't take a chance if she thinks it'll hurt them or herself. And if she sees they're goin' to be all right, I'll bet she leaves 'em. Be interestin' to see how she figures it out."

Slim knew that the wolf has about the largest vocabulary of any wild animal. He had heard them when he was certain they were actually conversing. Contrary to general opinion, wolves do bark. Slim had heard them, particularly females. Their bark, as clearly defined as that of a dog, is their warning to their cubs to go into the den at the sign of danger. He had heard their gathering calls, when the old lobo called his hunting clan together in the fall, the call of the pack in full hunting cry, the spine-chilling call of the kill. But now he was to hear something new, a mother talking to her sons.

The wolf called from the darkness, and the three young ones and the dogs stared at the spot from where the voice came. A moment later, the wolf spoke again, and the voice came from a different spot. The dogs turned their heads sharply to stare in the direction of this new source. So did Slim. The cubs never moved. For almost half an hour the she-wolf's voice seemed to move about from place to place in the darkness. Only by the closest observation of the cubs did Slim finally decide that she had not once moved her position, but that by some vocal trick had placed her voice where she wanted to with ventriloquial elusiveness.

She left silently and unseen. The cubs, receiving her inviolable instructions, curled up again and went to sleep. The dogs were restless at this strange happening they neither knew nor understood. It was a long time before the rattle of their chains quieted and they stilled their nervous throaty growls. Slim sat for some time watching the embers of his fire glow to death, thinking of how very little man knew about the world in which he lived.

The same thing happened the next night, and for several nights more. Just at deep dusk, when shadows began to blend with the dark, the she-wolf came and "talked" to her cubs. "Sentimental thing," Slim thought, and began to realize that she was teaching them. Slim watched the cubs, their noses pointed toward the heavy brush back of the camp, their spike ears sharply up as if to catch every guttural sound and whine, so soft that it was all that he could do to hear. He had never heard such voice control. "Tellin' 'em to be good wolves, I guess. We'll see how well they mind her," he said to himself. Then came an evening when at the appointed time the cubs didn't move. Heads down, they turned their blinkless stare at Slim. The she-wolf had given them her final message, and she never came again.

Slim tried with infinite kindness, patience, and understanding to befriend the cubs. Only one of them responded. The other two developed the surly antagonism of the breed. One day he carried his rifle and took the two bad ones by their chains. "I hate to do it, little fellows," he said as he led them snarling and snapping back into the brush. "If my plan's goin' to work, I got to get you two out of the way so your brother here won't get your disposition, and I can't turn you loose to grow up into killers."

Slim didn't like killing. No bushman or trapper does. They hunt for food. They trap fur for grubstake and supplies. With them it is a livelihood, not a sport.

The one remaining cub he named "Hoppy" because of his funny little habit of jumping up and down on the tiptoes of his forefeet whenever Slim brought his food. He was a friendly little thing, yet Slim knew that behind the inscrutable stare the reasoning of his wild heritage was going on. The question was whether to trust the outward show of amenity or to look upon it as a clever cover for treachery. The eyes showed no emotion. There was recognition but never the twinkle of loyalty he saw in the eyes of the dogs. When he touched the wolf, there was stiffening and quivering of muscles. Day after day he worked with Hoppy, and very gradually the evidence of the wolf's instinctive distrust disappeared. However, one thing remained. Whenever Slim would touch him, Hoppy's first reaction was a bristling of hackles and a short gruff expression that was neither a subdued bark nor a growl.

Bit by bit too, the wolf was moved closer to the dogs. Slim thought he had achieved a major victory when he moved Blizzard up one stake and chained Hoppy between the leader and the second dog in line. Blizzard made his position known to the young interloper by parading his size and growling his voice of authority. Hoppy was still small over-all, but his feet and bone structure showed promise of great size.

The summer fell into a pleasant pattern, and at the earliest touch of fall Slim had a well-trained young fivesome of pups that made up in eagerness what it lacked in experience. The young dogs had been as apt pupils as he had ever had. They had developed well, and were strong.

Young Hoppy had been accepted with certain reservations by the dogs. He had filled out and lengthened. He was almost as tall as Blizzard. Slim had already accustomed him to harness. He was very smart, quick to learn, alert, but headstrong. Slim didn't yet dare team him with one of the dogs. This would have to wait until the wolf showed that he could be trusted to run with a dog without attacking it. Slim still had a lot to learn about the animal's temperament. This was the first wolf he had ever seen captive.

Slim spent his spare time in laying up a winter wood supply. His traps were ready. He'd made a good supply of snares. He had scouted his trails and tentatively planned his winter trapping. He had his affairs under control.

About daybreak one morning he received a shock. First he was wakened by Blizzard's voice. As Slim came out of the cabin to investigate he saw the big dog pointing his nose high in the air and heard the final long, mournful wail that announced tragedy. It was the call of death. Slim hurried to where the dogs were chained. They were all on their feet, as was Hoppy, nervously pacing, and panting, all but one. One of the swing pair of the big team lay still. The dog was dead.

Slim examined the body. There was not a mark or other evidence to show what had caused the dog to die. Slim knew that death came in strange guises in the North. There was no answer for this visitation. He took the body far into the brush and buried it, then he pulled the dog's stake, boiled and stored the chain, then dragged fire over the place where the dog had lived. He did all he knew to eradicate completely every scent that the dog might have left. When he finished, the other dogs and Hoppy seemed satisfied. They quieted down and went peacefully about their daily stint of waiting for food and tomorrow.

At sundown of the day the dog died Slim realized that something else strange was taking place. He had finished his supper and was sitting on the cabin sill whetting his axe blade. The dogs, who had been fed and watered, had been walking about, yawning, stretching, and pawing. Suddenly everything seemed too quiet. It was almost as if the slight breeze rolling gently down the mountain slope and through the valley had blown all sound before it. There was complete and absolute silence. Birds were stilled, the gentle moaning soughing of the spruce was stopped. Slim looked at the frothy cascading river and wondered why he didn't hear it. It was eerie. It was death-like! Then he looked at the dogs. They appeared like statues. The nine dogs and the wolf, motionless, their heads turned toward the mountain trail, staring. Slim turned quickly to see what they were looking at. The trail was clear. He could see no movement. Then he looked back at the dogs, and as he did so, he felt cold, like a chill wind was blowing upon him. He found he was holding his breath as he saw the dogs, in unison, move their heads as they watched *something* come down the trail toward the camp. Their eyes followed *it* through the camp, along the aisle between the two lines of stakes, and to where it apparently disappeared along the river trail downstream. In all it may have taken about a minute, Slim didn't know.

Then as suddenly there was sound and motion. The river, the trees, the birds, the North was again alive. The dogs took up their activity as if nothing at all had happened. Slim wiped sweat from his forehead and his upper lip and looked at his hands.

What had happened? he wondered. Or had anything at all

happened? Had he only imagined it? He put down his axe and hone and went to examine the trail. There were no tracks. Yet he was convinced that the dogs had seen something come down that trail, pass between the two lines, and take the river trail out of sight.

He thought a lot about that experience. All the next day he wondered what senses a dog has that made such a thing, whatever it was, possible. He wondered too if it were not true that the Indians and Eskimos, uneducated, untutored in the processes of formal education, did not also have this extrasensory ability to see things that could not be seen—like the Indians and their "little men of the flat country." Who was there to say that they hadn't seen these people from the other side of the mountain without leaving their own wigwams or igloos?

The same thing happened the next day. Just at the beginning of dusk the dogs quieted, their hackles bristled, the world stilled, and Slim once more experienced feeling the presence of, and of watching the dogs see, a ghost. Slim had never heard of such things as psychic phenomena, or metaphysical manifestations, but he was convinced the dead dog, still alive in some form beyond his own comprehension, but clear to the animals, had walked slowly down the trail, through the camp, and out of sight, bringing with it the sense of mortal death.

The next evening it happened again, and the next. For four evenings in a row the same performance took place. The dogs looked up one trail, then the next night another, but their actions were identical, and there was no doubt in Slim's thought that these dogs knew what they were doing. Then it was over. The fifth night there was no activity. The episode was ended, except that Slim wondered.

Slim built himself another sled to replace the one he had left at Gud-le-ta's village, a small sled about twenty-two inches wide and seven feet long. He was enjoying the brittle beauty of fall when, with a snap that he could hear, winter cracked down. It took over as it did every year with a dramatic show, the overture of which was a blizzard featuring the shrill of the wind and the timpani of sap freezing in the trees. For about the next seven months, the Northland would be shrouded in white, sealed with cold.

The first cold held, and before too many days the river ice was safe for travel. He had already made one trip to establish his trail for the trap lines, and early in the morning he carried the harness to the big dogs to go over the line again.

Once the trail was made, the leader would keep to it. This trail followed the river downstream for several miles, then cut inland up the mountain slope through rocky cuts and finally along the tundra floor of the valley. It was about a three-day run from the time he left camp to make the loop and return. His absence would cause the other dogs no hardship, for with a good feed before he left, and since they were not working, they could go as long as four or five days without food and feel no discomfort. The same was true of Hoppy.

Usually excited about the prospect of a run, Blizzard now leaped, rolled, and cringed to resist Slim's effort to harness him. He added warning growls to emphasize the fact that he did not want to go.

Slim stepped back. "What's the matter with you, Blizzard?" he said. "You like runnin', an' it's a good day for the trail." No amount of talking or urging could kindle the slightest interest in the dog. Slim finally gave up. "All right," he said, "I'll give the little fellows their first run on the snow."

Ordinarily Slim would not have used the dogs for so long a run, but it was easy going, the snow was light, and the temperature just above zero. It would also give the young leader a chance to show what he could do. The pups were anxious and took to the trail like seasoned veterans. It had blown, and there had been little snow since Slim's first trip with the big team, so there was a hard surface. They jogged along at a fair pace of about eight to ten miles an hour. Slim was as happy as a kid with a shiny toy. His young leader was working, keeping the other dogs' traces taut and all of his team leaning into their collars. The weight of the light sled took little effort, so the dogs were having a great time, too. Their bushy tails curled over their backs bounced like fluffy puffballs. Slim kept up a running conversation with his dogs, telling them how good they were, how beautiful, and what a fine sled team they made.

The trail ran close to the shore, the ice was barely crusted over with snow, and smooth. About five miles down from camp, they had just rounded a tight bend, when Slim saw a bit of excitement 150 yards ahead. There stood a cow moose and her calf. When these two heard and saw the dogs, they took off along the river, the calf in the lead and the cow urging the awkward gangly youngster to greater speed.

The dogs sensed the chase, and Slim let them have their heads. They yipped and yapped like school children let out for recess, and took after. The moose also sensed a game and seemed to be enjoying the fun. Running with her long loping stride, she swayed from side to side as she made astounding speed. She kept looking back first over one shoulder and then the other to gauge her lead. The yearling ahead of her kept his bony legs churning for his full worth to stay ahead of his mother.

Slim had his work cut out too. The light sled bounced and skittered over the icy trail, and he ran his best to keep up with the chase. He figured it would do no harm to let the youngsters have a bit of fun, and after a good run he would stop them for a rest and give the moose and her calf the opportunity to get away. He didn't want them.

Just then the calf fell. Immediately the cow went sprawling after it. Slim saw the signs. They had hit glare ice, the most dangerous thing on a river trail. He called to the dogs, but he might have saved the effort. They were no longer sled dogs, they were puppies and having fun. Older dogs would have instantly obeyed the command, but these young ones had let their training go with the excitement. Slim tried to slow the sled but there was no brake, and holding to the handles and dragging his feet was of no help. His moccasins slipped and skidded like skis.

When they were about fifty yards from where the moose went down, Slim saw the next step to disaster. Two great splashes of water shot into the air, and the moose went out of sight. Open water! Slim saw the cause immediately, but this did nothing to ease the situation. A fast stream joined the Chitina at that point, and the junction of these currents created an eddy with force enough to keep the boil from freezing over. His dogs and sled were headed directly for the opening and apparently no thing on earth could stop them. There was one hope. Quickly, with a sharp jerk on both handles of the sled, he flipped it onto its side. His rifle went skittering across the ice toward the shore. He hung onto the sled, legs spread and feet braced, and yelled at the dogs with all the sound his husky voice could make, but it was hopeless. By then panic had replaced their excitement, and they clawed with all their strength but could find no purchase on the smooth glistening blue, greaselike ice.

Slim's efforts were as impotent as the climax was inevitable. The weight of the sled swung it ahead, taking Slim. He hung onto it like one mesmerized. He didn't know when he let go, but he knew he must have when he saw the sled slide slowly from him, gaining speed, and tumble off the ice into the swirling churn of the water. The dogs followed.

Slim's body was still moving. Carried by the momentum, belly down, he was gradually but certainly slipping toward the opening. He tried to make himself heavy, his moose-hide mitts clawed and pressed the surface, the toes of his moccasins tried to dig in. The glare ice, wet by overwash, sloped downward toward the water. Slim's efforts were useless. He closed his eyes and prayed.

He was not conscious of the fact that he had stopped sliding, but he had. When he opened his eyes, the lip of the ice was less than four feet away!

He had seen the sled and the five young dogs drawn under

133

the ice. The calf was also gone. But the cow was still struggling in the icy whorl that was about twenty feet across. As the moose, pawing and churning the water, was swept past him, her head was on a level with his and she looked straight into his eyes. In that one instant he thought he saw fright, pleading, hope, despair, and the next second she too was sucked under the ice, and he was alone.

He dared not move. He was afraid that the slightest effort on his part would start him sliding again. The sound of the water was hypnotic, the rushing current so near his face seemed almost a force to pull him closer. He tentatively moved one hand. Nothing happened. Then inch by inch, more carefully than he had ever moved before, he reached to the back of his belt. He knew he would have to work fast if his plan to get out was to succeed. He was getting cold, and being wet, there was a danger of his freezing to the ice. But he dared not hurry. Therefore, as fast as he carefully could, he gently pulled his knife out of its sheath and brought it in front of his face. He held it point down against the ice and gradually, barely exerting pressure at first, he shoved. He increased the force little by little and his body moved—backward. A few inches at first, then with longer stronger shoves, a foot or so at a time, he shoved himself away from the brink. He was at least twenty-five feet from the hole before he dared flex his legs or move his body. Then he sat up, and as he always was after the danger had passed, he was scared, cold, panicky.

When he could, he crawled over to his rifle. This gave him a little feeling of security again. Then he built a fire and dried and warmed himself. Next began the seemingly longest trail he had ever walked. It wasn't hard going, it was the thought of losing another team, by accident, to water.

As he plodded along, his mind was filled with self-condemnation mingled with self-pity. Hard luck dogged him, but most of it had been due to his own mistakes and misjudgment. He had loved those little dogs, and they had trusted him, and he figuratively had killed them. But reason told him there was no way of knowing of the air hole or the conditions that set up the tragedy. Air holes, he knew, could blow through surface ice anywhere at any time the pressure underneath became great enough. This hole might not have been there an hour before, and might be frozen over again with safe ice by tomorrow. This accident had just happened! And that's all there was to it. It was strange, he thought, that in his years in this vast land of mountains, glaciers, ice, and snow, his worst losses had all been in water.

Other thoughts came to him, thoughts of people. He wondered for instance, had he slipped beneath the ice, if anyone in the world would ever know or care. He thought about Linda with yearning and a sense of loneliness. Somehow he couldn't exactly define the emotion. At that moment she seemed very close, and it comforted him to think about her.

When he was about a half-mile from the camp, he heard Blizzard whining and barking. How, Slim wondered, did the dog know he was coming? The sound of his moccasins on the crusty snow couldn't possibly travel that far, nor could scent be taken that distance on the air. Yet Blizzard knew, and when Slim walked into the clearing, the dog went into a frenzy of joyous welcome. He jumped and pawed and whimpered and fawned. Slim stood before him and stared for a long time. "Blizzard," he finally said, "you knew something was going to happen today, didn't you? How did you know there'd be danger on the trail? You didn't want to go this morning, remember? An' now you're so gol-hanged glad to see me you're just the tickledest dog I ever seen. It's like you didn't expect me to come back at all." Slim paused and roughed the big dog's head with his mittened hands. "How you do it, I don't know, but you do."

The accident really unnerved Slim. More than anything since he had been in Alaska. His nerve was shaken. It took him several days to get on top of it. Even then he had a feeling of emptiness and insufficiency, almost as though he had lost something within himself.

·10·

In that vast white world where the silent sky
communes with the silent snow,
In hunger and cold and misery
I wandered to and fro.

Slim felt sorry for his little dogs. He felt sorry for the cow moose and her calf. He began to feel sorry for himself when he suddenly remembered something Big Ed had once told him. One day, as they were watching the line of bedraggled sourdoughs, Ed said, "Look at their faces, Slim. Look at the discouragement and, Slim, most of it is brought on by self-pity. It's the thing that when a man's alone will eat holes in his guts. If you ever begin to feel sorry for yourself, there's only one cure. Go to work!" Slim thought about Big Ed and his wise counsel. Then he smiled, and reached for his axe.

He started to build a new sled. He selected young trees, and even then it was no easy chore to handle the frozen wood, but he was both an expert and in no hurry. He chose his wood carefully, trimmed, cut, and fashioned the beams and spreaders, steamed and formed the runners. Then began the weaving of the intricate basketry out of raw hide which formed the actual structure and bound the sled together. There were no nails or screws or bolts in these Eskimo- and Indian-style sleds.

Things went along smoothly and well during the next year. Slim's traps produced. In the summer he prospected the creeks, but again decided that his traps were more dependable for a steady income. Late one afternoon that next winter, he was busy in camp working over a sled and he heard dogs yelping somewhere along the river trail. Before long a team pulled in sight and he heard a hail.

"Hallooo, Slim!"

A few moments later he was helping to put the dogs out to stake and giving them a good feed of fish.

"Hadn't seen you for a long time, Slim, and just thought I'd run up for a visit," the newcomer said.

The visitor was Charlie Gunther. Not as tall as Slim, he was well built, clean-shaven, clear-eyed, with a quick smile.

Slim felt good over seeing his friend. He had known Charlie for several years. He had met him first in Fairbanks on mail runs, and although there was a wide difference in their background and education, the Great North was the common leveler that gave them a solid basis for friendship. Their paths had continually crossed, and today Slim was especially glad that some apparently strong urge had prompted the trip up the river.

Slim motioned toward the cabin, but Charlie was staring at Slim's dogs. "What in the name of the devil is *that?*" He pointed to Hoppy. "Is that a wolf?"

Slim nodded. "He's just a little fella, cub."

"Have you gone crazy, putting a wolf in with your dogs? That thing'll be twice the size of your dogs in a year and he'll kill 'em like they were rabbits."

"I don't think so," said Slim. "I'm figurin' on matin' him with one o' the females."

"Now I know you're out of your mind. You can't mate a wild animal, a killer like a wolf, with a tame animal like a dog."

"I wouldn't say for sure," said Slim quietly, "I never tried yet."

They moved on into the cabin where Slim set out cups and made a pot of tea.

"Glad to see you, Charlie," said Slim, motioning to his friend, "sit on the bunk, it's better'n these stools I made."

"You got a bad cold, Slim?" Charlie asked.

Slim shook his head, and explained his voice.

"Maybe a good thing I came up to see you, then," said Charlie with some concern. "Somebody told me you had this layout up here on the Chitina, and I thought I'd like to talk with you."

"You're gettin' as bad as an Indian," Slim told him.

"What's the matter with Indians?" Charlie said.

"Nothin'," said Slim, and poured tea, "just interestin' how an Indian'll do what he wants to do, no matter how much trouble it is, and won't do what he don't want to do no matter how easy it is. How far is it from your camp here?"

"About a hundred miles."

"That's what I mean. Two hundred miles, up and back, just because you want to visit. Like an Indian. If an Indian didn't want to, you couldn't hire him to walk from here to the river, but if he got a notion he wanted to see somebody in Nome, he'd go the thousand miles and think nothin' of it."

Charlie smiled and nodded, then pointed to the pile of stripped raw hide on the floor, "Where did you learn to weave a sled, Slim?"

"Eskimos over near Iditarod. I did some trappin' in there when I was runnin' mail."

"Ever see one of those new 'Yukon Sleds' they're making in Seattle and shipping up here?"

Slim shook his head.

"Just no good at all. They're bolted together and you couldn't drive one ten miles without it knocking itself apart. Just like those fellows in the States trying to guess what Alaska's like and dreaming up a monstrosity like that."

"The more a sled can be twisted, the better she is," Slim agreed. "The last one I made, you could weigh down the back end and twist the front end all the way over. Good sled."

They were quiet for awhile. Slim knew that his friend had

138

not made the trip from the Copper River to his camp just to make friendly conversation, but it would not be polite for him to ask the reason.

"Slim," Charlie finally said, looking almost too serious, "I got a proposition for you."

Slim waited.

"How'd you like to go into a trading post deal with me? You wouldn't need any money. I got that." Charlie began a patient explanation. "I've had a good trap line over on the Tonsina, and I've panned enough in the past few years so I've got maybe $50,000. So, I'll tell you what I want to do. I'm going to open a trading post at Taral, right where the Chitina runs into the Copper. There's lots of trade there. And how would you like to come down there with me? You're one of the best trappers in the country, you know fur, and you get along with Indians just fine."

Slim grinned and nodded.

"And besides that," Charlie edged forward, "I'm going to get married. You know the girl too. I'm sure you saw her in Copper Center last spring. Her name is Annie."

Slim lost his grin. After a moment he shook his head slowly. "You ain't goin' to marry *her?*" His voice was low.

"Why not?" Charlie was quick with the question. "She's a fine girl. Pretty as any picture and as sharp as a barrel of needles."

Slim was a bit on the grim side when he said, "But she's only a little kid, and besides, she's an Indian."

"And as bright an Indian as you ever saw." Charlie replied. "What if she is only seventeen years old, she's smart. And you two would get along fine. I could take care of all the business, and teach Annie to work in the store and handle the trade goods. She knows fur and we'll just do fine. How would you like to come in with me, Slim? It's a great chance." Charlie sat back, smiling his satisfaction.

Slim looked at his friend sadly. "That what you come for, Charlie?"

Charlie nodded. "What do you say, Slim? You'll get rich."

Slim shook his head slowly. "Not in business with an Indian, Charlie, even if she is your wife. It won't work. You been to college, ain't you?"

Again Charlie nodded.

"And you come from a fine family. You're maybe forty years old?"

"Thirty-eight."

"You're thirteen years older'n me, and you ought to know that you can't change the Indian's religion, their thinkin', or their way o' livin' to yours, but *you* sure could be changed to theirs. I'd rather stick to my own trails than to go into it with you, Charlie, much as I like you and as good a friend as you are." The two were silent for a moment, then Slim repeated sadly, "It won't work."

"But isn't that just what you're trying to do, Slim?" Charlie argued. "Mate a wild animal, the wolf, with your tame dogs? You claim that will work."

Slim shook his head. "I don't claim anything, Charlie, all I say is I never seen it done, so I don't know. But I have seen white men marry Indians in this country, and I know that won't work. Different about wolves and dogs. Nobody's told them how to think."

Charlie smiled kindly, yet just a bit condescendingly. "Trouble with you, Slim, you've never been in love."

Slim looked at his friend, got up and refilled the empty cups, sat down and took a long swig of the steaming liquid. Love. This was the first time he remembered ever having heard the word spoken. Slim gave his friend a long thoughtful look before he answered. "Yes, I have, Charlie. I am in love," he said, and surprised himself when he did so. He had suddenly come upon a most awesome discovery. He had been in love since his first summer in Alaska—the first time he saw Linda. Then, he didn't even know what love was. Maybe he didn't even know now, but she was the one girl. And that seemed to be all there was to it.

Charlie hesitated a moment, then asked, "Why don't you go and see her then? Why don't you tell her?"

Slim shook his head. "I guess maybe I want to some time. Maybe I will. But that don't fit into my plans now, Charlie. I still got that urge to go and see things. Sometime, maybe, but not yet. And, Charlie," Slim paused, "she ain't no Indian. You marry Annie if you want to, that's your business, but don't expect too much."

Slim looked at his friend, at his shaven face, his good clothes and nice appearance. He had always admired Charlie for his neatness. The news of his coming marriage was something of a shock. No more was said about the business venture or the wedding plans and during the rest of his stay at camp, for a couple of days' rest, they resumed their former level of friendship.

After Charlie had gone, Slim examined his own thoughts more closely than he ever had. He had made a very profound discovery—that what he told Charlie about his feeling for Linda was true. It was equally true that at the moment he would do nothing about it. "This ain't no life for a girl like her," he told himself, "even if she would look at me. I better wait." He wondered what it would be like to hold her in his arms.

Slim finished the sled and went about his business of trapping. It was more than a year before he decided to go to Taral to see how Charlie was making out.

They greeted each other warmly. Charlie was demonstratively glad to see Slim, and showed him the trading-post store, his well-stocked warehouse, and home with a great show of personal pride. Then Charlie became expansive and exhibited his son. Slim looked into the crib at the little brown-skinned, moon-faced baby. Its black beady eyes sparkled, equaling the joy of the toothless grin. Annie was nowhere to be seen.

Charlie was every bit the proud father. "There he is, Slim. My son! He'll have the best of everything. College and all."

Slim nodded. "And how's Annie?" he asked.

"Oh, fine." Charlie was almost too positive. "She's fine. Of course she's got a lot to learn, and she's young, but she's coming along. Not quite as fast as I'd hoped, but she's fine. Next year I want to take her and the baby back to the States and show them off to my family. We're just going to have this one baby," Charlie announced knowingly, "I've talked that all over with Annie."

"Where is she now?" Slim asked.

"Oh, we just got in some supplies that came up the new river trail from Valdez, and she wanted her family to have some, so, like a kid, she loaded a packsack and went to see her folks."

"Potlatch, eh?" said Slim.

"Oh, no," Charlie shook his head, "she isn't potlatching. It's just for her own folks."

Slim knew the pattern. The signs were all there. Charlie wasn't shaved, a two- to three-day stubble on his chin. His clothes were dirty. Even the post store and warehouse, with as much valuable stock as they held, looked shoddy and ill kept. Annie and her trip to the family with gifts was only the forerunner of continuous giving, the Indian custom of potlatch—the giving-away of all personal possessions following any great ceremony, such as a funeral, for a full year. Since potlatch established personal importance, Annie undoubtedly assumed that her wedding was equal to a funeral. She had achieved sudden riches—food and traps, guns and ammunition, clothing, and everything that an Indian could want. They were hers, and with them she could have an all-time potlatch, as long as the stock lasted. Why should she learn the white man's way of buying, selling, trading? Her Indian way was much simpler and far better. Give it away! Potlatch! Charlie didn't fool him. Slim had caught the doubt in his friend's talk and actions. But he was not feigning his love for the little half-breed baby, who, no matter what the father's plans might be, would grow up to be an Indian.

Slim stocked up with ammunition, trail food, and a supply of trade goods, especially tea and plug tobacco.

"Where you taking all this stuff?" Charlie asked, helping Slim lash it in a tarp. "And you don't use plug tobacco."

"I may do some tradin'," Slim answered, hefting the weight of his purchases.

"Eskimos like that plug. You going to the North Pole?"

"Why not?" Slim grinned ingenuously, "I never been there yet. Maybe sometime I'll get me the idea to go see them fellas, and when I do I don't want to waste no time in getting ready."

Charlie busied himself with the kettle and tin cups. Soon the two were sitting over a pot of tea. Slim studied his friend. He knew that Charlie had talked himself into his present situation and was trying to justify his decision. Slim knew Indians better than did Charlie, but he had also long since learned that a man's thoughts are singularly his own, and therefore he rested on one of his virtues, that of minding his own business. He would let Charlie wrestle with the problem. He felt sorry for Charlie, but he could never tell him so.

"You know, Slim, I'm kind of sorry for you," Charlie leaned his elbows on the table, holding his teacup between his hands, "always on the trail, most always alone. Don't you care anything at all about settling down and making money?"

Slim squinted and scratched his chin with a thumbnail. "Fellow asked me almost that same question the day I landed in Valdez eight or nine years ago," he answered slowly. "Said I was crazy for not wantin' to get rich."

"Oh, maybe not getting rich, Slim, but look at all the opportunities right now. Valdez is busting its seams. Must be close to fifteen hundred living there now, not counting prospectors. They're building a wharf. Down at Cordova there's an Irishman named Heney building a railroad to haul out copper from the Kennecott mine. The trail from Valdez to Fairbanks is open summers for horses. New gold strikes at Fairbanks and there's a boom there. They're finding gold on Slate Creek, and Chisana. And you want to go north of the Circle."

"You ever hear of Barrow?" Slim asked.

"Sure," Charlie nodded, "up on the Arctic Ocean."

"Ever been up there?"

Charlie shook his head.

"Neither have I," replied Slim, "and I'd sort of like to, wouldn't you?"

"Can't say that I would exactly. Why?

"Well," Slim drawled, "they're the real Alaskans, those Eskimos, and I'd sort o' like to see what they're like and what their country's like up there and how they live. I heard lots of stories, but I'd like to see for myself."

"But that's almost two thousand miles of the toughest winter trail in the world!"

"I wouldn't know," said Slim, "I haven't been on it yet. All depends on how bad a fellow wants to get some place as to how bad the trail generally is."

"I think you're crazy, Slim. You're a hard worker, you're honest, you don't drink or mess around with women. A fellow like you has got all sorts of opportunities right here, and you walk out on them. You said you had a girl. Why don't you marry her and get yourself a stake and settle down? Look how well I'm sitting here. It's just right. It's the only way, Slim."

Slim sipped his tea. He couldn't explain that his "girl" was no more than a dream, and it was hard putting the romantic soul of a vagabond into words, but he tried. "I guess we all ain't the same, Charlie, and it's up to every man to do as he likes. I work. And when I work, I work hard for the privilege of doin' what I want to do. There's lots o' fellows like me who do things just for doin' 'em." He held out his cup. "Pour me some more tea, will you?" He stared into the filled cup for a moment, took a gulp of the steaming beverage, and continued. "I don't know what I'd do if I had a lot o' money. I couldn't buy the things I want, like goin' to places or seein' other things. A man's got to work this all out for himself."

Slim paused and looked out the window toward the

Wrangell Mountains. When he spoke again it was as though he was talking to himself. "They got railroads and cities and all that in the States. If I wanted those things, I'd go back there. But what they haven't got is things like those mountains over there. I love this country, Charlie, the bigness of it, the wilderness, and I don't think I'll ever live to see all I want to of it. So what good's money to somebody like me who don't need it? It can't buy the way a fellow feels inside."

The two looked at each other across the table, the materialist and the dreamer, separated by the chasm of their philosophy. Charlie shook his head slowly. "Yes sir, Slim, I feel sort of sorry for you."

Just as Slim was leaving Charlie's trading post, he saw Annie. She had come back to replenish her stock of "gifts" for her family.

When he arrived at his camp, and chained and fed his dogs, he stood in front of Hoppy and looked thoughtfully at the wolf. "You an' me, I guess, is quite a bit alike. Maybe we're the ones that mostly walk alone and like to be free. Only difference is, you got caught, and that's the end of the trail. I ain't figurin' on gettin' caught, not yet for a while anyway."

The wolf's unblinking stare seemed to satisfy Slim, for he smiled as he turned and walked toward his cabin.

Hoppy exceeded Slim's expectations. A year later the wolf, fully matured, weighed close to 180 pounds. He had developed into a magnificent animal, aloof, minding his own business, responsive to Slim's offer of friendship, yet with always a barrier past which no familiarity was permitted.

Hoppy completely ignored the first two of Slim's three female dogs, but the third apparently took his fancy. The result was twelve pups as perfect as Slim had ever seen. They grew fast, and by the time they were ready for weaning, they were more than the mother could handle. They were rough, and they were tough, and mostly wolf.

Hoppy tried his best to get to his youngsters. Wolves, the same as dogs, like little things. Hoppy wanted nothing more than to appropriate his twelve and start their education in wolflore. He was a born predator; although his own primary instruction had been missed, he felt by instinct the latent urges.

In about three months Slim was able to cull the litter. Some showed too definite and active traits of wolf. Others were more doglike. He saved nine of the most promising and began their training. His wolf-dogs would be ready to work when they were nine months to a year old; by that time his older team would be well past the practical age for sled work. For some time the urge to go beyond the Arctic Circle had tugged at Slim, not only to see the country, but to learn more about the little-known Eskimo. If his young wolf-dog team developed as he hoped, he would use them. He also planned to rebreed some of these half-breeds both with dogs and with other wolves, thereby varying the percentages of the individual strain in the hope that he might find the one right proportion for his "perfect dog."

Hoppy, therefore, having served his purpose, and since inbreeding was out of the question, would have to be killed. His older dogs would have to go, too. There were no places for these faithful animals to be "turned out to pasture." They could not be left to run the bush and fend for themselves. That would result in the cruelest death possible. Dogs were no match for any of the predators. Nor would Slim turn Hoppy loose to live out his span with whichever murdering pack might accept and adopt him.

Destroying the dogs was an act of merciful and practical kindness, but to shoot these loyal, courageous dogs was the hardest thing Slim ever had to do. He kept the leader. He didn't have the heart to kill him.

The nine young wolf-dogs more than proved his premise, having every attribute he had hoped for—wide shoulders, deep chest, big bones, huge paws, stocky, sturdy, heavy, weighing about ninety pounds, and apparently tireless. One big male turned out to be a good leader, and if he had a fault it was his almost obstinate independence. He stopped at a strange scent on the trail until he had investigated and satisfied himself, then he would again become a leader. It took all of Slim's infinite patience to overcome such inherent traits as this. But since the dog assumed the lead position with regal confidence, Slim gave him the name of his predecessor, Blizzard.

Slim studied his new team as he trained them. He watched for predominant habits, and planned ahead for the next mutation. These that he had were not perfect, but they represented the first step.

It was the fall of 1910. The pups were not quite a year old when Slim closed his camp on the Chitina. His sled held a good supply of dog food, a trail outfit for himself, his rifle and ammunition, and the trade goods he had bought. He went out of his way to give his old lead dog to Charlie.

The one-time route from Valdez to Fairbanks which began with the perilous crossing of the Valdez glacier, had given way to the Richardson Trail. This pack trail had been laid out under the direction of the War Department by Capt. W. R. Abercrombie. It had reached Fairbanks in 1904. Open for bobsled in winter and wagons in summer the trail was used to carry supplies to the growing number of prospectors working farther and farther inland.

Instead of taking this active thoroughfare, Slim held to the now nearly abandoned Millard Trail. This followed the Copper River, skirting the Wrangell Mountains, through the hazardous Mentasta Pass, crossing the Tanana River, and on to Eagle on the Yukon. This trail was the "back door" to the Klondike region. Although it was considerably out of his way, Slim chose this longer and more difficult route for two reasons. One was that if he went through Fairbanks he was almost certain to meet some friend who might succeed in talking him into taking a job, such as Windy Smith once had done. And that he wanted to avoid, since he had a definite project ahead. The other reason was that he wanted to keep his team of wolf-dogs as far from contact with other teams as possible until he was certain of their dispositions and his control over them. The Richardson Trail and Fairbanks would present too many possibilities for fights. The little-used Millard Trail [now known as Eagle trail], harder and more dangerous to himself, offered no such problems for his dogs.

From the beginning the young team worked like veterans. For Slim there were miles and miles of tedious breaking trail on snowshoes. There were blizzards, bitter cold, and blinding sun on snow—but these were normal conditions of winter travel for Slim, and normal to the heritage of his new dog strain.

He stopped briefly at Chicken, a gold town named by some prospector who sent out the rumor that the sands of the creeks thereabouts contained nuggets the size of chicken feed. The trail went on through Eagle which was the American town closest to the Canadian border on the Yukon River. From there on he followed the frozen Yukon Trail for several hundred miles through Circle, another gold town, named by some early prospectors who had misjudged the location of the Arctic Circle by fifty miles.

Ft. Yukon was at the northermost bend of the Yukon River, and was the earliest settlement in Alaska by the English. The Hudson's Bay Company established a trading post there in 1839 when the territory still belonged to Russia. The post was closed when the United States purchased Alaska. From there he made good time along the frozen Yukon. There was little snow and it was cold. Working in temperatures of forty and fifty degrees below zero was almost as enervating as the high temperatures of summer, and besides, there was always the danger of perspiring and freezing. He made frequent stops to rest, both his dogs and himself. He was in no particular hurry. There were several months of winter ahead, so the trail would be good for a long time. In the summer the Arctic tundra was an impassable muskeg, alive with scourging swarms of black flies and mosquitoes.

Slim had no map, but even without one there were two

things of which he was certain, the sun rises in the east and sets in the west, and from Texas to the Pole, Polaris marks the north. He knew vaguely where Barrow was located, and that to reach it he would merely have to follow the western Alaska coast line to its northernmost tip. He established his route as he had navigated the Bering Strait to Siberia. He had no fear of getting lost as long as the skies were clear.

He knew of a shortcut, and planned to take it. A trail led north from where the Tanana River joined the Yukon. A bit over a hundred miles north of this point was the gold camp of Allakaket. From there on there was no trail for the 350 miles through a mountain pass and on to the coast.

All went well during the first part of the trip. Game was plentiful, and he camped comfortably and ate well. His dogs were working fine and showed even greater promise. It was after he left Allakaket that he ran into trouble. He met the tragedy of hunger.

Night temperatures dropped to fifty, sixty, and seventy degrees below zero. In such cold nothing moved. The wind, during the day, was merciless, blowing steadily, with a force that pushed through parka and clothing to numb flesh and chill bones. Nights were still and brittle, and the overwhelming silence was broken only by the sputtering crackle of the camp-fire and the occasional long minor hunting call of a wolf. At such a call the wolf-dogs would tilt their noses to the sky and answer once, once only, then the silence folded in again. The velvety blue-black of the sky, gemmed with the cold brilliance of silver stars, spread over the whiteness of the mountains and snow, and the black of the spruce, a glimmering shroud. The only color, movement, or life, was the fire stabbing resentfully at the cold with orange-red flames. It was as though time had stopped, restrained by the Arctic's frozen grasp.

On nights when the Northern Lights came forth, mystic and majestic in the fury of their magnificence, the world about Slim was bathed in silver, red, green, and blue as the heroic shafts stretched from earth to zenith.

As the cold held, and game was nowhere to be found, Slim began to know hunger. He had no idea how far he yet had to travel to reach the coast, or even what he would find when he got there. His team was his first concern. Because of this he carefully rationed his dog feed. Days went by. He saw nothing moving. His progress slowed. At first he had been making a comfortable forty miles a day, but after five days without food he was grateful if he could cover as much as ten miles. His rests became more and more frequent. He withstood the reproachful stares of his dogs as he shared their dried fish, and when this was gone he began to wonder which would last the longer—the dogs, and he became food for them; or himself, and the dogs furnish the strength he needed. He lost count of days. He finally forgot the pain of hunger as he staggered behind his sled and the weakened dogs tried to pull the weight.

He made frequent stops to brew tea. He no longer wasted strength in unharnessing or chaining the dogs. They merely lay down where they stopped and stared at him. He tried to talk to them, but his voice was nearly gone. On one of these stops he again took his rifle and went to hunt food. He found a rabbit, a big fellow, lying at the base of a tree. It took considerable concentration for Slim to raise his rifle. His eyes watered and his sight was uncertain as he tried to aim. His tired muscles caused his rifle to waver. He was about to pull the trigger anyway when he lowered the gun, shook his head sharply, and laughed a little at what he had nearly done. Hunger, the dizziness of fatigue, and his blurred sight had confused him—they had almost tricked him into shooting a dead rabbit.

Slim had never heard of tularemia by name, but he did know that there was some disease or cycle that decimated the rabbit population every certain number of years, and that rabbits dying as a result of this supposedly became poisonous to anyone eating their flesh. But a starving man pays precious little attention to rumors of plagues. Slim took the rabbit and before long found several more. In his search for game he had overlooked these dead rabbits whose white fur made them almost invisible against the snow.

He skinned and cut up a few of them and tossed the pieces to the dogs. They ate them and slavered as they watched him prepare one for himself. If he was at all mindful of disease, it showed only in the length of time he boiled the meat. He actually felt the strength return to his body. He ate carefully, disciplining his urge to gulp and swallow without chewing. He had been hungry before. He brewed and drank tea. Then he ate more meat. Neither he nor the dogs found any fault with their fare.

The next day Slim felt fine, and the dogs yelped their eagerness to be on the trail. During the afternoon he came across some rock ptarmigan. These Arctic grouse with their white feathers were nearly as hard to see as the rabbits. There are two types of ptarmigan, the valley ptarmigan and the rock ptarmigan. The rock is the highland bird, smaller in size and wit than his lowland brother. It's a strange, stupid little bird, about the size of a spruce hen, and acts much the same. They have no fear, and are easily approached. Slim cut a stick and killed several of these little fellows with no difficulty. These gave him another good feed. He also found a few more of the rabbits which served the dogs.

When he reached a river, scenes became familiar to him. Although winter had changed the scape and definition, he recognized many landmarks that he himself had used. And when he came upon the remains of an abandoned camp, he was certain. He was on the Kobuk River. He looked up. There, towering white in its shimmering covering of snow, was his mountain of jade! It was like meeting an old friend. He grinned recognition. Reciprocally, the mountain was generous. That day he bagged a sheep.

·11·

On the wild, weird nights, when the Northern
Lights shoot up from the frozen zone,
And it's sixty below, and couched in the snow
the hungry huskies moan.

Slim followed the Kobuk River to the coast. He knew that by keeping to this and continuing north he would reach Barrow. There was no trail to follow. The course led northwest some 200 miles to Pt. Hope, then north about 50 miles to Cape Lisburne, and northeast from there 350 miles more. He guessed at these distances from what he had heard, no one seemed to know exactly, but a map would have shown him to be amazingly accurate. This was not country through which he could make good time. The surface was clear, and the temperatures not too severe, but after he turned the last point and headed northeast, he bucked winds off the Arctic Ocean that forced him more than once to seek what shelter he could find for protection. Winds of such force as to make progress all but impossible.

Another deterrent to speed was his entry into the area of Arctic "night," that period during which the sun is below the horizon. At Barrow the sun goes "down" November 16, and comes "up" January 26—seventy-two days of "night." Only through a few hours during the middle of the actual daytime was it light gray enough for travel, the hours usually between 9:00 or 9:30 and 2:30 or 3:00. The balance of the twenty-four hours was darkness. He came across Eskimo hunting camps, and sod-hut settlements where he traded for food. At any stop he would have been hospitably taken in, but all he wanted was food—fish for the dogs, and fish, seal, or caribou meat for himself. At one place he acquired a pair of much needed mukluks, made of seal hide. He stayed just long enough to make his trades and rest his dogs and himself.

The Eskimos were particularly interested in his dogs. The men gathered in groups and chattered, stared, and pointed. They had probably never seen dogs of such size or so nearly resembling wolves. Slim was careful lest the men get too close, for he was still unsure of his dogs' friendliness. Also, he was none too sure what the Eskimos' reaction would be if his dogs should tangle with theirs in a free-for-all. So to be safe, he kept his team well apart to avoid an incident.

Slim knew that on the frozen tundra wood was a scarcity. The Eskimos relied upon driftwood, scrub willow, and seal oil for their fuel. At any time of the year the wood was soggy and hard to burn, so before leaving timber Slim had loaded a supply of dry kindling, as much as his sled could conveniently carry, and kept his eyes open for any dry wood he could find. As he traveled up the coast, he was surprised to find that at some points Eskimos were burning coal. He learned that they gathered it in the summer from spotty surface deposits. These people were indeed richly blessed, for elsewhere throughout the Arctic piles of precious driftwood before the igloos of the more provident were often the accumulation of generations of beachcombing. Slim knew it would be unfair to ask these people to give up their precious wood. Therefore, he went into their country as well prepared with these essentials as his dogs could pull.

A few days over two months from the time he left his camp on the Chitina, Slim drove into Barrow. Although the group of igloos looked exactly like those he had passed along his route, he knew it was Barrow because directly beyond to the north the trail ended in mountainous ice floes cast on the shore by the wind at the time of the Arctic Ocean freeze-up. In every other direction was flat, frozen, wind-beaten tundra of the Arctic barrens. He had reached the end of the trail.

He was greeted with honest sincerity. These Eskimos, like others he had seen along the coast, appeared to be exactly like those he and Corks had known in Siberia, except for size. The Alaskan Eskimos were a bit taller, broader, and chunkier. Even then they were not large people. Slim figured that size seemed to be controlled by the North; like the dogs and the Indians, he thought, the farther south, the larger.

As Slim's dogs yelped their way into the settlement, the Eskimo dogs barked their greetings, and the men who had come crawling out of the tunnellike entrances to their igloos stood and grinned in equally enthusiastic welcome. None, however, made a move toward Slim until he called the team to a stop and walked forward and took hold of Blizzard's collar. Then one of the Eskimos, a little fellow, yet bulbous in his furred parka, pants, and mukluks, came forward and bent his neck to stare up into the face of this giant who had come calling at midnight. This Eskimo, who was more elaborately dressed than the others, and who, by coming forward, was evidently the head man in Barrow, grinned and bobbed his head. Slim had not spoken to anyone and received an answer since leaving Allakaket more than a month ago. He quite naturally assumed that there was no use in conversation, so he bobbed his head and grinned back. Soon the men crowded around like the little fellows had done in Siberia. He recognized their expectancy, so he released his hold on Blizzard's collar and charged the team to lie down. They obeyed. Slim went to the sled and unleashing a rope over the tarp covering, reached into the opening and pulled out some plugs of tobacco. He handed the first one ceremoniously to the man who had come to meet him. Then he offered a gift to each of the others. As if this were a sign, all the men returned to their igloos except the one before him, and this one apparently accepted him and from then on offered the full treatment of Eskimo hospitality.

The head man stepped toward the dogs, and before Slim could stop him, reached down and took firm hold of Blizzard's collar. The dog reared his head, curled his lips, baring long glistening fangs, and voiced a deep-throated growl of resentment. The Eskimo showed neither fear nor concern, and even before Slim could reach him, turned his back and still firmly holding the collar, led the dog away. Slim's mouth hung open as he saw Blizzard and the other dogs docilely follow. Slim had expected the dog to jump, rip, and tear, and he watched in amazement as the Eskimo chained and unharnessed the dogs. The animals acted as meek as kittens as the man fed them. Then the Eskimo returned to stand before him, smiling.

Slim looked from him to the dogs and back again and shook his head in wonder. "I don't know how you did it, little fellow," he said with full admiration, "but you just had a handful of sudden death. Maybe it's because you and Blizzard's got quite a bit in common. Only about half of you is tame. Anyway, thanks for puttin' my dogs out an' feedin' 'em." Even as he talked, Blizzard and his team had contentedly padded a circle in the snow and were already balled for sleep.

Slim's host pointed to an igloo and walked toward it. It was the typical Eskimo winter sod hut. They were all about the same size, ten by fifteen feet. The entrance was a long tunnellike passage. It sloped upward from the opening to where it met the igloo, to retain all the heat inside the dwelling and to provide drainage. Its open end was covered by a flap of caribou hide.

The Eskimo hunched down, pushed the flap aside, then with bottom tilted skywards he crawled into the entrance which was barely big enough to admit his body. Slim had trouble. His broad shoulders were a tight squeeze. He couldn't crawl on hands and knees as the Eskimo was doing, but had to lie flat on his stomach and scrunch himself up the incline with his elbows and knees. These igloos had been built for little people, he knew, and visitors of his size had not been imagined when they designed their homes. Another thing slowed Slim's progress through the dark: the entryway was also used as a storage space. He wormed his way over and past dog harness, part of a dead seal, bedrolls, and a Husky mother nursing her pups. His thanks for disturbing her was a snarl and a snap. Hot, fetid, stagnant air greeted him at the igloo entrance.

Once inside it took a few moments for Slim's eyes to adjust to the semidarkness. Light from the outside came as a yellowish glow through a small window of translucent seal bladder. To this a bluish tinge was added by a flickering seal-oil lamp, a stone bowl with twisted tundra moss as a wick. This, with their bodies, furnished the igloo's warmth. The roof and the walls were of driftwood slabs and whalebone. The over-all outside covering was layer on layer of tundra sod. Slits in the igloo's walls offered less than inadequate ventilation. The floor had been cut down a foot or more below the ground level, strewn with moss, and covered with hides. There was no furniture. Spears, harpoons, and a gun were leaning against a wall. On the floor in another corner was a great chunk of raw meat. Several walrus tusks showed that the Eskimo was an important and wealthy man.

Two women sat on the floor, naked to the waist. They looked very much alike, and Slim judged them to be either mother and daughter, or sisters. The older was suckling a nearly naked baby. They looked up at the big stranger and grinned a cordial welcome. His embarrassment burst into action. He dropped to the floor and crawled toward the opening of the tunnel. His exit was blocked by a pair of sturdy, fur-clad Eskimo legs.

Slim never knew exactly what took place during the next few minutes. He remembered tussling with the Eskimo. The little fellow was as elusive as a wet otter. Slim thought possibly that being overly tired from the long trail and coming into the sudden heat made him dizzy. The smell certainly hadn't helped him any. But whatever it was that happened, when his head cleared, he found himself sitting on the floor bereft of parka, pants, and mukluks. The Eskimo stood before him, smiling broadly, apparently well pleased with himself. He held Slim's garments over one arm and motioned with his other hand to the younger of two women. She bobbed her head and beamed with obvious anticipation.

Slim was mad, surprised, and now ready for a fight. He started to get up, but the Eskimo shook his head sharply and frowned.

"Gimme my pants!" Slim demanded. "I want out o' here!" He reached for the clothes, but the Eskimo pulled them away from him.

Slim had heard stories about the generosity of the Eskimos with their women, and he hadn't the slightest thought of becoming a party to any such relation no matter how much the man insisted, or how pleased over the prospects the girl seemed to be. If he tried to go outside without his clothes, he knew it would be like committing suicide, and it might be equally disastrous if he took the only other way that appeared possible for him to get them, to fight for them. He considered this for a moment. He knew that if these were Indians and he were a guest in the chief's wigwam and he should fight with the chief, he would not live to get out of the camp, the others would surely kill him. The allegiance of these Eskimos to their chief or to their medicine man might be as strong. He weighed the relative values of his sense of morality against the lethal allegiance of these natives.

He might have saved himself all this mental effort. When the Eskimo saw that Slim had somewhat subsided, he held up his pants and pointed to a jagged hole where he had evidently caught the fabric on some brush. His parka also had a bad tear. His mukluks were worn through. The man then handed the garments to the girl who giggled in apparent joy over being permitted to perform this act of hospitality—to mend the clothing and thus be of service to their guest. Slim suddenly realized that at no time had there been any other thought in their minds, and he began to laugh. Then they all laughed, all but the baby, who cried until his dinner, which had been interrupted by his mother's rocking with laughter, was returned to him.

These people were not immoral, Slim mused, their not wearing clothes sprang from no sense of indecency. They dressed or undressed depending upon which way they were more comfortable. Taking off their clothes was neither an act of immodesty nor an invitation.

As the girl sewed, the man shucked his heavy parka and mukluks and served up a steaming bowlful of unsavory smelling soup and passed it to Slim, along with a bone spoon.

Slim took it and dared not even guess what it contained. He tasted it tentatively. It wasn't too bad. It tasted like fish. The Eskimo watched him. "Areega!" he said, patting his stomach, "Ai-vek. Good! Wall-rus."

Slim looked up quickly. The man had spoken English words! "You talk States?" he asked.

The Eskimo nodded, "Me talk."

"Why you no talk?" Slim asked.

"You no ask," was the simple reply, and pointing to the bowl, "You eat. Good. Inside wall-rus."

Slim had heard of this stew made of the whole stomach of a fresh-killed walrus. It contained digested shellfish which was the creature's favorite food. It was undoubtedly rich in every dietary necessity, and after the first spoonful, Slim began to find it delicious. Here again he proved how unfaithful a thing an imagination can be.

By the time he had finished his meal, the girl had put fine leather patches onto his torn pants. He felt better when he had them on again. "Where you learn talk States?" he asked the Eskimo.

"Trade white man come boats. Trade white man." He pointed east. "Trade white man." He shifted his arm to the south.

"You head man?"

The Eskimo nodded.

"You got name?"

Another nod. "Aklak. You, States Injun, you got name?"

"Slim."

The Eskimo nodded, and tested the name, "Es-sleem."

Slim nodded. It was near enough.

Aklak pointed to the woman, "Agnak," he said. She did not acknowledge the introduction. He pointed to the girl, "Niveeaksee-kruk." The girl bowed her head. This was his family, his wife and daughter and his son whom he pronounced with great pride as *meklektuk*—a good boy, he translated.

When it came time to sleep, the Eskimos pulled their bedrolls in from the tunnel and spread them on the floor. They removed the rest of their clothing, lay down, and went to sleep. They paid no attention whatever to Slim. Again Slim realized that with these simple people there was no sense of nakedness. They were sleeping as the conditions demanded. In the heat of the igloo, if they slept with clothes on or unduly blanketed, they would perspire. Perspiration, either when they were dressed or undressed, was their greatest fear—perspiration meant wet clothing. If they went outside with wet clothing next to their skin, there was danger of freezing and certain death. Therefore, every night they undressed, hung up their clothes to keep them dry, and slept nude. Slim looked at the sleeping figures around the igloo, and took a deep breath. He shrugged, undressed, and went to sleep.

When Slim awoke, he felt as though he had been slugged or drugged, or both. His mouth was rancid. His head was in a fog of Eskimo-igloo stench. He had no idea what time it was, but it must be morning, he thought, for he was sure he heard birds twittering. He stretched, yawned widely, and sat up. The birds seemed louder. He shook the sleep out of his head and opened his eyes. The "birds" became people, little people. Four Eskimo children stood in front of him, their brown moon-shaped faces alight with merriment. There was no way of telling if they were boys or girls or some of each, for like their elders they were parka'd and panted identically. It seemed to be his beard that caused the excitement, for they pointed and chattered and laughed. It was joyous happy laughter, and infectious. Before he knew it, he was laughing too.

Aklak said, "They say you wear parka on face."

"Then we'll show 'em how we take the parky off," said Slim. He did not ordinarily wear a beard, but on the trail he usually let his whiskers grow because of the inconvenience of shaving. He had a most appreciative audience as he removed the two months' crop. The children, the two women, and Aklak stared unbelievingly as he sheared and shaved. Then he showed them his cleaned face. The children wanted to touch it. Then they scuttled out through the tunnel screaming with excitement to spread the amazing news of what they had seen.

For the next few days Slim adjusted to the pattern of the lives of these people he had chosen to visit. Although he had known Eskimos in and around Nome, and in Siberia, this was his first experience in one of their igloos, especially in a community where there was no access to trading posts for food or supplies. These people lived off the land and from the water. At first he questioned whether he could stick it out, but he had come a long way to learn about these people, so he decided that he could settle himself into their ways—that is, after he reviewed his reasons for coming to this desolate land to live in a foul-smelling hut. Granted that he had an insatiable curiosity, it was not with any reason of ethnological research or scientific exploration that he took these long trips. He merely wanted to go, and to see, and to learn what he could of this country and his fellow men who peopled it, to feed the gigantic question mark that gnawed on his mind like a relentless parasite, which, when fed and satisfied, digested and stored the knowledge, but with no practical purpose in sight. Slim just wanted to know things, about Alaska in particular.

He had long talks with Aklak. The Eskimo did his honest

best with a tantalizingly limited vocabulary to answer Slim's questions. Slim noted the almost identical features the children shared with Chinese and Japanese young ones he had seen in San Francisco and Seattle. Aklak was of little help in explaining this, never having heard of Japan or China and being sure only of his immediate forebears and the stories they had told which took the form of legends or fairy tales. Nevertheless, Slim was convinced that the people of Alaska, like its dogs, had originated across the Bering Sea.

As Slim became acquainted with the people of the village, one thing stood out especially. Eskimos loved their children. This was apparent in every group. Slim wondered if this expression of almost worship by the parents of their children did not have its basis in a belief similar to that of some of the Indian tribes he had known, wherein each child becomes the physical expression of some departed spirit, and the child is treated with great respect until he or she reaches an age where it becomes an entity unto itself. In the eyes of the Eskimo parents the children could do no wrong. And yet, like Indian children, these Eskimo youngsters were well behaved although there was no visible evidence of discipline.

In the barrooms of the gold camps Slim had heard weird, wild, and racy stories of the loose morals of the Eskimos. But he found no evidence of this among these people. Most certainly this Eskimo village differed in one obvious respect from the civilized towns and communities he had known. There were no public prostitutes. He asked his friend Aklak about this, and was told that it just wasn't done. True, the Eskimo said, girls of proper families sometimes erred, and if a baby were forthcoming as the result, she merely named the potential father. This responsibility the young man joyously accepted. A wedding, and thereafter the new wife's fidelity was unquestioned. Aklak said he had never heard of such things as 'lending wives,' or offering girls as temporary companions to transient wayfarers. Notwithstanding Aklak's insistence, Slim did notice more than one flirtatious eye among the maidens.

Things tallied with Slim's experience with Indians. He figured that the lives and habits of these races were somehow parallel.

Slim saw one very old Eskimo, and asked Aklak about the custom he had heard of called "rocking the old folks," which consisted of taking the old people, when they passed the age of productive usefulness, and sealing them alive in a tomb of rocks, there to die.

When he heard this, Aklak shook his head and vehemently denied any such thing. "Old stay alive long time," he explained, "last boy no marry. He take care old ones."

Akluk said that the custom was that the last boy of the family left unmarried, not always the youngest, must stay single to care for the parents. "No throw old people away," he said, "live long time. No throw away momma and poppa."

That explained one or two families Slim noticed, a young man and an old couple. And, different from Indians, the younger Eskimos showed great respect for the old. These people had no books, no records of any kind. Their only way of learning, therefore, was to listen to the experiences of the old. The older the Eskimo, the more wisdom he, or she, had. Old men and women sat with the others around council fires and gave advice as the younger ones listened with full attention. In this way their manner of life was passed from generation to generation.

"Eskimo no like kill. Momma go old, poppa go old. Die. Sometime baby die. No kill. Sometime man do wrong. Be bad man. No kill man." Aklak explained in as much detail as his limited use of English permitted that his people would not kill a fellow human being of any age for any reason. Murder, so Aklak described, was a heinous sin. The murderer, instead of being punished, was cast away to fend for himself until he had atoned naturally for his crime. When the murderer died, his soul then returned in the form of a dog, thus to live again in punishment. An Eskimo murderer, an extreme rarity as Slim found, was therefore his own punitive agent.

There was no judge or jury to pass judgment upon him, jail to hold him, or executioner.

For this reason the Eskimos would not kill a dog. It might be the soul of a friend or relative repenting, if not murder, some other crime. Slim had seen many old and feeble sled dogs about the village, and had asked Aklak why they were not destroyed as was the custom with the Indians and the white men to the south. Aklak was horrified. "No kill dog!" he said. "Dog grow old, die maybe," he nodded. "Dog go hungry, no eat long time, die," again Aklak nodded. "No kill dog. Dog maybe spirit somebody momma, poppa. Momma, poppa may do some bad, and die, then maybe come back like dog before he come back and be baby again." Aklak shook his head and spoke solemnly, "No never kill dog." Slim gathered from this that their belief of soul transfer of a dead spirit to a newborn baby might be interrupted by a return as a dog, if the person who died had a debt of honor to pay.

Another thing that interested Slim was a situation where one man obviously had two wives. This, Aklak simply shrugged off as a practical solution for barrenness. The main object of their lives seemed to be to get married and have children. If a man married, and after three years no children were born, he had a right, if he could afford to support another wife, to take one. The blame for infertility was always placed on the woman. Productivity was a byword in every home.

The longer he stayed the more he marveled over the placidity of these people. Never once was he aware of anyone voicing complaint. When they weren't smiling, their eyes showed the patience of eternity. All that they had, all that they ever hoped to have, came from the animals on land, and from the sea. Their food, their clothes, their tools, their weapons except for the white man's gun, all came as the result of their own ceaseless efforts. Whales gave them food, oil, bones for building. Walrus gave them ivory for spears and harpoons, meat, and hides that were the strongest leather on earth for boats and harness, and ropes. Seal gave them leather, food, and oil. Polar bear gave them food and fur. Caribou gave them food and hides. White fox gave them pelts to trade for the white man's tea and guns. It was a constant struggle just to be fed, to be warm, to stay alive. In the face of this, these people smiled and were happy, and were honest and good.

Slim never discovered their religion. He knew they must have one, because even the very smallest groups of Indians he knew had some sort of belief or superstition which could rightly be called religion. Some he had seen worshiped the sun, the moon, idols, or just had plain beliefs in a "power" bearing an infinite number of names. He had wisely observed that a man's religion is pretty much of a personal thing, so he didn't ask Aklak what these Eskimos thought, nor did the Eskimo ever mention it. There seemed to be no meetings or other ceremonies to be observed. He did see many pieces of artistic and intricate carvings, figures of men, animals, birds, fish, and delicately formed scenes and designs, each in walrus-tusk ivory. These may have been symbolic figures for worship, he didn't know, or they may have been only the result of a lot of spare time.

To many it might seem that these people were living in conditions that no human beings should endure. But Slim understood them. They didn't know it was dirty. They had never heard of the strict set of rules established by the white man about cleanliness, sanitation, and diet. They just didn't know anything different from the way their parents had taught them to live, so they went right on in primitive uncleanliness, and thrived.

One day when Aklak went hunting alone, Slim was left to his own devices. Not being able to talk with the other Eskimos, he walked around and looked. He noted how some people might believe that Eskimos lived in snow or ice houses, since the sod houses were snow covered and gave every appearance of being made of ice and snow. *Igloo* is the Eskimo word for "house." It is built over a framework, and covered with sod.

Underneath each frozen casing was a sturdy weather- and cold-proof building. It was true that the Eskimo hunters, if they were caught away from home overnight, would build a windbreak of blocks of snow. These sometimes took on the structure of a snow-covered hut, but these were temporary at best. Slim had used that shelter himself on his trip to Barrow, erecting a windbreak of snow against the gales off the sea. There was nothing that the Eskimos had or did that was not basically practical and useful for getting food, getting hides, or for keeping warm.

As he was returning to Aklak's igloo which had become his home by insistence, he saw the strangest contraption of dogs and sled he had ever seen. The sled was a regular basket sled such as he could make, but of unusual proportions. It was about four feet wide and six feet long. Eight dogs were fan-hitched, pulling the sled on which sat an Eskimo and three more dogs. Even as Slim watched, the driver reached forward and grabbed hold of one of the walrus-hide towropes fastened to one of the team. He pulled this dog backward toward the sled. When it was alongside the sled he reached out his foot between the dog's hind legs, and with a jerk and a flip the dog landed in his lap. In a moment he had unfastened the towrope from this dog's harness, and attached it to one of the extra dogs he had on the sled with him. Then, with another flip and a kick, he tossed this dog off the sled to land running and take his place with the team. The driver had a constant supply of reserve dogs. Eight were running, three resting. It could go on indefinitely, Slim guessed. Slim tried to talk to this newcomer, but again ran into the language barrier.

When Aklak returned from the hunt, unfortunately empty-handed, but glowingly hopeful for the morrow, Slim was able to persuade the singular dog driver, through Aklak's persuasion, to take him for a ride.

The sled, very light, and shod with walrus-tusk runners, with the eight dogs at full run, fairly skittered over the hard-crusted snow. Slim tried to master the dog change, but could not possibly equal the kick-flip technique of landing one dog in his lap, and the flip-kick that put the spare back with a running start. The more he tried the harder the Eskimo laughed. Soon they were both laughing so hard that Slim just gave up trying to learn, and let the little man do his own dog changing. After they had ridden about five miles out, they turned and went back. Slim never before had seen such a dog hitch, or manner of driving. The secrets were in the button-and-eye arrangement on the pulling strap of each dog's harness and the precision kick-flip of the driver when he changed dogs. Slim was generous with his gifts to the driver for the experience.

Slim was an excellent shot. Aklak, therefore, was very proud to have so good a partner on hunting trips. Slim, too, was always glad to go. He thought he had learned patience from the Indians, but all the Indians he had ever seen could sit at an Eskimo's feet and learn the real meaning of patience. Aklak sat hour after fruitless hour staring into a hole cut through the ice, with fish spear or harpoon, waiting, waiting, waiting for fish or seal. That took patience. So did creeping foot by foot across ice to get close enough for a shot at a polar bear or a walrus. Always in the cold, usually in driving wind, the Eskimo fished and hunted day after day in his eternal search for food.

When Slim succeeded in bringing in his first seal, he was given the name of *Ankvek Angun,* the Big Man. He knew then he had reached full stature in their eyes.

He found himself fitting into the tempo of their lives and liking it. One thing he did miss was conversation, but this did not stop him from talking. In from a hunt, he would sit in the igloo and talk to Aklak. The women went about their own business of cleaning or skinning whatever the men might have killed that day. Sometimes they sat and sewed. Sometimes they sat and stared. The younger one generally sewed, using bone needle and thread of sinews. There were always mukluks and shirts and pants and parkas to mend or make.

As Slim talked, Aklak listened politely, nodded frequently, clucked a bit now and then like a contented hen, and went on about whatever he was working at. He probably understood very little of what was said, but since it pleased his guest to talk, he would at least be polite and listen. One evening he was weaving a whip. The Eskimos used long walrus-hide whips in driving their dogs, whips supple as a buggy lash, and fifteen to twenty feet long. They started with a short clublike handle, about the diameter of a broomstick, and smoothly tapered the plaiting to the cracking tip which was no thicker than a piece of twine. Slim watched as this master craftsman split tough walrus hide with his thumbnail, shaved and scraped the leather with his homemade tools, and wove the strands together to give a surface as smooth as though it had been carved from a single piece.

The driver never beat his dogs, but used the whips for steering and giving commands. It took the place of his voice. Running on a trail, with a wind which could swallow a man's shout, the dogs received their commands by the crack of a whip. The driver whipped the long lash ahead and cracked it like a shot on one side or the other of the leader's head to give the order to "gee" or "haw"; atop his head, he would stop. So expert were these men with their whips they could easily flick a dog's ear at whip's length. The secret of the whip lay in its tapered balance given by the expertness of the weaving.

Dog harness, towropes, and harpoon lines were also made of walrus hide. Some were single strands, others woven into rope an eighth or even a half inch through, pliant as a lamp wick and with almost the strength of a steel cable. Slim had never known a walrus-hide towrope to break. He had used them on freight hauls where twenty-five dogs with a lunging start would jerk loose a ton or more of load with the sled's runners frozen fast. The single-woven, walrus-hide line would twang like a bass guitar string, but never break.

As Slim watched in admiration the intricacies of the weaving, he kept talking. He said, "You know, Aklak, I wasn't quite sure at first what you people were going to be like, and I wanted to find out. I know lots of people, important people likely, explorers and things, have been here and seen you people and studied you and written books about you, but I don't read much, and I don't know whether I like all I read." Aklak nodded, clucked a little, and grinned.

"Now you take Dawson, for instance," Slim said. It didn't matter that Aklak had probably never heard of Dawson or of the gold strike there. Slim went right on, "I know fellows there who write things and send them to newspapers out in the States, and send out stories about what's going on in gold camps and such, most of which maybe they never seen, and those fellows, a lot of 'em, are just about the biggest liars I ever saw. Now if I was in the States and was to read the things they write, I'd have the gol-hangedest cockeyed picture of the Yukon and Alaska you ever heard tell of. Only one fellow I know of over there who knows what he's really writin' about. A young fellow. Works in a bank. Writes poetry. He's just all right, that young fellow. You ought to read some o' his stuff sometime, Aklak."

Slim paused long enough to cut a piece of meat from the carcass of the seal and chew it thoughtfully. The girl stopped her sewing to look at him and smile.

"You're a purty thing," Slim told her, "too bad you can't talk English. I'd sure like to know what you're thinkin' about."

She dropped her eyes back to her work and Slim turned his attention back to Aklak. "That's why I don't put too much into what somebody else writes about a place or about people I never seen. Maybe they're tellin' the truth, maybe they ain't. Anyway they write what comes to their thinkin', and that may not be the way I'd see it at all. So when I heard about you people, and folks began to tell me all about you, I began to wonder, especially when I found out that about half the people who were tellin' me about you had never even been up here to see you. So that's the reason why I come up. Now I know what you're like, and I know what your country's like, and they can write all the books they want to, but I'll always know what I see myself."

These soliloquies clarified Slim's thinking and catalogued his impressions. He had wanted his facts first hand, and the only way he knew to get them was to go after them himself. He hadn't the slightest idea what he would ever do with them, but he did know that if anyone ever asked him a question he would be able to give him an honest answer.

Slim slowly began to realize that he was facing a problem. Here he was, a white man, living in the igloo of the head man of the village, which was something unusual to the rest of them. Also, since he seemed prepared to stay indefinitely, questions were bound to arise. If they were ever voiced, Slim never heard them, and if he did he wouldn't have understood, since he had yet to learn a single word of their strange dialect. His first clue came when Aklak suggested that he might want an igloo of his own. He would keep Slim in his own igloo as long as Slim wanted to stay, but this interest in home building flashed a warning in Slim's mind. Also, the daughter was permitted more and added privileges in waiting on Slim, in preparing his food, and taking care of his clothing. Slim, naïvely pleased with the role of a popular young man, had thought they were merely being extravagantly nice to him, especially since he was bringing in his share of provisions for the home.

Slim noticed the men talking with Aklak and looking and pointing at him. His suspicions were really roused when one day Aklak showed him a good place to build an igloo, nearby his own, and offered to give him driftwood and whalebone and even help in the building. It snapped into Slim's mind that Aklak was not too subtly offering a dowry. This became certain when he told Slim that his daughter would make a loyal, faithful wife, and give him many fine babies. A man, he said, should have children and grandchildren.

Slim had seen all this before. He remembered the little Siberian Eskimo girl who had been offered to Corks. They too had probably held a council and decided Corks was a good trader with lots of goods, and if he married one of their girls he would never leave, for no Eskimo ever leaves his wife or home after his marriage. Likewise these people of Barrow had seen his trade goods, judged that he was a good hunter, and would make a fine husband for Aklak's daughter, especially since she seemed to be thoroughly in favor of the idea.

Later in the igloo, Slim noticed that the girl had finished her sewing on an exceptionally fine parka, decorated with parts of the finest pelts they had, and was beginning to fashion tiny mukluks and softly furred garments such as infants wear. Then he could clearly see the trap that he had almost stepped into. The girl no longer lowered her glance when he looked at her. She now looked him fully in the eyes, and there was no mistaking her thoughts this time.

"You sure ain't keepin' it a secret any more what you're thinkin', are you?" he said to himself. "I guess maybe everybody in Barrow's thinkin' the same thing, except me. And when I look at you and you keep lookin' purtier'n' purtier to me, it's just about time I got back where I come from before I learn some more about Eskimos." He closed his eyes and tried to conjure the vision of lovely blonde hair, pink-and-white skin, and the clean sweet smell of soap. But when no familiar thought could penetrate the smell of the igloo, he knew it was time for him to go.

There was no denying that he had become genuinely fond of these people. True, he had not fully accustomed himself to all their ways and habits, but he had accepted as many of them as he could. For the food he had acquired a taste, and he had never felt better in his life which could partly have been attributed to a diet of raw meat, fish, blubber, and an assortment of stews. One thing he had not been able to adjust to was the smell of the igloo. That alone was enough to blot out all thoughts of a future life among these people. However charming a bride Aklak's daughter might be, or what she promised notwithstanding, Slim made his plans to leave.

"You're still purty—for an Eskimo," he told her, "and you'll find a good Eskimo boy to be the poppa of your babies."

He explained to Aklak that he had to go back to his own people, and that by leaving now, just before spring arrived, he would reach the trails to the south before breakup and before melting snows would stop travel by dog team. Aklak understood, as one who lived or died by the weather understood. Slim was sorry to leave. He knew that he had made friends, and that no matter who might try to convince him otherwise, his three months of living in an igloo with these Eskimos had shown him their true characters and their genuine goodness. He never could have learned any of these things out of a book. He left his trade goods with them out of sheer gratitude for their kindness to him, and as he bade them good-by he knew that their sorrow in seeing him go was genuine.

His dogs had been well worked, and were able to take the pressure he put on them. His fight now was against time and weather. He wanted to reach the Yukon before breakup. He drove hard and long, and the dogs were more than equal to it. Here he was seeing the practical application of his crossbreeding. The dogs recuperated remarkably fast after a long day's run and were ready for more after a short rest. He examined them every night. There was no apparent soreness of muscle, and the pads of their feet showed no wear. This was particularly the mark of the wolf. A dog's pads were quick to become sore and were the usual cause of trail delays. These things he mentally catalogued.

What he hoped for now was to find a location so that he could continue his breeding, crossing again with wolf, and also with other dogs. As yet he didn't know what breeding habits his present dogs had inherited, whether wolf, or dog.

Although surface snow was going fast under the daytime thawing heat of mid-April, the streams were still ice-locked. This was what he had counted on. Also, instead of returning the way he had come north, he decided to strike south from the Kobuk and hit the Koyukuk River and follow it down to its junction with the Yukon. If luck were with him, he could cross the river there.

This time his luck held, strangely enough. Although the shore ice was mushy, and in many places honeycombed, the big river seemed to hold safe surface ice. Slim held his breath, mushed his dogs, and made it across with no more difficulty than a splash-wetting to the knees.

From then on he was in no hurry. Now that he was south of the big Yukon, he could go just about where he pleased for his next experiment with the dogs. At first he thought he would go east and back to his Chitina camp, or even go to Valdez. Just as he started in this direction he met an old friend of his from his mail-run days. This man, whom Slim knew only as The Dutchman, was camped beside the trail, and told Slim of new activity to the south.

"You vas to de Iditarod vunce," he said, "dis is goot blace now. Some beaple name Guggenheim is bringing out golt, und two men name Beaton und Dyckman is making strikes oop and down de Iditarod Creek mit golt like you don't see vunce."

Slim had heard rumors before he left the Copper River country that a gold rush was in the making and if what The Dutchman said was true, that the Guggenheims were interested, it must be a good one. The Guggenheims, whom Slim had heard of as having about all the promotion money in the world, were already backing the Kennecott copper production in the east. He thought he might as well spend some time in the neighborhood. He had already trapped in the Iditarod country, so it would be familiar to him, and besides, who knew, he just might pick up a stake.

He outfitted with food and supplies and set out for the two-hundred-mile trip along the floor of the Kaiyuh Mountain Valley. There was still snow for travel, but Slim took it slowly and easily, feeling the full impact of the beauty of the mountains and the trees, of birds, and of things growing. This was the Alaska he loved, and he felt good just being alive in it. What a contrast, he thought, from the eternal bleakness of the arctic shore he had recently left; there where life was the exception, here where vivid, vital beauty was all about him. Several times he stopped his dogs just to listen to the songs of birds and the wind in the trees. His world was again filled with the harmonies of the music of the wilderness he loved. So different from the somber minor monotone, varying in pitch with its viciousness, of the constant wind of the Arctic.

Late one afternoon he saw smoke ahead, apparently from a campfire. As he drew near he saw a man running through the brush, not toward him, but in the opposite direction. Slim thought this strange enough to investigate. He stopped, tied the sled, and walked toward the smoke.

As a boy in the Southwest, during the sheep and cattle wars, he had first learned the lesson never to walk unannounced into a strange camp. He purposely made noise in walking, and called a greeting. Before walking into the clearing, he stopped. He saw a well-made, neat camp. A fire was burning, and there was a good stock of wood. Standing near the fire was a man, and Slim assumed this was the man he had seen running. He was long-legged, very thin, and probably fifty-five or sixty years old. He had scraggly gray hair, and was more than shabbily dressed. He was holding an axe.

Slim said, "Hello, friend," starting into the clearing. He took no more than a step or two, and stopped.

The man let out a yell that just about raised Slim's scalp, and swung the heavy, double-bitted axe above his head. "Stay right where you are!" he yelled. "You move an inch, and I'll split you in two!"

Slim looked straight into the man's eyes, searching for reason in their glassy stare. He believed the man meant exactly what he said.

·12·

There are strange things done in the midnight sun
By the men who moil for gold;
The Arctic trails have their secret tales
That would make your blood run cold.

There was Slim, face to face with trouble again. His gun was a couple of hundred yards away on his sled, and his two big fists were of precious little use against an axe. Slim looked at the man hard. His eyes were steely, certain with determination. Slim thought fast, but acted slowly, for if the man were startled, he'd swing the axe as sure as Slim was scared.

Slim had often evaluated this thing called bravery. He had brushed with death many times, and had always stepped aside with deep respect to let it pass rather than rush headlong to meet it. He had seen men, who called it courage, hurry in to tangle with death and be killed for their trouble. Maybe they had been afraid, maybe they hadn't, Slim wouldn't know, but in his own experience he admitted to being afraid, but not to being a coward, not a weakling certainly, but afraid to the point of being careful and cautious rather than reckless and foolhardy. With the odds of the chance figured, his fear disappeared, and he would and could hold his own against terrible odds. But to walk into this man of uncertain thinking, to try to take the axe away from him, bordered on stupidity. Slim knew he had made many costly foolish mistakes, but this would not be another of them.

It was Slim's keen sense of observation that got him out of this predicament. Although the camp looked in good condition, Slim sensed something lacking. It dawned on him there was evidence of neither food nor cooking. There was no crane over the fire, no boiling pot. He also could see no rifle. These things gave him his clue, and he asked as matter-of-factly as he could, "Have you got any grub?"

The man squinted his eyes and stared at Slim. "There's an enemy I haven't seen for more'n a week," he yelled, then quickly lowered his voice to a whisper. "Have *you* got any grub?"

"Well, not right with me," said Slim, "but I got some at my camp, and how about goin' over there with me an' havin' a feed?"

The man cocked his head and continued his squint-eyed stare, then slowly began to lower the axe, very slowly. Slim didn't move.

"Thought you was an enemy spy," the man said. "I'm captain o' this brigade, and we ain't had no grub for more'n a week. Our ammunition's gone too. Good thing you came. Where's the grub?"

Slim relaxed. The man leaned against the axe handle for support, and continued his conversation on the condition of his troops. He had obviously been without food, for he swayed back and forth as he stood. His recent physical effort had taken just about all the strength he had left.

"Eight days," he said, "I tabbed 'em off, every one. Eight days I ain't had a bite o' food. A man could starve in eight days, but I didn't. Now come on, soldier, where's the rations at?"

"You just follow me," said Slim, "and you better let me carry your axe. It must be purty heavy." He cautiously reached for it.

The man studied Slim for a moment, then slowly handed him the axe. Slim then started off toward his sled. Behind him the man was still loudly deploying platoons and directing skirmishes.

This man was not crazy, he was "wild." Slim had seen men like this before. In gold camps he'd seen them come staggering in from their diggings, wild-eyed and raving. He'd seen them on the glacier at Valdez on their way to the outside. "Wild men" they called them, "bushed." They were different from the Jorgensens, the ones who completely lost their minds. These fellows, living alone, let their imaginations get out of control. The result was they began to live in this other world. Slim himself, as has anyone who lives too long in the wilderness alone, had been "wild." Having reached the limit of being lonesome, the man then enters the antisocial state of actually dreading to see a fellow human, even to the point of going to considerable trouble to avoid it; in the last stage he begins creating his own world. It was a temporary thing, a frothy realm of addled thinking that took time to repair. Apparently the man was playing soldier and fighting a war. This didn't bother Slim so long as he wasn't drawn into the battles.

When they reached the dogs and sled, Slim made a quick camp and first of all cooked a pot of rolled oats. He fed the man a spoonful at a time, almost having to hold his hands to keep him from grabbing it away to gulp it down. He told him it would be suicide to eat it fast. After a while the man slept. Slim watched him for a few moments, then figured it would be safe for him to lie down for a bit of rest himself. He had no sooner stretched out than the man began splitting the air with yell after yell which bounced off the mountains and up the valley. Slim woke him out of it and fed him again. The next time they lay down to sleep, Slim tied the man's wrist to his own, and each time the yelling started Slim just jerked him by the wrist and pulled him out of it.

The next day Slim left the man alone in camp for a few moments while he went to pick up wood. When he came back he found the man had opened the food sack and broken out a five-pound bag of dried apples, and with each hand full was stuffing them into his mouth as fast as he could. In one jump Slim was on him, knocking the apples out of his hand and shaking him to get them out of his mouth. A starving man with a stomach full of dried apples was as good as dead.

"You gol-hanged fool," Slim shook him again, "you get a belly full o' those apples and you'll puff up and bust wide open. They'll kill you!"

Instead of being belligerent, the man suddenly quieted, and meekly apologized. "I'm very sorry," he said in a soft, well-mannered voice, "I had no idea I was taking such chances. And would you mind telling me who you are and what you're doing here?"

The man had come out of it. As quickly as that his mind had cleared, and he was as rational as could be, and of a character completely unlike that which he had assumed. Slim shook his head. "That's the way it does, sometimes," he said to himself, then told the man who he was. He told him none of the experiences they had just been through. The fact that he had been found and fed seemed to satisfy the stranger.

From then on improvement was rapid. Slim stayed close to him, fed him a little at a time, and often, until the man's stomach began to accept food in quantities and he could be trusted to feed himself. Finally Slim took him back up the trail to Koyukuk and turned him over to the men in the village. The man was effusive in his thanks for Slim's care and kindness.

Back on the trail Slim pulled up for the first night's camp. The snow had been going fast and the trail was becoming spotty with bare rocks and moss. He started talking to his dogs while he unharnessed and fed them. "Bet you the next time I'll mind my own dang business," he said. "Get caught up with a 'wild' one and waste pit' near a week gettin' him sane enough to travel alone. And of all the gol-hanged fools I am, I don't even know what war he was fightin', and hang if I didn't forget to ask him what his name was. Well," he finished with his usual philosophical summation, "somebody has got to take care o' fellows like that, so it might as well be me, and it don't make a lot o' difference anyway what his name is."

The next day Slim took to the trail early, and mile after mile gloried in the beauty of the country, the mountains, the trees, the sky. He hadn't a care in the world. The dogs too seemed to feel the lack of any pressure. They ran freely, with their bushy tails curled and waving over their backs in rhythm with their perfect stride. "Them's awful good dogs," said Slim. His world was a wonderful place.

Ever since Slim arrived in Alaska, it seemed that the very moment he became pleased with life, and complacent, another emergency arose. This one took the form of a silver fox. Directly ahead, not over fifty feet in front of the dogs, a fox appeared out of the brush, scented and saw the dogs, and took off through the undergrowth. Things happened fast. The lead dog left the trail with a bound and started pursuit with eight eager yelping dogs behind him. Slim, unprepared, was thrown off balance and fell. Luckily he grabbed the trail rope dragging behind the sled and hung on. This rope, being a sort of safety brake, was attached to the handle bars of the sled and Slim's sudden weight tipped the sled on its side slowing it enough to allow him to scramble to his feet.

"Whoa!" he yelled as loudly as his foggy voice would let him. "Whoa, you dogs! WHOA!"

But the dogs paid no attention. Filled with the wolf-urge for a kill, they tore through the brush until their harness tangled in a downed tree and jerked them to a stop. Slim surveyed the shambles with complete consternation. His sled was broken, his pack split open, and his supplies scattered. He walked up to where the dogs were now lying down, quietly, tongues lolling out as though nothing out of the way had happened. He stood and looked at them and shook his head. In spite of the damage, he had to smile. He had been caught off guard. Had he been alert, he might have prevented all this. So, rather than being angry with the dogs, he was ashamed of himself. He said to the leader, "If I'd been watchin', I could have stopped you. I can't get mad at you for what your poppa bred into you. But from now on, young fellow,

178

I can't trust you to be boss of the team, you're going to have a new leader. You half-breeds are all right for workin', but I'm going to have a full-blood dog for a leader, somebody I can trust." He stopped and stroked the great head of the dog. "You wouldn't understand punishment, would you? So, I'm not going to punish you. If I gave you a grown dog, you'd kill him. So I'm goin' to get you a puppy. A little baby puppy dog, and you wolves with your love of young ones will raise him, and you'll like him and he'll like you and you'll get along so well the first thing you know he'll be your leader."

Slim got busy and mended the sled, picked up and packed his scattered belongings and got back onto the trail.

Before many days Slim was in familiar surroundings. The holdover of the original strikes and rush of 1906 was great, and even now, five years later, prospectors were literally crawling the creeks. It was a stampede all over again. Usually when a strike was made, one sizable enough to attract such thousands as in this neighborhood for instance, Slim was either too late or too far. And when he did arrive the panic was in full force. Habitually he had followed the urge, then when he arrived he was, as always, disappointed. It was the same story over again. He felt no urge to joint the pick-and-shovel panners. He just didn't like crowds. Of the thousands, perhaps a very few would gain enough gold to show any profit. Not that there wasn't plenty of gold, there was, millions and millions of dollars worth of it. But the precious yellow metal taken from the creek beds slipped as easily and quickly as yellow oil through the fingers of those who found it.

There were those who were always present to catch that flow of wealth, the saloonmen and the gamblers. These smelled gold finds as they were made, and with unerring accuracy, as if by second sight, had their establishments ready for the take before the prospecting horde arrived. Slim had known since he was a boy that the dollar he didn't work for was a dollar that bought only grief, and he didn't call prospecting work.

Of those who did find gold, only a few had richly profitable claims. The prize was very great, but the odds against success were amazingly high.

So Slim analyzed this gold rush. But he was there so he might as well stay. If he joined the others, he might spend a few years panning creek beds. Being frugal, he would surely pan enough to buy supplies, and show some profit, but the odds were thousands to one against his making a rich find. Besides, Slim had never been happy in the monotony of one job. How then could he put all this activity to his own good use for the time being and still do what he wanted? Here Slim called on his experience. One thing these prospectors needed and would pay for was meat. Slim decided to make a camp in good trapping and hunting country and supply the demand. This was his "sure thing." Let the prospectors dig; whether they found gold or not, they still had to eat.

Slim found dogs in Iditarod, and after careful inspection bought a fine young male puppy. A full-blooded Malemute. His wolf-dogs immediately took to the little fellow, for the dog half reached out to dog, and the wolf half, with its love for all young things, accepted it protectively. Then he bought supplies, loaded his sled, and went into the mountains. After about a week he found just the place he wanted. There was a stream of clear fast water with lots of fish. There was plenty of evidence that it was a good trapping country. He had also seen some game, but not too much. And most important, he had seen no prospectors, so apparently he would be well away from their activities.

He set about putting up a lean-to and establishing a permanent camp. He watched his dogs play with the new puppy. It seemed that each of the big dogs tried to outdo the others in gaining the favor of the little puppy. They seemed almost human in jealousy if the puppy favored any one especially. They were almost ludicrously gentle with the little fellow.

He was just comfortably getting settled after returning from a trip to Iditarod where he spent his last money for more traps and supplies, when a young stranger walked into camp. He was younger than Slim, six inches shorter and about forty pounds lighter. A good smile broke through clear blue eyes. The two men gauged each other for a full minute. The newcomer stuck out his hand.

"My name's Eddie Cooper," he said. "I been in the country three or four years and I heard about this Iditarod strike a year ago and decided to come over."

"You a prospector?" Slim asked cautiously.

Eddie laughed and shook his head. "Are you?" And when he looked around Slim's camp layout, he said, "I see you ain't, so it looks like you and me have got the same idea. Let them dig for it, and we'll feed 'em. I been lone-wolfin' it, so when I saw your fire smoke, I thought I'd come over and see who you are. I know the bush, and I'm willin' to work if you want a partner, but I warn you, I'm broke."

Slim laughed. "Nothin' so wrong with that, so'm I," he said. "Guess we'll both have to work. I'm Slim Williams."

Wilderness friendships are based on elementals, like a common cause, mutual trust, and a willingness to work. These were the essentials. Over a pot of tea and some fried fresh grayling the two made their deal. They joined forces to hunt and sell meat to the prospectors, and to trap. Probably all that Slim would ever know about his partner was what he had already been told, that he was a good bushman, and that his word was as good as his aim. That was enough to satisfy Slim, for that was relatively no more than he would tell Eddie about himself.

Eddie started over to see the dogs, but as he neared them he was stopped short by a snarling rasping growl. He jumped back.

Slim laughed. "They won't hurt you," he said. "They're all wolves, half-wolves anyway, all but the little puppy. He's a dog. He's their new leader."

"Their what?" Eddie asked incredulously. "That little puppy goin' to be a leader in that wolf-dog team?"

"That's right," said Slim, "those wolf-dogs will take in that little puppy and let him grow up with 'em, and will accept him as a leader when he gets grown. It's the only way you can put a dog as leader in with crossbreeds. Put a grown dog in, they'd kill him."

"You know pretty much about dogs, don't you?"

"I worked with 'em ever since I been in Alaska. That's a good many years."

Eddie looked at Slim closely for a minute or two. "Williams," he mused, "Slim Williams." Then recognition came. "Say!" he said, "Now I know who you are! The way you talk about dogs. You're *the* Slim Williams! You once drove a team of fifty dogs."

Slim nodded.

"All in one team, one hitch?"

Slim nodded again.

"Seems impossible."

"A fellow can sometimes do an awful lot if he wants to, and there's an honest need for doin' it," said Slim. "I didn't drive 'em far, I guess not over fifty miles. I drove 'em from Nome out to where a fellow was goin' to board 'em for the summer. That was quite a few years ago. I suppose any good dog man could ha' done it."

"And you were running mail on the Dawson-Nome trail?" Eddie asked.

"Lots of fellows made that run," said Slim.

"But didn't a fellow named Slim Williams make some records for the run? Like drivin' dogs the two thousand miles from Dawson to Nome and back with more'n a thousand pounds o' freight an' doin' it in sixty days?"

Slim grinned. "Some things sort o' slip my mind, Eddie."

"Well, I heard you did. As the dogs tired you changed teams, you had to, but nobody changed off with you, you made the trip goin' and comin'. I heard fellows say there ain't another dog man in Alaska could do it. I heard a fellow even wrote a book about your doing it. Is that so, Slim?" Eddie didn't wait for the answer that probably wouldn't have come, but went eagerly on, "And I heard about the time you bucked a blizzard for more than fifty miles, all alone, to bring out a fellow who'd shot himself by accident. Fellow you didn't even know. I heard about that in Fairbanks, even talked to the fellow whose life you saved, big fellow, weighed more than two hundred pounds. Shot himself in the belly by accident. Fellows say nobody else would even try to go after him. And I heard . . . . " But Eddie had lost his audience. Slim had picked up his axe and started off. "Come on, Eddie," he called, "better get started makin' ourselves a camp to live in. First thing we better do is build ourselves a shack." Slim completely dismissed the recounting of his past, nor did Eddie ever succeed in getting close to the subject again.

Eddie couldn't help but look admiringly at this big, easy-moving, modest man who had established records over many trails for strength and stamina, who seemed willing to let them live in silent memory instead of in conversation.

By fall their camp was well formed. Slim had chosen the spot wisely. There was plenty of game, and they had done well with their sale of meat to the prospectors at Iditarod. After the trails were snowed down, Eddie watched with open admiration as Slim handled the team. "You're the best man with dogs I ever saw, Slim," he said, "I don't know how you do it."

"It's not so hard," Slim explained, "if you only give the dog credit for thinking. Trouble is when a man tries to do the thinking for the dog, that's when things go wrong. Dogs are smart, they think, and they know. And the more you give 'em credit for it, the better dogs you got. There's nothin' in this world a dog wants more than to make somebody happy. Now look at those dogs." They looked across the camp clearing to where they were chained. They returned the men's stare. "Purty, ain't they?" Slim commented quietly. "They know we're talkin' about 'em, and you can see in their eyes that they're thinkin'. It's knowin' how they think that makes it easy to get along with 'em. Sometimes I look at them and they're dog. Sometimes, like right now, they're pure wolf. Maybe it's because it's fall. We'll never know all about 'em. But a dog is the most tickledest when he knows he's doin' what you like."

"That little dog's going to make a good leader," Eddie commented appreciatively.

"He's awful young yet," said Slim, "but he's awful smart. His bein' with the wolves, you see how they take to him? They'll follow him anywhere. I'm not puttin' any weight to him yet, just lettin' him take his place at the head so he'll learn, and they'll do what he tells 'em. I think I'll call him Buck, the way he holds his head up like that. He's a good dog. He knows he's special, too, bein' the only one we don't keep on a chain."

Freeze-up came fast. Both men worked hard in laying out trap lines and setting snares and deadfalls. Slim found his partner was apparently tireless in the bush, and was a good and careful trapper. They each knew that they had reached the point of good partnership when they could go sometimes all day without talking. Like the Indian who is a poor conversationalist, he'd always thought that silence was a mark of friendship and understanding; rather than talk extravagantly about the beauty of a mountain, the Indian knows that you see the same mountain and yet has the politeness to let you think your own adjectival description. He sees it, you see it, so why talk about it. Slim had acquired many of these really admirable traits from his Indian friends. They were never ones to argue, each man, they felt, should do his own thinking. Talk, to Slim, was more often than not a filler of time for lack of thinking. Silence between friends was more important than words.

One night the deep cold took hold. The temperature dropped fast from late afternoon to black night. Sap froze and snapped riflelike in the trees, the wind was stilled as though the North were holding its breath.

Slim and Eddie were rolled in their blankets. Slim watched the lights cast from the fire in their little stove as they danced merrily on the logs of their shack. Suddenly from the night outside came the call of a wolf. One lone, long howl. It was the voice of a monarch. It was a command! It sounded nearby, but it might have been a mile or more away so clearly did sound travel in the clear night. Slim knew the call. He had heard it many, many times before. It was the gathering call of a leader to his pack. As the sound died out there was sudden commotion outside the cabin. The dogs rattled their chains restlessly, and there came an answering call. Slim knew that voice. It was Blizzard, pouring into his wail all the longing and yearning of a wild thing for its own. One sad, heartful cry. Then all was still again.

It was a strange winter. Trapping was good, hunting was bad. The fur-bearers were on the move, and Slim and Eddie were kept busy skinning, fleshing, and stretching pelts. Although Eddie was adept at the work, he soon acquired expertness under Slim's skillful tutoring. They knew they would show a splendid profit from their winter trapping, but they still hoped to sell meat to the prospectors. They hunted, but game was not to be found in quantities that would make a trip to prospectors' camps a profitable venture. There were times when they themselves had to be satisfied with meager meat rations.

One morning Slim told Eddie he was going hunting. "All we've done is to take a gun on our trap-line runs," he said. "I'm going over that next ridge and see what I can find. There's got to be game somewhere, and we'll find it."

"All right, Slim," Eddie agreed, "You do that, and I'd better take a look at the downstream trap line."

Slim hunted hard and far. With all the cunning he had, he tried to locate game, but for some reason it seemed that the big animals had disappeared. Slim knew they did this at times because of food, but he was hopeful that in one of the valleys, or along a ridge, he would see at least evidence of food game. He was disappointed.

By the time he started back to camp, he realized that he had stretched his hunt too far. Dusk was rolling in, and the cold was dropping down. He felt all right, he had eaten, but the more he walked the more he wanted to sit down and just rest. He was getting tired. Once he sensed this, he drew himself out of it quickly. He would not sit down to rest. That urge was the first danger signal, the warning to stay on his feet and keep going.

Cold is an insidious and treacherous thing. Cold at first may seem to offer exhilaration and a sense of joyous, vital activity. But cold is tiring. It dulls and deadens senses until every muscle movement becomes a conscious effort. Cold is also a liar. The senses cry out in pain at its first touch, but it quickly dulls these senses by the same touch that caused the pain. From then on cold is a murderer. With the senses no longer aware of its presence, it chills and freezes until the only thing that can share it is death itself.

Slim was conscious of the cold. And when the urge came to rest, he drove himself on. Reason would have dictated building a fire, but Slim was no longer reasoning. The cold had passed the physical to touch the mental. His hands and feet and legs went through the first biting, stinging signs of being cold, but he accelerated his gait and these signs passed. He felt his cheeks and chin for the telltale hardened patches of freezing, and when these came he warmed them with his bare hands until they tingled their thaw. Finally even this no longer seemed necessary. Strangely enough he finally no longer even *thought* of cold. He had no idea what the temperature was. The world about him was the eerie blue-white of early night, and still, very still. He reached the comfortable stage of having no sense of body. His feet were no longer heavy to lift. Yet, although he seemed to walk without effort, he was tired. His one thought, and it became an obsession, was sleep. He wanted more than anything to lie down in the trail and rest, and sleep. When he awoke, he would go on to the cabin, refreshed, and tell Eddie of this amusing experience, how joyous it was to walk in the cold without feeling it, and to have a good refreshing sleep, a good long sleep.

Slim finally decided there was no reason why he shouldn't lie down and rest for just a few moments, so he did. One minute he was standing, the next, without any conscious move, he was lying down. A misty, vague thought tried to tell him this was not the thing to do, that it was dangerous, and that the cold instead of being kind to him and numbing him past the point of pain, was actually killing him. He got to his knees. That was right. He must go on. There was a trail ahead of him, he knew, and he began to crawl hoping that he was on it. Once he stopped to catch his breath and he looked back. There behind him perhaps ten feet or a little more was a rifle seemingly suspended in air, following him. He had never seen such a thing. He laughed. He laughed long and hard. He called to the rifle and told it that if it wanted to be shot to come up close to him and he would shoot it. That's what rifles were for, he told it, to shoot. Little by little as though moving cautiously the rifle became clearer to Slim, and he was surprised when he found it in his hands. He laughed again and patted it, then pointed it in the air and pulled its trigger. Then he lay down on the trail and quietly went to sleep. If it became a thousand degrees colder and remained so for a thousand years, Slim would have known no difference. Held thus in the embrace of cold, Slim had actually frozen to the point of death.

Slim was awakened sharply by pain. He tried to raise his head, but each time that he did he was struck down again. He opened his eyes and saw two great shining eyes close to his own, staring at him. A beast with great sharp paws clawed at his face. Wet ran down his cheeks and into his eyes and mouth, but he neither knew it was blood nor felt the gashes in his scalp and face from which it flowed. He knew he had to get away from the creature somehow. He raised his hands to ward off the blows and tried to strike the shaggy face that leered so close to his own. He shook his head. He could feel no more pain, but once more he was fully awake. The thought came to him strongly now that he should be on his way to camp, that he must move. Laboriously he got to his hands and knees and began to crawl. The animal hovered near, but made no effort to touch Slim as long as he was moving. Slim had gone no more than a hundred yards, sightless from the blood and cold, when his arms could no longer hold his weight. He tried with the utmost of his will to lift himself. But he fell forward into the snow. He concentrated on raising his arms. There was something solid ahead of him that barred his way. Feebly he tried to push it or to beat it away with his hands, but it was no use. This final effort cost him his consciousness.

That which barred his way moved. It was a door, and it opened to show light and give forth warmth. Eddie stood in the opening. He looked down at the form lying before him. He had heard a muffled tapping and had opened it to investigate. He recognized his partner lying there. He carried Slim's unconscious body to the bunk. The parka hood had been clawed off. Slim's scalp and face bled from long deep gashes. His cheeks were frosted gray. But his chest rose and fell in full regular rhythm.

Eddie went to work deftly and expertly to care for the all but frozen man. He spoke quietly, "A Frenchman I knew in Canada would call you *L'Homme du Nord*, 'The Man of the North.' And if you're not a Man of the North, you'll do until one comes along. Thank God, Slim, you're still alive."

·13·

Can you remember your huskies all going,
*   Barking with joy and their brushes in air;*
You in your parka, glad-eyed and glowing,
*   Monarch, your subjects the wolf and the bear?*

The following several days were tough ones for Slim. Fortunately there was no "black freeze" on any part of his body, no frozen dead flesh that turned black and indicated almost certain amputation. His feet had been well protected by his using the Eskimo precaution of lining his mukluks with dry-grass insulation against cold. His hands were saved by covers of four-ply knitted wool mitts under moose-hide mitts. Although he had been chilled beyond sensitivity and feeling, he was very fortunate that the results were not serious.

His thawing-out was a painful process. Eddie had seen cases like this, as had Slim, and they both knew that a gradual defrosting was essential for the preservation of tissue as well as for the tiny surface blood vessels. When the frost-bound nerves began once more to warm to body heat, they screamed their resentment. They tingled, itched, ached, and altogether made Slim as miserable as he had ever been.

"Just what were you trying to do?" Eddie asked him a few days later when Slim seemed willing to talk a bit. "You're no Eskimo, you know."

"Eskimo'd have more sense," Slim growled. "It just goes to show how stupid a fellow can be when he don't pay attention to the lessons he's learned." He spoke with difficulty through swollen split lips, just healing. "You'd think I was a cheechako, and yet it fooled me. I thought I was ahead of the cold all the way, and then when I knew it had caught me and I was goin' to sleep, it was too late for me to do anything about it. I should have lighted a fire when the idea first come to me. I pit' near died, maybe I did, I don't know. Just lucky, I guess."

Eddie brought him a cup of good thick caribou broth. "I found out what it was clawed you up," he said.

"I don't remember much about that. All I know is it was a big animal with claws a foot long tryin' to take my head off. Maybe a big wolverine."

Eddie shook his head. "Ungh, ungh, wolverine wouldn't even o' left your head on you. It was your own pup, Buck."

"Buck?" Slim said incredulously.

Eddie nodded. "All I got to say is it's a good thing you leave him off the chain most o' the time."

"How do you know it was Buck?"

"Because he's got part o' your parky hood over his chain post. He won't let me go anywhere near it. He's guardin' it."

"So it was Buck. I guess I don't remember much about it." Slim closed his eyes and lay back for a moment. "Hm," he cleared his throat, "Buck saw me in trouble and figured he had to get me up. I don't remember even gettin' to the door. Buck must have kept at me until I did. And you say you heard me knockin' on the door?"

Eddie nodded.

"Don't remember it. But I remember somethin' about shootin' a rifle. You didn't hear my rifle?"

"Sap in the trees was poppin' all over the place, freezin', sounded like guns, so if you did shoot yours I wouldn't of heard it."

"But maybe that was what Buck heard, the rifle, an' come to find out what it was. Found me layin' there and went to work gettin' me up. He didn't know he was hurtin' me. He was doin' the only thing he knew."

"Well, it did the business anyway," Eddie agreed. "Now all you got to do is take it easy for awhile until you grow back together."

Slim sighed. "And my dog done it," he mused. "Guess maybe I'd ha' froze to death if it wasn't for him, wouldn't I? You know, Eddie, it just shows there ain't anything in this world much better'n a dog."

Slim was a poor patient. He had always been able to take care of himself, and capably. But this was a new experience. He was confined against his will and he didn't like it. The cabin was kept darkened until his eyes could readjust to bright light. Layers of dead skin sloughed off with the growth of new. His head and face wounds healed. All this took time. He fretted like a baby, complained like a spoiled child, and groused like a lumberjack over Eddie's ministrations, the applications of cool tea to his cold-burned skin, and poultices of tea leaves on his eyes.

"Where'd you learn about this, Slim?" Eddie asked.

"Indians," said Slim. "They use a herb but tea's just as good."

Eddie was a stern handler. "Trouble with you is," he told Slim, "you don't know when you're well off. Anybody that's got no more sense than to go to sleep in a snowbank ought to be kept in cold storage. Instead of that here you are not liftin' a finger, bein' fed an' waited on like a bride, and look at the thanks I get for my trouble. Now here's your dinner. Tonight you get rolled oats and tea and sourdough biscuits."

"All you feed me is gol-hanged soup and rolled oats. How long you goin' to keep on feedin' me this baby food?"

"Until you grow up. Now shut up and eat your supper before I give you a lickin'."

Slim grinned at his partner, who grinned right back. "You're a good boy, Eddie," said Slim, and wasted no further time in talk. He cleaned up a second bowl of the steaming hot porridge before he sighed deeply and leaned back in his bunk.

Muscles began to loosen, nerves quietened, and Slim was

once more on his feet. The first time he stepped out of the cabin, he called Buck to him. The dog came bounding across the clearing, reared, and with paws on Slim's shoulders almost knocked him off his feet. The dog then pranced around, bounced, and yipped and barked. In every move and sound there was the full expression of joy. "You remind me of a little dog I used to have over on the Chitina, Buck. He used to get just about as tickled as you are right now, but not quite. You're out-ticklin' him, that's sure. And I'm glad to see you too, fellow, and I want to thank you kindly for savin' my life." Buck looked into his master's face and barked.

When spring came, just before breakup, Slim and Eddie held a "business meeting."

"How would you like to take our fur and sell it, Eddie?" Slim suggested. "Take the dogs while there's still ice, and bring back our summer grub? These dogs know you well enough so you can drive 'em."

"Don't you want to go 'out'?" Eddie asked with just a bit of surprise.

"No, Eddie. There's nothing out there I want that I haven't got better and more of here."

"All right," said Eddie, "then is there anything special I can bring you? Something to eat maybe? I'm not forgetting I treated you pretty rough when you were going through your spring thaw."

Slim thought for a moment, rubbing his thumb against his chin. He nodded. "Eggs," he said simply, "if you can get some eggs and potatoes, bring 'em. I like boiled eggs and mashed potatoes; eggs nice and soft, then break 'em onto the potatoes and mix 'em up. That's good eatin'."

"Eggs it'll be, Slim, if I can find 'em in Iditarod."

"Or some maple sirup, so we could have some good flapjacks and sirup. Never did have enough flapjacks and sirup."

Their winter catch of furs brought banner prices. The sled was packed high with pelts when Eddie waved to his partner and mushed off down the creek.

Ten days later Eddie returned, the sled packed this time with supplies. After unloading, and a good hot meal, Eddie was eager with conversation about the new happenings at the towns of Iditarod and Flat, and the dramas of the creek placers. A huge powered mechanical dredge was being assembled on Flat Creek to dredge the creek bottom, to pan and sluice the sand automatically, by the ton! he said. Slim muttered something about "civilization crowdin' in."

As he unpacked the supplies, Eddie held up a sack. "Eggs," he announced. "I had to talk fast to the restaurant man, he didn't want to sell 'em, but I got you a dozen. I don't know what hen laid 'em, where, or when, but they're eggs, and a dollar apiece. And here's a sack o' potatoes to go with 'em. And a tin o' sirup. Now you can have yourself a feed."

Slim almost drooled as he grinned and accepted these treasures from his partner.

The eggs, as Eddie had said, were of doubtful vintage, but they were nonetheless eggs, highly tasteful, acridly aromatic, sulfurously flavored, but—eggs. Eddie passed them up, so Slim enjoyed the questionable pleasure of eating them all. It took him just one meal to accomplish it. After this feast he sat back and sighed with satisfaction.

"Well," said Eddie, "now that you aren't exactly suffering from hunger any more, how'd you like to know how we come out on our furs?" Eddie reached into his packsack and brought out a paper-wrapped package.

"I hadn't been thinkin' much about it," said Slim, "I been pretty busy myself."

As Slim watched, Eddie counted and stacked up two identical piles of bills. It was a one-for-you-one-for-me division. When he finished, he shoved a pile toward Slim. "After buying grub and supplies, we come out with three thousand dollars apiece. That's pretty good, Slim."

"Mm hmmm," Slim nodded and picked up the bills. "You did all right, Eddie, you made a good sale."

"I thought so too, Slim." Eddie was obviously pleased.

"Three thousand dollars apiece for a winter's trap's good money."

"Never paid much attention to money," said Slim as he stored the bills away in his packsack. "Money to me's always been something I had to work for to trade for something I needed. I guess it depends on what you think you need and how bad you need it whether you got a lot o' money or not. I carried mail at a dollar a letter, and freight at a dollar a pound. But I turned right around and traded that money for better dogs or a better gun, or axes or grub or whatever it was I needed. Now if I was plannin' to go out, back to the States or some place, why then maybe I'd want money. But I ain't plannin' to go any place but to stay right here in Alaska, so money don't seem to matter so much to me. I don't put too much store in it."

Slim had lived a pay-as-you-go existence. He had never saved, it didn't seem necessary. That, to him, was like anticipating needs before they arose. He'd always been taken care of somehow, and he believed that he always would be. His credit was undoubtedly good with any trading post in Alaska, but his life of trade and barter was of the moment, and debt to him was a bad habit, one he had never acquired. Money, therefore, was only money. If Eddie had brought back twice the amount for their furs, it would have made little difference to Slim. His needs would have been the same.

When he had his share tucked away, he said, "Now come on, and I'll show you what I got while you were gone."

Ten minutes later Eddie questioned him, "Aren't you taking on quite a bit, Slim?"

"No, I don't think I am," said Slim, looking at the assortment of animals he had caught and chained. "Those two bear cubs won't give us much bother. But what I was really after was wolves. Of course, its early for 'em, but I thought maybe I could find a den."

"What do you want wolves for? You already got a team o' half-wolves now."

"Sometime I'm goin' to breed and rebreed these dogs and wolves to try the different proportions to see where I'll get the best sled animals. If I could get some cubs, then I'd try to breed a male with one of these females and see what three-quarter wolf-dogs would be like. I'm goin' to try it sometime."

"Take a long time to find out," said Eddie.

"Be worth it," argued Slim, "if we get a top dog. Take about four years each time. Three years for the wolf cub to grow up to become a man, and about a year to see what the pups would be like. I'm going to try it sometime, though." Slim was a man of determined temperament. Although at times he seemed to act on impulse, like his trip with Corks to Siberia, he nonetheless was positive in following the line of thought in which he believed. The progressive mutation of sled dogs from crossbreeding with wolves was one of them.

Eddie could not help but agree with the very sound reasoning of this man whose experience with dogs topped that of anyone he knew. Then he looked at the two black, roly-poly balls of fur, and pointed.

"But I can't understand what you want with two bear cubs."

"I don't want 'em," Slim shook his head. "Second day you was gone, I was just comin' out of the cabin and there was this bear, big one, standin' right across the clearing. She come for me, and I shot her. Then out of the woods comes these two little fellows. They was her babies and I'd killed their momma, and look at 'em, Eddie, ain't bigger'n a cat. I couldn't kill them too."

Later in the spring Slim and Eddie began laying out new trap lines. Eddie had been away for several days. When he returned, he and Slim sat in the cabin. As they talked, Eddie stared at something on Slim's bunk. Two very bright eyes stared back at him from the blankets. Slim saw, and explained, "That's Raffles. Wasn't there a fellow named Raffles somewhere who was supposed to be pretty fast with his fingers in pickin' people's pockets and stealin' and like that?"

"Yes," Eddie nodded, "I read stories about him. He was a crook."

"But nothin' mean about him, except stealin'. That's why I named this little fellow after him. Got the slickest little way of gettin' what he wants without your hardly knowin' he's gettin' it." Slim went to the bunk and carefully shoved his hand under the blanket. "He likes it under here, it's warm." In a moment he drew out a tiny ball of bushy red fur. It had a sharp, pointed black nose, beady eyes, and it was nibbling at Slim's fingertips. "It's a baby red fox. Cute little fellow, ain't he? Of course, if he was a silver he'd grow up to be worth a lot of money, but he's just goin' to grow up to be a red and won't be worth a dime, but I kept him because he's such a cute little rascal."

"Where'd you get him?" Eddie asked.

"While I was wolf-huntin'." Slim tossed the tiny fox back on his bunk and the wee animal immediately dug himself out of sight in the blankets. In a moment the black tip of his snout pushed out and two bright little eyes stared at the men.

"And you brought back a red fox?" To Eddie it was undoubtedly a waste of time and effort.

Slim looked a bit sheepish. "His mother is a beautiful silver. I saw her and figured she had some pups, so I started callin'. I learned that from the Indians a long time ago. Takes a lot o' practice, but you listen to her talk, and you get so you can mimic her, then you can call pups right up to the mouth o' the den. But only this one come up, and him a red. She crossed with a red somewhere and that's what she got for it. That's how I found Raffles, so I just brung him along back with me. I never seen her again. That's about all there is to it."

"Well, it's another addition to your menagerie. What are you going to do about feeding this zoo?" Eddie asked.

"I'd thought of that," Slim explained. "We got lots of fish for the dogs, and the bears'll eat what's left from everybody else. They ain't so fussy, they'll eat anything."

"And how about your friend Raffles, here?"

"Oh, him," Slim laughed and looked toward the bunk at the unblinking stare of the tiny animal. "That little Raffles. He can just about nibble his way along with you and me. Tickles me the way he'll try to get into your pocket to see what you got. I always wanted to see if I could tame a fox into bein' a pet." He shook his head. "Cute little fellow, likes to get under the blankets and nibble at my toes to get me up in the morning."

"How do you think your happy family is going to get along together?" Eddie had seen the dogs' hackles rise when they looked at the bears, and heard their gruff resentment.

"I'll have a talk with 'em," said Slim. "We'll all get along all right."

Slim had been right about the unity of the camp with the assortment of animals he had brought together. The bears and the fox were purely for pastime and entertainment. His wolf-dogs were a necessity, as was Buck. The bears were playful nuisances, the little fox a prankster. The dogs minded their own business.

Eddie looked at him and shook his head. "Thirteen assorted animals to feed and take care of. Slim, you're going to be a busy man."

Eddie was right. Slim was busy, but it was the sort of busyness that he liked. To Eddie it would have been a chore. Slim suggested, therefore, that Eddie could well spend the summer in putting up some lean-to shacks along the trap lines. Slim could work closer to camp so as to take care of his animal problems. By fall, things would be under control, and the two could once more devote a winter to trapping.

Of all the animals in camp, the one that gave Slim the most trouble was Raffles. He became a docile, friendly, companionable pet. But his mischievousness was beyond control. Slim kept him in the cabin, and it took no more than a lesson or two and a few days to housebreak the little fellow. He seemed eager to learn. That's what got him into trouble. He learned where Slim kept the things he liked to eat. He learned that by sitting on Slim's lap when Slim was eating, he was quick enough to rake his foreleg along the table and brush things to the floor. This he learned after Slim had cured him of sitting on the table during mealtime.

Raffles was better than an alarm clock. At exactly dawn each morning he crawled out of his little blanket bed that Slim had made for him, and jumped on Slim's bunk. If Slim's blankets were so tight he couldn't crawl under to nip his toes to wake him, he sat on Slim's chest and stuck his cold little soapy-wet nose in Slim's eyes until they opened. Then he started a play scamper around the cabin until Slim gave up trying to catch him. He was like trying to thumb down a flash of red light. Raffles was an expert at hide-and-seek, and peek-a-boo. He sometimes played like a kitten, sometimes like a puppy, but most generally like a little red fox. He had the run of the cabin and the camp. He never tried to run away, and he knew to the very inch how far the chains would permit every animal in camp to move. He teased the other animals unmercifully. When Slim went hunting in the bush, Raffles followed him like a dog. Slim discouraged this, not because he didn't like his little friend's company, but because he was afraid that some harm would come to the youngster, who was unaware that danger lurked in a world unknown to him. His mother had not taught him to hunt or to beware of his enemies. To Raffles the world consisted of a big man who fed him and played with him, and an assortment of chained-up animals which were not to be played with.

Slim's chastisement of Raffles consisted of sharp finger raps on his nose. The fox learned quickly, and remembered. He'd stand disconsolately in front of the cabin when Slim told him to stay home, and stare at his master as he strode off along one of the hunting trails. Then he would dart into the under-brush, and parallel Slim's course. Some miles from camp he would put in his appearance on the trail ahead of Slim and wait for him. When Slim saw him, the mock penitence and the act of great remorse over having disobeyed overcame any thought of punishment. By then they were too far away from camp for Raffles to be sent home. He loved Slim, and asked no more of life than to be allowed to spend it with him.

The bear cubs were different. They grew up to be bears. As cubs they were also delightfully playful, but before many weeks they had grown to such size that it was no longer exactly safe to play or scuffle with them. It is possible that a bear has no idea of his own strength. Whatever it is he wants to do, he does, and seems to have the power to do it. Slim had seen the big fellows in action. He had seen one blow of a paw crush the skull of a moose. He had seen a bear, looking for grubs or ants, with no show of effort lift a rock weighing hundreds of pounds with one paw. A playful tap of a paw could easily break a man's bones.

Slim had never known a bear to be tamed. He had seen them chained and submissive, but he was certain that the volatile nature of the animal was lightly covered, and that just under the docile surface was a fury that could never be fully leashed, always ready to break loose at the slightest provocation. Indians said, "Never believe bear, bear all time thinks kill." Perhaps they were right that a bear's thoughts were always lethal, no matter what he looked like or how he acted.

Bears are smart. In Slim's estimation, the wolf and the bear share the top spot for animal wisdom and sheer natural shrewdness. One thing they have in common, they are killers. One difference between them, however, is that the wolf will not attack a man unprovoked or without reason; the bear will attack a man if he feels like it.

The little cubs grew fast. Slim kept them chained, and increased the strength of the chain as they developed in strength. Here, too, were two untutored youngsters of the wilderness. Ordinarily the mother bear stays with her cubs for two years, during which she prepares them for a life of survival against natural enemies, and teaches them how to secure food. Slim wondered just how much of this was instinct and how much they learned from the maternal instruction. He could not keep these two indefinitely, and as they grew in size their demands for food increased. They were no longer playful, and had long since grown past the stage where Slim's sympathy for their orphaned helplessness affected his judgment. One day he took them across the creek and far down the valley, and there turned them loose.

For more than a week Slim kept close watch lest the bears return and make a wreck of the camp in search for food. He discouraged this by putting food out for them at night, each night leaving less and placing it farther from camp. One morning he found that the food had not been touched. The bears were on their own. Except for occasional visits, which Slim assumed to be thoroughly friendly and inquisitively exploratory, he saw very little of them for the rest of the summer.

His dogs were no problem. Sled dogs in the summertime do nothing but eat and fight flies. Slim kept his dogs purposely underfed. With no running or even exercise, it would have been easy for them to put on weight; and this fat would have been a dangerous acquisition by fall, when it would have to be dissipated, worked off. A dog, perspiring through his tongue, finds difficulty in losing weight by that method. Muscular exercise, running at top speed for long periods, instead of causing weight loss affects the lungs, and a fat dog easily becomes wind-broken and useless. The control of food is the control of fat. Therefore, Slim watched fatty-food consumption by the dogs without even knowing that such a thing as a calorie existed. He gave them what food they needed, but just enough to keep them alive. By fall they would appear scrawny, but they would be healthy.

The scourges of the North in summer are mosquitoes and black flies that cloud the air in unbelievable swarms. The bites of the flies are maddening. Slim had known of men losing their reason because of them. The flies also attacked the animals, and noses, ears, and eyes were turned into swollen, bleeding sores during the short but dramatically violent visitation of the insects. Nothing that Slim had ever found proved a preventative against them. Netting over the bunk was his protection, but his heart ached because of his inability to help the animals. During flytime it was best to let the dogs alone. Their suffering made them irascible and cranky. These animals could not reason the source of their torture, and even Slim's efforts toward kindness were looked upon with suspicion.

The fly season ended when the first nip of cool came and brought with it the giant dragonflies. These flying bombers of the insect world with their iridescent diaphanous wing structure were the sign that the flies and mosquitoes would be gone. Within a day or two the bites and stings stopped.

It was one day during the fly season that he heard what sounded like heavy blasting. There was one extremely heavy charge shortly after noon, one that caused the ground to shake. Another came three or four hours later, not so heavy as the first, but still a big explosion. Both came from the same place somewhere to the south. The next day the air was filled with a strange dust. His shovel and tools and things around the camp appeared to be covered with copper. The sun shone through a reddish haze. This lasted for several days. Slim put it down to the blasting and air conditions and went about his work.

Buck had developed beautifully, fulfilling every promise of his puppyhood days. Slim was training him to be a first-class lead dog.

Little Raffles began bit by bit to realize that he had a heritage to fulfill. Things in the underbrush began to interest him, things like field mice. Slim watched as the fox stalked a mouse and pounced. His hunts became daily adventures which carried him farther and farther from camp. At first he returned each night, but as fall came on, he went wider afield, until finally his visits were rare. After the first snow, there were often tracks in the morning to show that during the night the little fox had prowled in the camp with friendly familiarity. But his days of being a pet were over. Slim was sorry to see him go, but he would have taken no pleasure in keeping him tied or penned up to serve no more purpose than amusement. Slim only hoped that Raffles' juvenile trickery would develop through his inherent instincts to become adult cleverness.

Two friends did return, however, with positive decisions to spend the winter. The bear cubs, grown to considerable size, selected the camp as a fine place for hibernation. One of them found a potential cave at the root of a downed spruce and dug himself in. The other crawled between uprights and clawed his way under the cabin where he proceeded to sleep the winter out. These selections of winter dwellings were made while Slim and Eddie were away from camp. When they returned, they read the signs.

"What are we going to do about the one under the cabin?" Eddie asked.

"You want to tear up the log floor and kill him? It's the only way you'll get him out. When he goes to sleep, he sleeps."

The bear gave audible testimony of his full abandon to sleep. All winter long the trappers were serenaded by an almost continuous assortment of snores, grunts, whines, and snorts.

"Don't know why he couldn't have picked a tree-root cave like his brother. He snores almost as bad as you do, Slim," Eddie shook his head and grinned.

"Then the three of us must make a purty good trio," said Slim. "You ain't exactly a cheechako at snorin' yourself. You just hope you don't wake that bear up and make him mad at you for spoilin' his dreams. He'll come right up through the floor after you."

One night when the deep cold had set in, the two partners were sitting in the cabin, just sitting, each in the luxury of his own thoughts. Slim sighed deeply. "You know," he said quietly, just to himself, with no thought of disturbing Eddie, "I wonder what Raffles is doin'. I hope he's all right. He was sure a cute little fellow."

·14·

To pitch my tent with no prosy plan,
To range and to change at will;
To mock at the mastership of man,
To seek Adventure's thrill.

Slim and Eddie were good partners. Each gave the other the privilege of thinking for himself, talking when there was something to say, each doing nothing to make conversation. Long evenings were sometimes spent together with no word spoken.

Eddie was sincerely interested in Slim's theory on dogs. One evening he asked Slim about it.

"There's one thing about half-breeds, Eddie," Slim said in answer, "they've got speed and power, and I bet they could run forever. You know how dogs will start out and just burn up the trail until you have to stop and let 'em blow and get their wind? After that they'll hit a stride. But the half-breed does like the wolf, spurts for maybe a quarter-mile to limber up but not enough to lose his wind, then hits a stride he can hold all day. A wolf doesn't burn it up the way a dog'll do. What I want to do, like I told you, is to take half-breeds, and crossbreed them with another wolf and with another dog. One mating will give me three-quarter wolf and one-quarter dog, the other three-quarter dog and one-quarter wolf. Then see what those pups grow up to be. Somewhere there's got to be just the right mixture. But always with a full-blood dog for the leader. I'm sure even if there'd be the slightest strain of wolf in a breed, there'd be just enough so it might crop out at any minute. You couldn't predict what they'd do.

"Tough thing, o' course, gettin' the wolf cubs, and raisin' 'em, an' then killin' 'em. But somehow, Eddie, it don't bother me killin' wolves. They get a bounty on 'em for good reason, they murder meat animals by the thousands. But dogs is different. When my teams get old and I have to do away with 'em, it's almost more'n I can do. I always give my leader away. I won't kill him. I give him to maybe a prospector or somebody like that who ain't got a dog."

The trees outside were popping their resentment at the dropping temperature. "Listen to them things snap," said Slim, "always a wonder to me how that sap freezes and they bang away like that all winter and it never hurts the tree. Speakin' o' bangin', Eddie, last summer over where you was workin', did you hear any blastin'?"

"Yes, I did," he said. "Let's see, that was about in June. I was over past the far ridge working on a lean-to, and I heard two blasts, and then the next day there was all that dust and the red sky. I thought maybe it was blasting, but there was only the two shots. Then I wondered if it wasn't maybe a volcano."

"Volcano popped open over in the Wrangells, used to smoke a lot. Never saw it blow up, though, but it give out a lot o' gray smoke, and the dust was gray, and it didn't make much noise or explode. Besides I don't know of any volcanoes in this part of Alaska, do you?"

Eddie shook his head.

After a moment or two, Slim said, "Funny thing about this country though, Eddie. I been purty much over it. There's not many trails I haven't followed, and I'll get on those too, but just when you think you know what to expect of Alaska, she surprises you with something new. I'll bet there's a good reason for those explosions, too. We can find out about it when one of us goes out."

It fell on Slim to take the creek trail to Iditarod for supplies. He pitched a camp at the edge of town and staked out his dogs. He planned to stay in Iditarod just long enough to make his purchases and to pick up the latest rumors and news of Alaska. He picked up most of the general gossip from the friendly, fat, and garrulous man who ran the restaurant adjacent to the saloon. This man, who said his name was Harry, developed great respect for Slim's appetite, for on the third visit his first day in town, Slim was heartily greeted.

"Come on in, Slim. I got a idea I know just what you want."

It was early for supper, and Slim was the only customer at the moment. He slid onto one of the counter stools and leaned one elbow on the counter with his forearm straight up and fingers extended. "I want a stack o' them flapjacks just as high as from my elbow to the tip of that longest finger, and about a half a gallon o' sirup."

Harry laughed, "If you ain't the gol-darndest flapjack eater I ever saw! I knew that was what ye wanted."

"I hope you beat up some extra batter, 'cause I don't want you runnin' out again like you did this noon."

When a steaming pile of batter cakes was well doused with sirup, the proprietor stepped back and leaned against the back shelf.

"I got some kids back where I come from, and I write 'em about things I see here in Alaska, but danged if they won't think I'm a lyin' fool when I tell 'em about you eatin' hotcakes. You sure do like 'em, don't you, Slim?"

Slim's rhythmic chomping and his sticky sirupy grin would have pleased any cook in the world. When he could eat no more, he sighed.

"Harry," he asked, "who owns that big machinery dredge in Flat Creek?"

"Fellows named Guggenheim from the States," his cook friend told him. "They got a load o' money and promote things all over the world, I guess. That dredge works the bottom o' the creek and it sludges and handles the sand by the ton. I hear they took out about a half-million dollars in gold in three months this summer. Pretty close to that much anyway."

"Beats swishin' it out of a pan," Slim observed. "Get those things around on creeks, and the placers'll be out o' business. Maybe a good thing, seems like there's too many of 'em most times anyway. Don't know which is worse, them, or civilization and machinery."

Slim drank another cup of coffee. "Say," he suddenly remembered, "did they do any blasting around here last summer?"

Harry shook his head. "Not that I remember," he said. "A volcano blew up south o' here last summer that made quite a bit of noise, but I don't remember any blastin'."

"What volcano?"

"The thing hadn't done nothing for as long as anybody remembers, and one day it blew the top right off itself. It's called Mt. Katmai. It's down on the Alaskan Peninsula. Indian was in here right after it happened. Said the whole top o' the mountain lifted off and blew a hole eight miles around. More'n that, about seventy square miles o' hell blew up through a valley, burnt it out and busted it full o' holes, and there's hot water and steam squirtin' up out o' the ground up to one thousand-foot spouts. Indian said *Windigo,* Evil Spirit, make Valley o' Ten Thousand Smokes. Scared that Indian so he was headin' north and I bet he ain't stopped yet."

"About how far away would that be?" Slim asked. He was intrigued by the description. Here was something he wanted to see.

"Oh, maybe 250 or 300 miles, I guess. Over a tough range, so the Indian said. It almost blew the Alaska Peninsula right off'n Alaska." Harry turned around and scanned the wall behind him whereon were written names, places, dates, messages, and an assortment of general memoranda. "I got it down here some place," he mumbled. "Never was a hand to remember real good, so I write it down." He stabbed a spot with a pudgy forefinger, "Here it is, June 6. See? I got it wrote right here, 'June 6, 1912, Mt. Katmai blowed up.' I always put things like that down so's I won't forget 'em."

There was the answer to the "blasting." "No wonder it made a lot of noise," Slim commented. "A whole mountain blowin' up. Do you know how a fellow could get there?"

"Heard some fellows talks about a boat goin' out of Seward that'd drop you off. Been to Seward, Slim?"

Slim shook his head. "But I know where it is," he said.

"Down on Kenai Peninsula. Indians say overland to Alaska Peninsula is tough. If I was goin', I'd go by Seward," said Harry.

While he had been eating and listening, the lunchroom had filled, and Harry became too busy with hungry men to carry on more conversation. Slim paid his tab, took his parka from the wall peg, and shrugged into it. Just as he reached the door leading outside, he heard Harry behind him announce somewhat proudly to his customers, "Know who that fellow is? That's my friend Slim Williams."

When Slim returned to camp, he brought Eddie up to date on news, and related Harry's description of the Mt. Katmai eruption. "I'd sure like to see it, wouldn't you?" he said.

"Not especially," said Eddie. "I've heard about those mountains not having any trails across 'em because there's no reason to go down to the peninsula. Mostly rocks, from what I hear."

"But I'd sure like to see that valley with all those little steam funnels shootin' up in the air. Maybe I'll go down there some time just to see it. It'd sure be interesting."

That year the trap line continued to produce, but not in such profitable quantities as the first year. Hunting improved, however, and the combined income from the fur pelts and the sale of meat continued to make their venture profitable.

Spring broke, the hibernating bears came out, and with no more than a surly show of the evil tempers they had developed through the hunger of a long fast, went their unpredictable ways.

After supper one evening Slim looked at Eddie and asked, "You sure you don't want to go see Mt. Katmai?"

Eddie looked up sharply. "I'm not even thinkin' of it," he said.

"Thought maybe I would," said Slim.

"What's so interesting about a blowed-up mountain?" said Eddie.

"Nothin' very much, I guess," said Slim, "except that I never seen one. I think I'll go look at it." Slim packed a light trail pack.

"You go ahead then, Slim, you go look at your mountain. I'll stay here and feed the dogs." He waved his hand and watched Slim take the trail to the east.

That was spring, 1913.

That fall, about three months later, Slim walked back into camp. "Hello, Eddie," he said.

"Hello, Slim," Eddie greeted his friend as though he had seen him a day or so before, "been expecting you. Say, have you lost weight or are you getting taller?"

"Maybe a little o' both," Slim laughed. "Been on a long trail."

"See your mountain?"

"That's what I went for, Eddie. Tell you about it soon's I say hello to the dogs."

The meeting was a happy one. Buck almost twisted himself in two, and the big wolf-dogs pawed the air in welcome. Slim had a greeting for each one, and there was no hiding the fact that they were glad to see him.

"You know something, Slim?" Eddie had come up beside him. "Those dogs told me you were coming. That's why I wasn't surprised to see you. They've been watching the trail for a good two days."

Slim nodded. "I know," he said.

After a good feed Slim recounted his trip. "When I left here, I headed east to hit the McGrath Trail over the range and then I had water to get me down to where I could get to Seward. There's a place got almost as many mountains as Valdez. That's where I found the boat. Little boat named

Dora. Supply boat for the peninsula. They's a little native village where they stopped. I forget the name of it, but it's on the peninsula right across to the west of an island they call Kodiak. I found out when the boat'd be back again, and I got off and looked around. It's quite a country, Eddie. You never saw anything like that Valley o' Ten Thousand Smokes. It's a good country around there. Lots o' mountains. Lots o' timber, and good lakes. I bet there's a thousand lakes, and some of 'em awful big, lots of fish. Maybe not a thousand, but seems like everywhere you look is a lake. And from what I saw, plenty o' fur. Lots o' game. And that Mt. Katmai is quite a mountain."

"Did it really blow the top off itself?" Eddie asked.

"It's got a hole in it about three miles across and about three-quarters of a mile deep. She just gutted herself clean out. And there's streams there with water as cold as ice, and some with water like out o' a boilin' kettle. And that Valley o' Ten Thousand Smokes is about seventy square miles o' hell with the lid off. Steam and water is spurtin' out o' little holes and cracks and what looks like li'l bitty volcanoes. There ain't a thing growin'. It's all mud, an' it looks like the mud itself is boilin'. I'll bet there's a million o' those spouts spoutin'. When Mt. Katmai blowed up, what didn't blow out o' her, blowed up through the floor o' this valley, and she's still spurtin'. And funny thing, too, the mud's in colors. All kinds o' colors, where this steam and water shoot up. Not the steam or water is colored, just the mud. And it bubbles. Red, blue, yellow, brown, all kinds o' colors. It's the gol-hangedest thing you ever seen. You ought to go see it, Eddie."

"Anything to do there?" Eddie was being practical.

"Nothin' except if a fellow wanted to trap in the nearby area. Lots o' fur."

"How about getting in and out?"

"That'd be the trouble," Slim nodded. "That little *Dora,* the boat I went over and back on from Seward, she makes the trip around the peninsula, but there's no good trail out to the north and not a place I could find out about where there'd be supplies or tradin' except that little village, and only a few Indians livin' there. I waited around there till the little boat come back, and then I come on up here. Quite a trip. Not bad at all. I may go back again sometime."

Thus Slim summed up as succinctly as only a bushman could a summer sight-seeing trip of a thousand trail miles or more.

The two were quiet for a while, then Eddie said, "Funny about fellows, isn't it Slim? Take you and me, for instance. We get along just all right together. But different as can be. You like to go and see things. I'm pretty satisfied with a good layout once I got it. You like to travel and roam, don't you?"

"Yes, I guess I do, Eddie," Slim said thoughtfully, "I guess I like the trails, and to see what's on the other side of the mountains, and there always seems to be a mountain on the trail ahead o' me."

"And you'd like to keep on movin', wouldn't you, Slim?" This was more of a statement of agreement than a question.

"Maybe I would, Eddie. You know while I was gone this summer, I got to thinkin' maybe it was time for me to go back to my camp over in the Wrangells. I been away a long time, and there's people and things over there I want to see. And you been thinkin' the same thing, Eddie, that it's time we sort o' split up an' went our own ways for a while."

"How'd you know that?"

"A fellow gets to know," Slim said quietly. "Livin' with somebody you get purty well acquained with the way they think. I think maybe it's a good thing to break apart and go on our own. But I'll sure miss you, Eddie. You're as good a partner as anybody'd want."

Eddie sighed, "I was almost scared to tell you what I was thinking, Slim. It's like you say. And I'll miss you too. A fellow never had a better friend than you, Slim."

"Well," Slim drawled, "we'll go right on and see that it sort o' stays that way. Bein' good friends don't depend on bein' together. If it did there'd not be many friendships. Where do you think you'll go?"

"I've heard you talk so much about the Wood River area, thought maybe I'd go there for awhile."

"It's a good country." Slim agreed the move would be a smart one. "Me, like I said, I'll go back to the Wrangells. I may even go down to Valdez."

"Linda?" Eddie smiled.

Slim nodded. In moments of confidence over the time these two men had lived in harmonious partnership, Slim had told Eddie a little, very little, about Linda. There was so very little to tell.

"Well," said Eddie, "maybe a good thing if you would go down and see her, Slim."

"Yes," said Slim, "maybe so, Eddie. I just been countin' up. I been away from my camp on the Chitina three years, too. And that gets to be a pretty long time."

These two men, who had met by chance, had shared their intimacies of thoughts in perfect understanding. This could not have been possible if each of them had not had years of preseasoning in living alone in the wilderness. There they had learned the essential lessons of minding one's own business, and respect for the right of the other to his moments of solitude, privacy, and to his own thoughts. Slim and Eddie were friends because they knew that the friendship each had was not his to give; it was, instead, the privilege of the other to take. In this Slim had found the key to understanding.

Slim was the first to leave. His sled was loaded and his team was anxious and eager. Slim pointed to the leader, "Look at Buck, Eddie, ain't he a purty dog? See how proud he is? He knows he's a good leader. Just a dandy. An' them other dogs know it. So long, Eddie."

"So long, Slim, good luck."

"Our trails'll cross. Be good to yourself." Then with no more formality, Slim turned his full attention to his dogs. "Mush," he shouted. "Mush!"

·15·

It's the great, big, broad land 'way up yonder,
  It's the forests where silence has lease;
It's the beauty that thrills me with wonder,
  It's the stillness that fills me with peace.

The dogs ran well, but Slim was in no hurry. He figured he had about a thousand miles to go, so he paced each day for a minimum run. He took the trail from Iditarod west to Anvik on the Yukon River, then followed the Yukon up to and over his old mail route eastward. He branched off where the Tanana River joined the Yukon, and followed this river trail cutting south of Fairbanks to meet the Richardson Trail. This was familiar ground to Slim, like getting home.

About a month and a half after leaving the Iditarod camp, Slim drove into Taral. This had been an exceptionally long bit of travel for Slim, but he traveled as he wanted to, and he enjoyed to the utmost being on the trail, and being alone. Often, after he built a good fire, fed the dogs and himself, and stretched his bit of canvas windbreak, he lay in his bed-roll and watched the sky. Slim never tired of looking at the night sky. It didn't look like a dome to him, with stars set against it. Instead it seemed to have no substance at all, it was infinite space, and the stars just hanging, some near, some at the other end of eternity. Overhead it was dark and the stars were just *there*.

More than once on the trip he had remained camped for

an extra day, just because he wanted to. At one point he stopped for almost three days. But that was because of a storm. One day the mountains began to "smoke." As far as he could see into the distance, the outlines of the mountains were lost in the cottony fuzz of blowing snow. It looked exactly as if smoke was lifting from the slopes. "Wind," he said to himself; then to the dogs, "Maybe blowin' up a storm, you dogs. Whoa! While I take a listen." The dogs dutifully stopped. From far in the distance came the high-pitched whine of the wind. It was faint, but it gave Slim the warning he needed. First he saw to his dogs, that they were well staked. Impervious to wind or cold, curled, with noses tucked in their tails, they would snug out the worst of storms.

For himself, Slim borrowed from the bears, the rabbits, field mice, and others of the wild who turned to nature for their protection. It seemed strange that comfort and warmth and safety from cold could be found under the snow. But it is true. The animals find warmth and safety blanketed by its heavy insulation.

Slim dug a cave in a heavy bank of snow. He made it generously oversize so he could move about comfortably, with room enough to lie down, and with plenty of air space. Once inside he closed the opening with loose snow, leaving just clearance enough for air to prevent suffocation. A fire was out of the question, but he had dried meat and fish. Snow would quench his thirst. He could last out the storm. Fortunately it wasn't too cold, about ten or twenty below zero. It was nothing like the still, killing seventy below of the night he had frozen.

The low moan of the wind grew in intensity to a roar, and held without change of pitch or tempo for two days and nights. It blew snow before it, but not too much, for this was not so much a blizzard as it was a gale. These frequent winter windstorms defied any living thing to stand or move against their pounding power. But Slim was sheltered, and comfortable, and warm.

The wind stopped. It did not gradually fade out and sigh

away. One moment it was there, the next moment it was gone. It was as quick as that. In its place was silence, silence that was heavy. It was a positive silence, and weight. Slim strained his ears to listen for sound, but all he heard was the silence. He had experienced this strange phenomenon many times before, and always it was the same. After the cacophonous roar and timpani-like pounding of the wind, he listened to the beauty and solemn dignity of silence.

Coming out of the darkness of his snow cave was a painful process. It was day, and the brilliance was almost blinding. He wore his Eskimo-fashioned "glasses," a piece of bone which covered his eyes, tied on with leather thongs. Thin slits cut through the bone permitted him to see but kept out the blinding glare of the snow. Even through these the light was at first painful. It took several moments to adjust to this. He found his dogs through the simple method of looking for mounds of snow. They bounded out of their secure protection and quickly responded to his offer of fish after their two-day fast. Slim cooked a good meal for himself, and cleared his sled from its snowdrift, and took to the trail again. These were not hardships to him; they, like the weather, were the normal expectancies of living.

At Taral Slim planned to pick up supplies and go on up the Chitina to his old camp. When he drove into the settlement, he headed directly for Charlie's trading post. Slim had often thought of Charlie during the years he had been away and had been looking forward to a good visit with his friend. He wondered if he had taken his young Indian bride and their son "outside" to meet his mother as he had assured Slim he would. Slim pulled into the compound beside the post store, and tied his sled. He thought it somewhat unusual that no other teams were there, for it was the time of the year when the midwinter trading should be going on. Also, Slim read signs that showed there had not been too much sled traffic around the post, nor moccasin or snowshoe trails to the store itself. It was strange too, he thought, that there was no evidence of a good woodpile. Charlie was a good bushman, and that was one thing he would certainly have taken care of. Slim looked up at the thin wisp of gray smoke coming out of the chimney, shrugged his shoulders and went inside.

As he closed the door behind him, he heard what sounded like field mice scuttling around the floor, and squeaking. In a moment it stopped. He looked around but no one was in sight. The place was a mess. The shelves were all but bare. A few cans were set about indiscriminately, a half-unrolled bolt of yard goods lay tumbled on a counter, torn and dirty. The racks that had held saw blades and axe handles and the pegs where traps had hung were all empty. The place was dirty with filth and torn paper and broken packages of food. It was more than disorder, it was absolute wreckage.

In a shadowy corner he saw movement. There sat a dumpy, fat Indian squaw. The movement Slim had seen was the wiggling form of the baby she held in her arms. He walked toward her. She didn't look up at him or move, or change her expression. He stared. He could hardly believe what he saw. It was Annie. All of the youthful prettiness of six years ago had gone. Her hair was matted and stringy, her pudgy face was caked, and twin drools of snuff marked her chin. She was filthy dirty.

"Hello, Annie," said Slim. "Where's Charlie?"

She raised her dull eyes and stared at him for at least a full minute, then shrugged.

"Is he here? Is he in the back where you live?"

Again the shrug.

Slim knew that Annie could speak English if she wanted to. He also knew that she recognized him. But he had no idea how to make her answer. Again he tried. "Charlie go away?" No answer. "Charlie come back soon?" No answer. Slim heard the scuttling and squeaking sounds behind him again, and turned quickly. He saw several little black-haired heads, bright-eyed, peeking at him from around the end of the counters. Including the one Annie held, he counted six. He spoke to the children. "Come on out," he called as happily as he could, "I won't hurt you. Me friend your poppa."

He was not able to induce the young half-breeds to quit their hiding places. One baby a year, he thought, and Charlie had assured him that his first son would be the only one. Slim finally left without getting more than a shrug from Annie. Self-indulgence, constant pregnancy and lack of all interest or pride had made her a slattern at twenty-three.

In the little settlement Slim found a young Indian he knew, one of Gud-le-ta's band, and went with him to the one-room shack where he and his squaw lived. Slim wanted to find out about Charlie.

"Good see you," the Indian said, and made tea for his guest. "You go see Gud-le-ta? He like see you. He say, 'You see Sleem, you say come Gud-le-ta.' You go see Gud-le-ta."

Slim said that Gud-le-ta's village was on his way to his own camp, and he promised a visit. The Indian nodded.

Then Slim asked about his friend Charlie. The Indian shook his head. "Charlie no more."

"Charlie go away?" Slim asked.

"Squaw no good. All time potlatch. No Indian trade Charlie. Charlie got no more money. Squaw potlatch. All time got baby, all time drink. Charlie got no more money, squaw got no more potlatch, squaw got more baby. Charlie got little gun. Charlie take little gun, go river, walk in river, shoot little gun. Me see trail. Read sign. No find little gun no more. No find Charlie no more. That's all. Charlie go 'way. Squaw no good. No Indian take squaw."

The rest of the visit was brief. Slim listened to the not-too-surprising story. Charlie had been consumed by something he did not understand, the Indian. Little Annie, cute and clever and pretty, had played upon Charlie's sympathy and his passions. Once he had succumbed wholly to her wishes and will, he was as doomed as a man sentenced to die. She had pot-latched, given away everything he had. Even the Indians had lost respect for him and would no longer trade with him.

Finally when his money was gone as his self-respect and standing among men had also gone, he took his revolver, waded into the Copper River and ended, for him, this unhappy and sordid experience. Annie would live on in the trading post, eking out an existence from the dregs of what her own family might give her. She had lost her standing among Indians because her time of potlatch was over, she had no more to give; and because of her marriage to the white man and bearing him a child each year, her band would not take her back.

There were marriages between white men and Indian girls that had been successful, but this one followed the more common pattern. The exceptional case was a man of understanding and will, who could meet and overcome the Indian girl's basic racial traits, habits, and customs by domination. But Slim knew when Charlie told him of his marriage to Annie that it was to be a failure. Charlie was too good and trusting, too kind, and too emotional.

Slim stopped to see his friend Gud-le-ta. The old man was genuinely glad to see him. Things were very bad, he said, his boy was sick and the medicine man had not been able to heal him. Would Slim look? Slim remembered the boy from his last visit to the village.

Now a lad of about eighteen, he had been accidentally shot. It had been merely a flesh wound, but the difficulty was the infection that followed, and not so much the wound itself.

"Medicine Man make big medicine, no get well. Now Medicine Man say boy die."

In the shack where the young fellow lay on a bunk, the medicine man had brought the coffin. When the medicine man decided that any case was beyond his control to heal, he moved a coffin into the shack or wigwam and waited for the sufferer to die.

"You make good medicine, Slim, you make my boy get well." Gud-le-ta turned and left Slim alone with the boy.

Slim knew nothing about medicine or surgery, but he had

worked on himself on various occasions, and had pulled some of his dogs through moments of sickness. He had no alternative here. He would have to try. If the boy died, at least they had expected that and would not blame him. If by equal chance he lived, then they could all be grateful, and the medicine man would claim he had made powerful medicine. He knew that the first thing he must do was to clean the boy up. At least cleanliness would be a great help toward a possible healing.

More to have room to work than for any other reason, Slim moved the whipsawed coffin outside. Then he started with warm water to wash away the clotted blood and dirt from the wound and the boy's body. The boy lay very still, breathing evenly and deeply. He showed by an occasional catch of his breath that a moment of pain had been felt, so Slim knew that he was conscious. It took time, but finally Slim was satisfied. The wound was clean. The flesh looked redly healthy as he bandaged the side with cloths that he had boiled. A little later he took some caribou broth to the shack. The boy was awake and his eyes showed recognition, and gratitude, as Slim had seen in the eyes of his dogs.

The recovery was rapid, and Gud-le-ta offered Slim great rewards. Slim shook his head and told the old chief that the good medicine in clean water had helped the medicine man.

Gud-le-ta told Slim that more disaster had befallen him. He took Slim to the rear of the village and showed a fine shack he had built.

"Good trail e'rywhere now. Indian make good trade, get plenty e'rything. You make fish weel, we get plenty fish. We get plenty eat. Dog get plenty eat. Me go big place. See e'rybody got big horse. No more dog. Me trade. Get horse. Me bring horse here. Make big house for horse. Put horse in house." Gud-le-ta shook his head sadly. "Horse die. Horse no eat. Me fill box full e'ryday. E'ryday fill box full fish. Horse no eat. Horse die. Horse no eat fish. Very sad. Horse no good. Dog eat fish. Dog more better."

Slim shook his head. "Too bad," he said in honest sympathy for Gud-le-ta, and the horse.

Slim decided he would be on his way to his own camp, but Gud-le-ta tried again to dissuade him. "You good man, Sleem. You good States Injun, you be good man my village. You come here live. Build good house. Me good chief. You be big man. You wait."

Gud-le-ta stalked pompously out of the shack where he and Slim had been talking. In a moment he was back. With him was an Indian girl. Gud-le-ta pushed her ahead of him into the shack, and stood proudly behind her.

"This Ya-tee," he announced. "She my girl. You make my boy well, me give you my girl."

Slim looked at this slight little girl. She was about sixteen, he guessed, and she must have been one of the many children working and playing around the village the summer he had spent there, since she was Gud-le-ta's daughter.

Here was the familiar pattern. Little Ya-tee, dressed in beautiful white, unsmoked caribou leather, richly and extravagantly decorated. Her clothing a masterpiece of their craft. Her hair greased and shiny. She was ornamented like a Christmas toy, and she was pretty. Strange, thought Slim, how pretty these little wild things are.

"You stay. Me give you Ya-tee. You marry. She be good squaw."

Slim knew again that this old chief in all sincerity was doing a great and generous thing. He was offering his daughter in an extreme expression of friendship and gratitude. Slim didn't want to hurt the old man's feelings, or to shame his friend. He therefore pretended to think seriously about the offer.

"Gud-le-ta," he said finally, "maybe more better I wait. I have many things to do away from village. Maybe not ready to live in village. I go away now and when I come back maybe we talk some more. More better we wait."

The old man knew that Slim would keep his word about returning. He furrowed his brow in deep thought.

Meanwhile Slim looked at Ya-tee. "Little girl," he said, "you're about as purty as anything I ever saw."

She grinned. Here was temptation and invitation in a most enticing form. Slim thought of the little Siberian girl, and the little Eskimo girl, and Annie. He thought about Linda. Then he said to himself, "Ya-tee, I better get out o' here before you stop lookin' like a Indian."

Gud-le-ta nodded. He had apparently made a decision. "Good," he said to Slim, "you go. Bimeby you come back. You stay, you be big man my village. Ya-tee be good squaw." He nodded emphatically as an indication that in his mind this conclusion had already been reached.

Slim looked from the chief to Ya-tee. The two Indians beamed their satisfaction over the prospects. Slim had his doubts.

Within a few minutes he was on the trail.

·16·

This is the law of the Yukon,
and ever she makes it plain;
'Send me not your foolish and feeble
send me your strong and your sane—'

When Slim drove away from Gud-le-ta's village, he wanted to see Linda. As a matter of fact, any white woman would have served his purpose for comparison, but as usual whenever he thought of a woman, she always turned out to be Linda. He had only seen native women, Indians and Eskimos, for almost three years, and this most recent erotic experience told him it was time for him to return to his own kind before he made a serious mistake. So, instead of his camp, he headed for Valdez. He drove his dogs hard and made excellent time.

As he arrived in Valdez, he received a shock. Valdez had burned. Practically the whole business section and many of the homes had been destroyed. People were still raking cindered ruins in the hopes of finding possessions. A tent city had been raised, and the cry "Rebuild!" had found many willing workers. The new plans for the town apparently called for a proper layout of streets and sidewalks, and the work was well under way.

Many of the inhabitants, especially women and children, had left, and more were leaving to go to Seattle to stay until new homes could be provided. Slim thought of what a difference thirteen years had made. From the tough, disorganized gold camp of 1900, it had attained the stature of a town. The people were no longer pioneers, in-and-out prospectors, gamblers, and such, but were business folk, homemakers, who were establishing the stability of the new land.

Slim's first interest, of course, was to determine if the little schoolteacher was still in Alaska, or had she already gone. There was a ship in the harbor, and he went to the shore to search among the crowds there for one familiar face. He looked at those saying their farewells, and he saw her. There was no mistaking the blonde loveliness. It was Linda without a doubt, and she was dressed for travel. In the years since he had seen her she had fulfilled her youthful promise of becoming gently and delicately formed. Her face was more beautiful than he had remembered. He felt a surge of excitement as he saw her, once he was certain she looked straight at him. For an instant her blue eyes were on his, and her face seemed to glow with joyous recognition. She waved. Slim started to raise his hand in answer and almost stepped toward her, when suddenly he realized that her eyes were not on his, in fact she hadn't been looking at him at all, but had recognized an older woman who was standing behind him and who walked toward her at her signal.

His thoughts were strangely mixed. In the first place there was no reason why she should recognize him. She had never known him. It was he who had built the structure of their intimacy and friendship out of his own imagination. She didn't even know he existed. It was a strange kind of self-consciousness he felt. He seemed completely detached from this whole experience. It was as though he were standing apart and watching his own uncertainty and confusion. He could not feel himself as a part of it. Nevertheless his emotion was very real and sincere.

Final good-bys were said. Slim heard Linda's laugh as she told her friend, "Don't look so sad, I'll be back by spring." He stood until the ship was well up the narrows. He wondered if he would ever see her again, or even if he wanted to. It was hard for him to analyze his feelings. He didn't know what he felt. It was like pain, and yet it wasn't. But whatever it was, he couldn't understand it.

His immediate answer to such problems was always the same. Work. He took a job helping with the cleaning up and the building.

Just before breakup Slim went back beyond the mountains toward his camp. As he promised he would, he stopped by Gud-le-ta's village. The boy was well, fully recovered, and all, including the medicine man, were very happy. He saw little Ya-tee. Stripped of her finery and dressed in her everyday unadorned and shapeless garments, she looked like any other little Indian girl. The glow of her prettiness was dimmed. Her hair was stringy and matted, her face was very dirty, and she sniffled from a cold. In his thoughts there was no answer to the perpetual light of desire in her eyes. He was sure that before too long Ya-tee would succumb to any one of the several young eager bucks of the village. Slim told Gud-le-ta, "not yet," and continued upstream to his own camp.

He found his place in surprisingly good repair. He had built it well, and the years it had stood alone had done very little damage. Before long he had his affairs under first-class control, and for the next few years was content to find new trails and explore more of the Wrangell Mountains he loved.

On each trip he made to Taral or to Copper Center for visits or supplies he saw new evidences of the approach of civilization. The Richardson Trail had been widened and graded and became the Richardson Highway. A few automobiles and a truck or so were beginning to make their appearance. And wonder of all, there was even an airplane in the sky. The first time Slim saw it was when he was in Taral, and he stood with a crowd of curious, incredulous, and almost frightened Indians, staring upward, fascinated by the miracle of flight. After that he saw the plane from time to time, and learned that it belonged to a young prospector in Fairbanks.

Just after breakup in 1918, Slim planned a visit to

Copper Center. He made his usual little boat of willow wands and canvas, gave his dogs an extra feed so they could well wait out his absence, and started downstream. When he reached Copper Center, there was great excitement. An Indian friend told him there had just been an accident. "You only man, Sleem. You only man!" he insisted.

Slim wanted to know the what and where of the accident.

"Gakona," the Indian answered. "Right now. You go."

"But that's thirty miles north o' here," Slim said incredulously and questioned the excited Indian. "If it just happened, how do you know about it? How did you know they want me?"

"Me know." The Indian stared at Slim.

Here it was again, thought Slim, that impossible thing of the Indian, like the dogs, knowing something that had taken place miles away with no apparent means of communication. "Moccasin telegraph," the old-timers called it. It was as uncanny as it was incontestible. Slim had seen too many evidences of it to doubt either its existence or verity.

The Indian pointed northward. "Gakona. Fly man fall down. All break. E'rybody die you no hurry."

Apparently a plane had crashed at the settlement of Gakona, and a call for help had gone out to be picked up mystically by this Indian thirty miles away. But how, thought Slim, could the Indian be sure of what happened? Slim was the Indian's friend, and knew that the Indian wouldn't lie to him, there would be no object in that. He also doubted if the Indian imagined it, he was so demandingly certain. And Slim was too wise in the ways of the Indians to ignore it.

"You come," the Indian argued. "E'rybody die you no come."

"But somebody'll be there to help."

The Indian shook his head. "You big man, Sleem. You help my chief Gud-le-ta, you help my people. You help e'rybody. Come, now we go. You help. Hurry, before e'rybody die."

The Indian insisted so convincingly that many people would die unless Slim hurried to their rescue, that Slim finally nodded. "All right," he said, "we go." After all, thirty miles wasn't too far to go if there had been an accident and he was needed.

There was a new truck in Copper Center, and when Slim explained the emergency, the young owner was as eager to make the trip as the road was bad. It was all that Slim and the Indian could do to stay aboard the bouncing, rattling vehicle. Grades were up and down, curves were dangerously sharp. The driver had the advantage of having the wheel to hold onto. Just before they reached the trading village of Gakona, they stopped. A group of ten Indians and six white men stood along the river shore, talking and pointing. Slim looked, but he could see no evidence of any wreckage.

He joined the men and found one among them he knew, a man named McCauley, one of the early old-timers. Slim singled him out.

"What is it, Mac?" he said. "And where's the airplane?"

Mac pointed across the river. "He came down somewhere acrost that hell-boilin' river. Tryin' to land in that meadow over there along the road. Somethin' must've gone wrong. Anyway he shot up a little way sort o' like he was bouncin' an' come down in that marsh grass and muskeg over there some place. Right about opposite here. Me'n another fellow was walkin' along the road on our way to Gulkana and we seen it. We don't know if they're dead or what. All we know we ain't seen anybody since he come down. What we got to do is to get acrost this river and see. That's why I kind of sent out word by the Indians to see if anybody knew where you was at. I knew you was back, an' I figure you're the only man I know with nerve enough to try to get acrost it."

Slim looked at his Indian friend whose eyes seemed to say, "I told you so."

Slim regarded the river. It was the Copper, spring swollen, wide, and millrace fast. It was about a half-mile from shore to shore. The speed of the current made the river surface glassy smooth, and so swift was the flow that the level of the water at the river's middle was two or three feet higher than it was along shore. It didn't seem possible that anyone or anything could cross the river, or would even make an attempt. As he gauged the probabilities, he thought of his first experience with a boat on the Copper when he'd swamped running into a sweeper. He thought of smashing into the rocks in the Kobuk's white water. But this was no time to think of failures, he decided. There were dozens of successful trips he had made, and here in front of him were no sweepers, rocks, no obstacles, except the half-mile of rushing, powerful, dangerous water. He was not afraid, but he knew he would have to use all the cleverness he had ever learned; that, and all the strength he had. He watched the tricks of the current intently, then turned to Mac.

"Anybody know who it is?" Slim asked.

Mac supplied a guess. "Seem to think it's that young fellow who just come up from the States, lives in Fairbanks, an' he bought hisself this flyin' machine. Maybe he even had somebody with him. We don't know."

"Well," said Slim, "only one way to find out."

"How's that?" asked Mac.

"Go over and see," was Slim's practical answer. He turned again to look at the river and its treacherous current. "First," he said, "we got to get ourselves a boat. They ain't any here, so we'll have to make one. Who's got a piece of canvas?" A tarp was supplied from the truck.

Slim went to work, and with the help of Mac and his Indian friend, he began building his boat. He recognized the importance of making a boat better than any he had made before. He selected his wood with care, and wound the joints firmly. He stopped often to look at the river as if gauging its innate power against his own ability, then he jerked the lashings tighter. He took extra pains in fitting the canvas onto the frame. When finished, he had a boat about eight feet long and about four feet at the beam. The truck again met a need by furnishing a can of grease which Slim rubbed well into the canvas. Then he made two pairs of oars. When all was ready, he faced the white men, who had been watching but had said very little, and asked for a volunteer to cross with him. He knew it would have been futile to ask an Indian. Not one of the men moved or spoke. Finally old Mac stepped out. "I'll go with you, Slim," he said.

"Maybe I better have a younger fellow, Mac," Slim suggested.

"Looks like you ain't goin' to get nobody less you take me, Slim. Younger fellows don't seem to be willin' to take a chance. But don't let it fool you that I'm almost seventy, I c'n handle my own along with you. Besides, Slim, I pretty near see all they is to see, and I got no place to go, so come on, you'n me'll take this thing acrost."

Slim hesitated a moment, and looked from Mac to the other men standing by. He didn't blame these men for not wanting to go. It was a great chance they'd be taking, and probably a foolhardy thing. He didn't want to go himself, but somehow he had to. He spoke to the young truck driver. "You know where there's a doctor in case we bring somebody out?"

"I think maybe there's a fellow in Gakona. I could drive over and see."

"Suppose you do that," Slim suggested, then to Mac, "Come on, Mac, let's see what we can do about getting over that crest o' water in the middle o' this thing. Once we cross that we can just about coast downhill to the far shore. Sure wish we could stretch a rope across, but if we tried to tow a rope it'd whip us like a lash. We'll just have to paddle her."

It was dusk when Slim and McCauley took their places in the frail willow-frame canvas boat and shoved off from shore. Immediately the water churned and gurgled about them, snatched and buffeted the light craft as if to tear it apart. Slim's work had been well done, it held together and stayed tight.

There was no talk. These two men, fearless but not foolish, tested in the trials of the wilderness, pulled steadily on their oars. They worked the boat diagonally across the current yet with great care lest it be pulled broadside and capsize. Here Slim's long experience with these light willow-canvas boats of his making stood them in excellent stead. Of one thing he was certain. This time there could be no mistakes, not a moment of carelessness. Not only his own, but the lives of other people might depend upon him and his little boat. Slim and Mac fought the relentless river and climbed the curving crest inch by hard-won inch. Once past the middle they slipped down the far side, and yet it took all of Slim's skill with the oars to pull the boat out of the hold of the current and safely ashore. They stepped out over half a mile downstream from the point on the other shore where they had started. They looked back. The men on the far shore waved. Perhaps they cheered, but Slim heard nothing above the roar of the river. Mac had done his valiant best, but there was no doubt it was Slim's strength that had made the crossing.

They went ashore into what appeared to be a sheltered cove. Instead it proved to be a backwash channel with its other opening about a mile upstream. It was only a few feet wide, and wadable. The island it formed was nearly a half-mile across at its widest point. It was on this muskeg that they found the plane, hopelessly wrecked. There were two occupants, a man and a girl, both injured, but as Slim bent over each one he saw they were alive.

"We'd best take the girl first," he told Mac. "She's got her foot hurt purty bad under that piece there." He leaned down and pulled away a part of the fuselage that had imprisoned the girl's foot. "Purty little thing, ain't she, Mac? I'd say she's about twenty-five. Maybe we can make a stretcher out of this piece of wing to carry her," he suggested. Then as tenderly as a mother would lift a baby, he put his arms around her slight body and picked her up. As he did so, she opened her eyes and gasped sharply from pain.

"I know it hurts, but don't you worry, little girl," Slim said confidently, "you're goin' to be just fine. Got your foot hurt a little bit, maybe, but you're goin' to be all right. I'm going to get you across the river where there's goin' to be a doctor waitin' to take care of you, and don't you worry about a thing." The girl lapsed into unconsciousness.

"Mac," Slim called sharply, "go bring the boat up to the top o' this channel. This girl is hurt real bad." When Mac returned, he said, "You put that piece o' wing in the bottom of the boat. I'll hold her and put her in." This done, the men waded the narrow channel upstream to where it joined the big river, towing the boat in which lay the motionless girl.

When Slim took his place at the oars, he said, "Only room for two, Mac. I've got to get her across, then I'll be back."

"You'll make it, Slim," the older man nodded. "Good luck, boy," he said and gave the boat a shove into the current.

As he rowed, Slim kept his eyes on the still form of the girl. "I'll get you across," he promised through gritted teeth, "I'll get you across, and you're goin' to be all right." He hoped he was telling the truth. He put his back with all the strength he had into every pull of the oars.

He was still rowing hard when hands grasped the bow of his boat. The men on the shore had formed a chain into the water and caught his boat and pulled it to land.

The young fellow with the truck had returned with a doctor. A stretcher was improvised on the floor of the truck and the girl placed carefully on it. The doctor made a superficial examination. Slim stood by.

"Is she all right, Doc?" Slim asked when the man stood up.

"Can't tell. She's badly hurt. Probably her back. May be able to save her foot—if she lives." The doctor mounted the truck and said to the driver, "Let's go into Copper Center. And son, this girl can't stand a jiggle or a bump, so you drive this truck like we was running on eggs."

Slim stood and watched until they were out of sight. "Too bad," he mused, "I sure hope she gets to be all right—wonder who she is."

He made the crossing again. Mac was there to meet him and they towed the boat the length of the back channel, and put the injured pilot on a moss cushion. Once more Slim made the dangerous crossing. It took all the strength he had to make the pull across the river.

After each crossing, Slim went over the boat carefully, tightening the lashings, firming the canvas covering. The little craft was holding up almost miraculously against the vicious beating it was taking from the water. He had one more trip to make. He had to go back for Mac.

Mac was watching and waiting for him, and dawn was tinting the water when Slim pulled the boat to Mac's outstretched hands. He took a good rest. There was no hurry now. The emergency was over. The injured had been carried safely across, and he and Mac could make it back in their own time. Also, the river current had lessened. It would boil again when the daytime thaw fed the creeks, but the cold of night stopped the thaw and the river consequently dropped.

Nevertheless, the last crossing was not easy. Mac was old, and he had worked hard in the first crossing and in the long night's work. Slim was near exhaustion. His muscles burned like fire with each oar stroke, his head throbbed from the effort, and he barely knew when waiting hands pulled them safely onto the clay bank.

The injured had been taken away. Most of those who had gathered had gone about their own affairs. The few who had stayed to see them safely ashore soon left. There remained Mac, Slim, and his young Indian friend. Slim stretched out on the bank. He had had no food since the noon before. He had performed six impossible crossings of the swollen Copper River in more than six hours of constant, gruelling, punishing work.

Mac stood looking down at Slim. The Indian stood a few paces away.

"Slim," said Mac, "when you first said you was goin' to do it, I didn't believe you, only it was worth a chance an' I was with you. This night I seen with my own eyes somethin' that no man might believe if he heard it. I heard o' some o' the things you done, an' some o' the lives you saved, an' the way they was told me I clucked in m' cheek about 'em. No longer, lad. You're a man I'm proud o' knowin'. I seen lots o' things in the North, but none like this, and I know no other who could've done it."

"Just lucky, I guess," said Slim.

Just then the Indian stepped nearer, and bobbed his head. "Good you come, Sleem," he said, "you good man. I tell e'rybody e'ryw'ere you bes' man anyw'ere. You plenty good man, Sleem."

Slim smiled and went to sleep.

·17·

Of cities leaping to stature,
of fame like a flag unfurled,
As I pour the tide of my riches
in the eager lap of the world.

On his way back to his Chitina camp, Slim stopped at Copper
Center. He learned that the doctor had driven on to Valdez
to see that the girl was taken on the first ship to Seattle where
surgery might accomplish what they were not equipped to do
in Alaska. As far as anyone knew she was still alive. He bought
his coal oil and went on to his camp.

Things were changing in Alaska. The frenzy of the gold
rush days was giving way to more orderly, planned development. Following governmental territorial administration, the
first steps after the establishment of law and a sense of order
were transportation and communication between important
points of business. The Richardson Highway was already built
and a thoroughfare. A railroad was begun to connect Seward
with Fairbanks, 470 miles inland. Telegraph and telephone
lines were strung, commercial flying was cutting time and
distances. A university was planned and begun in Fairbanks,
newspapers were being published. Although there were spas-
modic flash rushes following every new gold strike, these had
lost their stampede force, mainly because the population of
prospectors had dwindled by one-half within the decade before
1920. Another reason was that gold mining had become a

232

business with most of the major properties owned and operated by organized companies. The lone prospector of the creeks with his shovel and pan was in danger of extinction, replaced by crews of specialized scientists and geologists.

Also, new industries were tending to shape the form of Alaska's future. The salmon-fishing industry was giving employment to native fishermen and taking out millions of dollars in fish. New lands were being opened for settlement and homesteading.

In 1867 it had been considered a prime piece of folly when William H. Seward, Secretary of State, paid Russia $7,200,000 and acquired this uncharted chunk of frozen wilderness for the United States. Within the short span of fifty years it was turning into one of the most fabulously wealthy assets the United States owned. "Seward's Folly" it was called, a "giant icebox." It was a political laughingstock until little by little its vast potential became known. Its nickname was changed to "America's Treasure Land of the North," with its gold alone repaying its purchase price fifty times over.

With a land of such promise, and so rich in natural resources, it was only normal that the boom give way to organization and development. Its administration had been under the War Department, Treasury Department, and Washington-appointed governors. In 1912 Alaska's status changed from a district to a territory and under this assumed a type of limited self-government. Business lobbies in Washington were also tending to lend it the stature of stability.

Notwithstanding the surge of "civilization" northward, there were still thousands of square miles of Alaska yet unknown. And there were men, like Slim, who lived in the wilderness for the sheer love of the country. But progress was a law not to be denied, and Slim even aided at times by hiring out to lay rails or to stretch wire; but these were but brief experiences. He didn't really turn his back on progress, he merely stepped aside to let it go on without any particular help from him.

Wherever he went, Valdez, Fairbanks, Copper Center, Gakona, Seward, Nome, anywhere that more than one were gathered together, there was talk of politics, growth, expansion, development, controls, and more politics. Slim listened to much of this, heard, but made no attempt to enter the arguments.

Slim was now about forty years old. Had he been younger, had he had formal education and training, or even had he had a liking for community organizational work, he might have taken a deeper and active interest in the affairs of these people he knew. But he was fitted neither by bent nor desire to become other than what he was. Let others take office and manage. He was a bushman, and other things being equal, he intended to remain one.

One day on a trail he stopped his team and pointed up to a plane going over. "See that?" he said to his dogs. "They can bring them things and railroads and automobiles and all the rest up here, and they may do all right in the summer, but in winter when there's work to do, this country will rely on dogs like you for as long as there is weather. Alaska just can't get along without you."

During the next ten years he spent most of his time in and around the Wrangell Mountains. He made occasional tries at gold panning, but as in his past prospecting he was disappointed. Once he split a claim with a friend of his—he was to take one side of a creek, his friend the other. All one summer they worked hard. Slim's pan never showed a single ounce of color. His friend later cashed in his side for better than $100,000. Slim tried other diggings from time to time until he was finally convinced that he was not destined to be one of the lucky ones. Most of the time he hunted, trapped, and bred dogs. He bred and rebred wolves and dogs until he proved to himself that the finest workable percentage with the greatest chance of producing pups of balanced dispositions and of the best working attributes was half-wolf, half-dog. The other percentages, leaning more to one than the other, seemed to breed into the predominant the weaknesses of the strain rather than the better qualities. Therefore, he settled on his teams as half-and-half, but he was still most particular of his choice of parent stock.

During one of these periods of planned breeding he had five wolf cubs. He spent one whole summer in satisfying his unlimited curiosity. He wondered if it would be possible to train wolves and to drive them as a team. He found out. First he spent hours every day near the cubs until they were used to him. He talked with them until they were well acquainted. He worked with infinite patience. There was never a quick move, never a sharp or angry word, and only very short lessons at a time. He gradually gained the confidence of the cubs. He worked one at a time, first accustoming him to the harness, then to the weight of the small drag sled. Then he coupled two together and went through the same routine day after day, with kindness and understanding. He handled them in training exactly as he had his first team of puppies at his Chitina camp.

Finally he harnessed all five, and fastened the towrope to the weighted sled. He had selected one sharp-eyed, spike-eared fellow for the leader, and now, with all ready, this wolf seemed to sense the importance of his position and stood statuelike, alert, waiting for the command. Slim had made a practice trail on the ground along the shore of the creek. Up and back they went. In perfect precision these five wolves, born to the wilderness, worked as obediently and as accurately as any dogs Slim had ever had. On the final run back to camp, after they had "gee'd," and "haw'd," "whoa'd," and "mushed" without the slightest hesitancy or mistake, Slim gave them their heads and felt the full potential of their power and ultimate speed when they should be grown. When they came to a stop at camp, there stood a man in the camp clearing. The wolves immediately froze, hackles bristling and throats rumbling. Slim ran to the leader and grabbed his collar.

"Hello, Slim," the man called, "heard you was back and come past to see you."

It was a man named Doug Bross, a trapper and a friend.

"Hello, Doug," said Slim, "better get over by the cabin there till I chain up my dogs."

"All right," said Doug, starting toward the cabin, and then he stopped short. "Did you call them things *dogs?* Them ain't dogs, them's wolves."

"Yeah," said Slim, unharnessing and fastening each animal to its stake, "but I'm usin' 'em for dogs."

"Wolves," Doug said, just about to himself, incredulously, "the guy is drivin' a team o' full-blooded wolves." Then he raised his voice, "Slim, are you crazy? You can't drive wolves. You can't break wolves to harness and drive 'em in a team."

"Maybe not, Doug," said Slim, "only these wolves don't seem to know that. Anyway I just done it to see if I could. It wouldn't be safe to use 'em on a trail, because if we come across another team o' dogs, there'd be a fight. Wolves'll take after and kill a grown dog anywhere an' any time he gits a chance. Even a wolf-dog breed you can't depend on, that's why a wolf strain can never make a leader."

"But aren't you afraid o' wolves?" Doug asked.

Slim shook his head. He had learned a great deal about these animals since the experience he had had with Corks. "No," he said calmly, "I never heard of a case where a wolf attacked a man." Slim squinted at his friend a moment, then said, "Ever know, Doug, that a wolf won't eat human flesh? A fox will, lots o' other animals will, but not any wolf I ever see, an' I seen lots of 'em. Ever know a Indian medicine man won't make his mask like a wolf? 'Spirits no afraid of wolf,' the Indian says. I ain't sayin' a wolf, an' especially a wolf-dog breed, ain't snarly an' might snap an' bite at you, even like a dog if he don't know you. But my wolves growed up knowin' me, an' we're friendly, but I wouldn't know for sure what they'd do if you tried to get acquainted with 'em."

Doug eyed the wild animals questioningly. "I ain't even

thinkin' o' tryin' to find out either," he said. "You can think what you want to, an' I'll think what I want. Maybe you're right, Slim, but to me a wolf is a wolf, an' he's dangerous, an' I don't want no part of 'em. But dogs is different."

The two talked dogs for a while, but regularly Doug looked to where the wolves were lying placidly at their stakes and shook his head in wonder. "I bet there ain't another guy in the world ever done that, drove a team o' wolves."

One spring just after breakup Slim was camped in the Slate Creek country. Indian friends of his in a little village had been having a hard time getting food, and he offered to help them. He talked with the chief.

"Medicine Man come," said the chief, "make medicine. Then you hunt. If Medicine Man make good medicine, we get food."

Slim agreed to await the arrival of the medicine man who would make 'medicine' and show them where the game was.

The Indian arrived and was ceremoniously offered the best hut. He disappeared inside with his pack, and in a short while came out dressed in his full official regalia to make strong "medicine." The chief had gathered the village together to await the appearance of the medicine man. Slim had seen strange things throughout the North, but no matter how strange they might seem to him, he knew the seriousness of these occasions to the Indians. Here came the medicine man, standing as pompously erect and tall as he could, stalking and posing and gesticulating with the greatest show of austere arrogance. He wore moccasins, a heavy suit of red woolen underwear, and a somewhat battered top hat. Slim dared not laugh, and he bowed his head to hide his grin. This the medicine man took to be a gesture of obeisance and singled Slim out of the group as being worthy of receiving the "medicine."

He gave strict and detailed instructions as to where a goat would be found. Slim followed them, found a goat, and returned with the meat. The following day more "medicine" was made, and Slim was directed to another point where he found another goat. All this was very mysterious to the Indians, for they were good hunters, and had been combing that very country with no sign of game. The medicine man's "pay" was a hind-quarter of a goat which he took back to his own village.

From then on hunting continued to be good. Here again Slim saw the actual practical result of the Indians' esoteric magic. Whether it was coincidence, chance, or "strong medicine," he didn't know. It was not infallible, but sometimes it seemed to work and when it did it was always dramatic.

He ranged to the north and east in his hunting, and one day was treed by caribou. It was difficult to see for any distance in the heavy timber, but Slim received his warning when he heard the rattling of caribou horns. He wanted meat, and if there were only a few, he could wait and pick one or two off and the Indians could come for them. But the longer he waited the louder and more general was the noise of the horns, and almost before he realized the danger of his position, he was surrounded by caribou. There was no possible way out. He could not shoot his way through, they would not be frightened away, and if he stayed where he was, he would certainly be trampled to death. There was only one direction he could go—up. He climbed a tree. He didn't have to climb far, perhaps six or eight feet off the ground, enough only so the antlers of the animals would not scrape him off his perch. Every head had a rack of horns, for both male and female grew them.

Slim had struck a caribou migration. Twice each year, spring and fall, once in each direction, the caribou traveled from the Arctic southward for rutting, then back north again. The trails they followed were sometimes as wide as a quarter of a mile, and there might be upward of twenty such trails to accommodate the possible fifty thousand of these animals. Slim remained treed for more than an hour while the caribou ambled their way past. Two of the stragglers added to his Indian friends' supply of meat.

Slim decided on one more day of hunting since he knew caribou to be in the vicinity. This time he hunted along a valley, and as he was crossing the meadowed floor, he found himself encircled by caribou. He stood still and looked around him. It seemed that the entire woods around the clearing was solid with them, and they were walking slowly toward him. He looked for a tree to climb, but the nearest tree was now at least twenty yards behind the advancing animals.

Again it would be useless to shoot. For lack of anything better to do, he sat down on a bit of windfall. It seemed obvious to him that the caribou could not trample him this time since they were coming from all directions converging on him. These animals are myopic, keen of scent, and stupidly inquisitive. They probably wanted to know what Slim was. There was neither sense of fear nor animosity among them. They approached to within thirty yards and stopped. Slim was solidly ringed by caribou perhaps fifty to a hundred deep. They stared, shook their great heads, making a sound with their horns like thousands of giant castanets. They blew and sniffed the air, and pawed the ground. Slim knew that if he shot one in an effort to frighten the others away, it might cause a stampede. This would have been fatal to him. Instead he did nothing, and waited. After about half an hour the caribou seemed satisfied that Slim was neither dangerous nor edible, and one by one they filtered back into the woods and out of sight.

So far as Slim knew, the caribou is the only animal that runs in packs or herds that has no leader. They seem to be prompted by a communal idea, and it is every animal for itself. If one should assume leadership, it is but for a moment; another might take the lead next, then another, until each was leading itself, yet all following the same group migratory pattern.

Slim went on to Copper Center to trade his furs and pick up supplies. As usual he stayed a few days to get caught up on news and rumors.

It was by no means strange that Slim knew and was known by most of the white and native population of the section. His travels through the years had taken him over trails that passed through almost every established settlement in the country. It was no wonder that Indian and white alike could say "Hello, Slim," to the familiar figure on a trail. One of his Indian friends stopped him as he was going through Gulkana on his way to his camp. "You in hurry?" the Indian asked.

Slim shook his head. He had long since adopted the Indian philosophy about a too rapid tempo of living. "You hurry," says the Indian, "you hurry to die. When you feel hurry, sit down until hurry go."

"No," Slim told his friend, "I'm in no hurry."

"Good. You come. We go fish. Go Big Charlie Lake," the Indian said, "beeg feesh. Ling cod liver. Good."

Big Charlie Lake, so-called by the Indians and lying some forty miles west of Gulkana, was a *Windigo* lake, and Slim was surprised that an Indian could fish there. He had heard that this *Windigo* or evil spirit was in the form of a huge black fish which lived in the lake. One time, so the my-poppa-say story went, five Indians built a "stick canoe," a raft, and on it took three caribou to cross the lake. Halfway across the big fish swallowed them, raft and all. Consequently, no Indian that Slim knew would go on Big Charlie Lake.

Nearly every lake, river, or mountain had some similar legend which the Indians passed down. They were usually stories of tragedy, and therefore attributed to the evil *Windigo* spirit. Possibly some accident had happened on Big Charlie Lake years back, and undoubtedly there were some very large fish in the water, but in the retelling the story assumed overly generous proportions. The result was that the Indians feared and respected such *Windigo*-inhabited spots.

"Windigo no eat if we no in canoe," the Indian told him.

Therefore, it seemed safe to fish from the shore.

When they arrived, there were other Indians there, throwing their hooks in from the shore. They used only a casting line with no rod or pole. Slim and his friend chose a promising spot on a flat rock overhanging a deep pool. The water was clear and deep. They dropped their hooks into the water and waited. Slim could see the fish swimming lazily about, and one that took the Indian's hook. Slim yelled and pointed, "Big fish." The Indian pulled hard on his line, felt the unyielding weight of the huge cod on his hook, and threw his line into the water and ran.

"Hey!" Slim yelled. "Come back here! No *Windigo,* only fish."

It took Slim considerable time to convince the frightened Indian that it was only a fish and not the raft-eating *Windigo.*

After that they caught many of the big ling cod (or burbot). They reminded Slim of catfish. They were grayish, with long slender tails, and marked by yellowish-white spots. These ling are the only member of the cod family known to inhabit fresh water, and, strangely, the only portion of the fish the Indians wanted was the liver. The fish, some as heavy as fifty or sixty pounds, had livers weighing up to ten pounds. Here again Slim saw the natural supply of dietary essentials. Cod-liver oil, fresh from the cod.

There by the lake Slim and the Indian had a good feed of fried liver, and had enough left over to pack nearly two hundred pounds of this greasy, succulent meat back to the Indian's village. There they had a feast. Slim noticed that particular attention was paid to feeding the juicy oily meat to the babies. These little fellows gurgled and smacked their pudgy lips with delight.

Slim moved his camp as trapping conditions warranted, but generally stayed within the trading area of Copper Center. One fall he had a specially fine team. In it were seven grown half-breeds and one dog, raised with them from a pup. The leader was a splendid big full-blooded MacKenzie Husky, and he was Slim's special joy.

"Finest leader I ever had in the thirty-two years I been in

Alaska," he told the trader in Copper Center. "He's so purty I just had to get a special name for him. I heard about a fellow who paints pictures, and if he ever painted a picture purtier'n that dog, I want to see it. So I named the leader after that painter. Rembrandt. And I call him Brant for short. There ain't a better dog."

It was during this conversation in the trading post at Copper Center, with the emphasis on sled dogs, that someone mentioned a man named Groshaw, from Nome.

"Goin' to drive his team o' dogs clear to Chicago. They're havin' a fair there or somethin'," someone said.

Slim was buying his winter supplies, but couldn't let this challenge pass.

"That Chicago's a long way from Alaska," he said, "and I heard about that Groshaw and his team. He's got Huskies. Gettin' so anybody with a li'l bitty wooly pooch under his arm thinks he's got the best dog team in Alaska. Huskies 'd never make that trip." Slim laughed, then sobered. "There's only one dog in the world ever make that trip, an' that's the wolf. I got the only team in Alaska that could do it."

There were about ten or eleven men in the post besides Slim. All had been talking about this trip. One of the younger men called to Slim, "You're so durned good, why don't you do it then?"

Slim put down his pack and turned to face the others. "I'm goin' to. What do you think I come out for? To get supplies, that's why, and I'm goin' back to my camp for my outfit, and I'm takin' the trail and headin' out for Chicago an' that fair just as soon as the snow gets good. I told you I got the only dogs that can do it."

Slim knew vaguely where Chicago was, but he had not heard about the Century of Progress fair.

He finished loading his pack and went back up the river to his camp. During the next week he was busy getting his traps ready for his winter trap lines and had already forgotten his bit of conversational bragging about his dogs. But someone had taken him seriously and pinned his loose talk together, for about two weeks later, when he decided he needed some more grub to see him through the winter and went back to the post at Copper Center, he was given the surprise of his life.

This time when he walked into the store he was greeted with silent awe and respect by some, and with shouts and backslappings by others. Tacked on the wall was the front page of a newspaper. The headline was big, black, and blaring—

SLIM WILLIAMS TO DRIVE DOGS
TO CHICAGO FAIR

There was more. It told how the word had gone out over the telegraph about Slim with his team of dogs and that the newspapers across the United States had front-paged the story of "Alaska's Most Famous Sourdough" and his proposed trip.

Slim read through the headline and first paragraph, and whirled to face the crowd. He was mad. "Which one o' you sockeyes done this?" He glared from one to the other.

"It's your own fault, Slim," the trader said. "You come in here puffin' about how you was the only man in Alaska could make the trip, an' either you are or you ain't." And he handed Slim a canvas sack. "This here's mail that already come for you, Slim. You may not know it, but you're a doggone international celebrity now."

Slim looked dazedly at the sack holding hundreds of pieces of mail, all probably having to do with his trip. He looked again at the newspaper on the wall. Then he faced the men.

"Well," he said, "I said I would, and in thirty-two years I never said I'd do somethin' an' didn't do it. But I sure opened my great big mouth wider this time than I ever did before in my life." Slim started for the door.

One of the men called to him, "Where you goin', Slim?"

Slim turned, and answered, "I'm just goin' out to tell my dogs what I talked 'em into. They don't know it yet, but I'm either the biggest liar or the gol-hangedest hero they ever saw!"

·18·

Searching my uttermost valleys,
fighting each step as they go,
Shooting the wrath of my rapids,
scaling my ramparts of snow.

Slim couldn't help feeling just a little important. Here all at once he had flashed into prominence, and had a front-page newspaper story and a sackful of letters to prove it. It still remained for him to justify all this by following through on his boast. He knew there was no backing out.

Among the letters he received were some from Donald McDonald, one of the finest highway engineers in Alaska. Slim knew McDonald. There were letters also from the Automobile Highway Association. These showed great interest in Slim's proposed trip, and suggested a meeting to discuss it. Slim next went to Fairbanks for a meeting in answer to McDonald's suggestion.

For some time there had been talk about the possibility of a roadway between Alaska and the United States. It was obvious that the thoroughfare would have to go through Canada, but the big question was, where?

McDonald had called together five men of the Automobile Highway Association to discuss with Slim the proposed dog-team trip out, and the best route to follow. He opened the session by introducing Slim to the other men, and concluded, ". . . and I don't know of any man in Alaska better qualified to make the try. A trip by dog team from Alaska through the ranges to the United States has never been done. Lots of men have tried it, but none have succeeded. Therefore, when I heard that Slim here had volunteered to make the try for the fair at Chicago, I was sure we had the man who could do it if anyone could."

McDonald clapped Slim on the shoulder. Slim didn't tell him that his "volunteering" was a matter for question. "I've known Slim for many years," McDonald continued, "and he always amazes me, because in the first place he's got more experience than any other sourdough in Alaska, and he has the courage and knack of trying things no other human would, and invariably accomplishes the impossible. So, fellows, I think we've got our trail blazer."

McDonald then went on to show that according to his best judgment, Slim's trail should follow the valley between the British Columbia coastal range and the Rockies. The reasons for this, he explained, were that the Japan Current along the coast tended to keep snowfall at a minimum, that the valley floor should form a solid roadway base, and besides it was the shortest. Other routes east of the Rockies would be long, probably over miles of muskeg, and as future roadways would be more expensive to build and maintain.

"Of course, Slim," one of the Highway Association men said, "we haven't the authority to appoint you an official representative of Alaska on this trip of yours, but we don't know of anyone better fitted. What we are anxious to determine is the practicability of this route McDonald has suggested through the mountains from here to the Washington state border."

These men were actually highly enthusiastic over the fact that Slim was going. "Also," said McDonald, "we're not in any position to finance the trip, but we do have this for you, Slim, from private contribution." He handed Slim $300.

Slim was embarrassed. "I'm sort o' not used to this," he said. "I can make the trip, all right, like I intend to, and

I'm sure glad to have the suggestion of a trail to follow, but I didn't expect anybody to pay my way."

"Let's say you're doing it for Alaska, Slim," said McDonald, "and we're all Alaskans and sort of in this together. But I'm sorry," he added, "there are no maps."

"I been travelin' Alaska without maps for thirty-two years," Slim said wryly. "Most of the maps I ever saw have a big space on 'em sayin' 'Unsurveyed' and that always happens to be the place right where I'm goin'. But you just show me on the big wall map there so I can get my directions straight, and I'll make out."

The line was pointed out from Whitehorse almost straight south and a little east. There was a natural high-level gully between the two coastal mountain ranges. Slim, whose memory automatically photographed trails, places, and landmarks, took in the full details of the pictured map and McDonald's explanation. Then he closed his eyes so his mind would do the developing and make a permanent record. Slim never forgot a trail once he had run it.

"Think you'll get lost?" one of the men asked jokingly.

"I learned a long time ago how not to get lost if I could see the stars and the sun. I've never been lost, but did I ever tell you about the time I lost the North Star?"

The man shook his head.

"I was runnin' mail down the Yukon," he said. "I hadn't been in Alaska long, wasn't more'n a kid, an' I was on the big turn where the river crosses the Arctic Circle. One night I tried to get my bearings and I looked for the North Star. I'd learned how to get my compass points from it when I was a kid in California, but you know I couldn't find that star? I went around and around the sky and it just weren't there. Some Indians was there and I told 'em what I was lookin' for. They pointed up. Sure enough there was the Dipper with the two 'pointers' and the North Star. That's when I found when you're standin' on the Arctic Circle, you don't *go* north, you *are* north. North is just about straight up!"

"How about your dogs, Slim?" McDonald asked. "The last team of yours I saw were pretty good."

"These are better," said Slim. "If you men want to see the team that's goin' to make this trip I got 'em tied right back o' the building."

The dogs took the examination with a bit of self-conscious fidgeting. Especially the young dog.

One of the men remarked, "They look like wolves, Slim, all but the leader and the little fellow."

"They are," said Slim. "This team's half-breeds. The little dog I had put in to fill up, and the leader is a full-blood MacKenzie Husky."

"They're certainly beautiful dogs," said McDonald.

Slim nodded with pride. "Took me almost twenty-five years to get 'em," he said.

"Twenty-five years?" one of the men asked.

Slim laughed. "To get what I wanted," he amended. "Did you ever see a wolf run?" A few of the men nodded. "It's about as purty a motion as you could find. Smooth, an' they run with no effort, an' don't seem ever to get tired. They're born to run. What I wanted was to breed that runnin' power o' the wolf into the sort o' civilized thinkin' o' the dog, so's I'd get strength an' toughness along with the kindness an' the understandin' o' the dog. So I got wolf cubs just when they was born, an' raised 'em with dogs until they was old enough to breed, three years for the wolf, an' only about nine months for the dog. Then I'd raise their pups an' see what happened. Then I crossbred them, some with wolves, some with dogs, an' out of every litter I'd keep some to train an' try out in harness. Too much wolf give me trouble, they was likely to be mean an' snarly. Too much dog didn't seem to give me enough of the wolf I was hopin' to get. So I finally settled for half-breeds, and they work out just fine. This team is two year olds, nearly prime. They're smart, strong, feet are tougher'n any dog's, don't know what it is to get tired. An' that leader is just a honey."

"Aren't they dangerous, Slim?" McDonald asked. "I notice you haven't got a whip."

Slim shook his head. "I never used a whip or a club on a dog, Mac. I train 'em just by talkin' to 'em, an' they know my voice an' they obey me. But I wouldn't want a stranger to get too close to 'em. They still think like wolves."

When Slim told them of his experiment of training and driving a team of full-blood wolves, some of the men eyed the team suspiciously and took a respectful step back.

"I thought wolves, even half-breeds, would kill a dog," said one of the men.

"Not if they're raised together, they won't, or if a dog is put in with 'em when he's a little puppy, they won't," Slim explained. "I learned that a long time ago from Indians. I had a wolf once I was goin' to breed, and a Indian friend o' mine and his squaw come by to my camp an' they had a little baby. When the wolf saw it he was about the excitedest animal you ever saw. He just wanted that baby. He wouldn't ha' hurt it, he just wanted to play with it. Of course I didn't let him, but a while later I was in a trading post and there was a doll, and I got it and took it back to camp an' gave it to that wolf just to see what he'd do. He was a big fellow, near two hundred pounds, but do you know he loved that doll? He carried it around and guarded it. He just thought the world o' that doll. Now he knew it wasn't human, or anything to eat, but it was something that looked like a baby and it was little. He kept that doll till it was just wore out. I found out that they was like that with pups. Put a grown dog with 'em and they'd kill him in a second, but wolves'll take a puppy and let it grow up with 'em. They'll even teach it to talk like a wolf. The leader there, Brant, went with 'em as a pup, like the little fellow too."

The men laughed about the wolf and the doll, but Slim insisted it was so. "That's the way most of us in the bush learned the things we know, by tryin' 'em. I been tryin' an' learnin' for a long time."

"And that's why I say again, Slim," said McDonald, "that if anybody is equal to the job of driving dogs from here to Washington, D.C., you're the man to do it. Good luck to you, my friend."

Slim looked up sharply. "Washington, D.C.!" he said. "I thought it was Chicago I was going to. Washington's where the government is."

McDonald laughed, "After you get to Chicago, Washington isn't much farther. You know Tony Dimond, don't you?"

Slim smiled. "They ain't a man in Alaska who don't, I guess."

"Well, he's in Washington, looking after Alaska's affairs for us, and you go to him and you can give him your report on your trip. Maybe you'll even meet the President."

Slim laughed, and shook his head. "Not much chance o' that, I guess. But I'll sure be glad to see Tony. I'd go to Washington just for that."

Thus Slim, with letters of identification and introduction, became in theory, at least, Alaska's representative to blaze the first trail of an international highway. What had begun as a stunt he had talked himself into, was to prove an important pioneering mission. He would be the first man to make the journey overland by practical transportation.

Blessed with semi-official recognition, and funds, Slim was ready to start. His personal preparations were quickly accomplished. He closed his camp, and exchanged his camp food for trail fare. For himself he carried twenty pounds of rice, twenty pounds of sugar, and plenty of tea, a rifle, ammunition, matches, no compass, no tent, no stove. He planned to live off the land and out of the streams. His little seven-by-nine piece of canvas would be his windbreak. The rest of the poundage on his sled was dog feed. He was leaving from Copper Center. There was no great excitement built up over these preparations; Slim Williams was merely going on a trail trip with his dogs. This was the white man's reasoning.

The Indians, however, sensed that something was taking

place that called for special action on their part. Before he could leave, he had to talk with several of his Indian friends, many of whom had come long distances when they had heard he was leaving. Mentasta Sam was one of them. He brought Slim a pair of moose-hide mittens heavily beaded. They were Sam's own mitts and had been well worn. He tied them to the handle bars of Slim's sled.

"You no take off," he cautioned Slim. "You go through Big Flat Country. You see Little Man. Little Man see you he want to eat you. Then Little Man see mitts. Little Man know me. He know you good man, I give you mitts. Little Man no kill you, he see this." Sam was very serious about this.

Other Indians brought similar tokens, one a beaded bag, another a belt, a pair of moccasins, another a pair of mitts. All of these had been worn or used, and each owner impressed upon Slim the danger of going through the country of the Little Man without these tokens to assure safe travel.

During his thirty-two years in Alaska Slim had become well acquainted with almost every tribe in the territory, but still many of their ways and thoughts, such as this, remained mysteries to him. They believed firmly that the Little Man was real. He was a spirit who had power for the maintenance of good fortune to those who knew him. Therefore, the tokens offered by the Indians were symbolic assurance of their prayers for Slim's safety on his journeys. He was sincerely grateful for this show of honest friendship from these people. He promised each one that these would remain as they were and that he would be very careful in passing through the Big Flat Country, the unknown country ahead.

On the morning of November 21, 1932, Slim left Copper Center without too much fuss or fanfare. It was forty below. And thus started the first leg of the longest and certainly the most hazardous trip by dog team ever attempted.

Luck rode with Slim on this trip, and most of it was very, very good, but when it was bad it rocked him back on his heels. His trail looped past the northern rim of the Alaska

Range. This rolling country led him over familiar ground, through the Mentasta Pass, Chicken, Fortymile, and to Dawson.

His first bit of misfortune met him as he was leaving Fortymile on the leg to Dawson. Because of his youth, the little dog was given special privileges. The pup was an eager and willing worker, but he couldn't hold the pace with the full-grown wolf-dogs and Brant. Slim took him out of harness about two hours at a time to let him run free and to give him a rest from the load. He'd scamper and run ahead and frisk like any pup, then he'd willingly take his place again for a spell at work.

During one of his "free" periods the dog was two hundred or three hundred yards ahead of the team when Slim saw him stop. Directly ahead, facing the dog, stood six or eight wolves. They were huddled together and Slim didn't get a clear count, but there were at least six. Slim saw disaster. He yelled at his dogs, urging speed. They did their best, but it wasn't good enough. The young dog could see no difference between these wolves and his own team, they looked alike, and talked alike. By the time Slim had come near enough for a shot, it was too late. Slim stopped his dogs, tipped his sled, and had his rifle out just as the dog reached the wolves. The wolves had waited until the dog was a foot or so away, then they lunged. At the same time Slim got off his first shot. He shot again, and again. He killed three. The others disappeared into the brush, but the dog was badly torn and dying. This left Slim with an unbalanced eight-dog team.

His way from Dawson led south over the old Whitehorse trail and on past the junction of the Pelly River. It had turned colder. He guessed it to be forty or fifty below, and was therefore glad that a prospector, living in a shack along the trail near the Pelly, asked him to take cover with him. The man was married to an Indian, and at first Slim hesitated, but once inside he changed his mind. The shack was as clean and well kept as any he had ever been in. The squaw was neat, nicely dressed, and turned out to be a wonderful cook. Unlike Charlie's experience with Annie, this was just one of those off-chance cases where a malleable Indian married a strong-willed white man and the white man took the trouble and patience to teach her. This fellow, Slim learned, was from Kentucky.

He stayed three days until the weather broke to a more comfortable twenty or thirty below, just good for travel. The Kentuckian had a little dog he'd sell to Slim to make up his team.

"I don't know," said Slim, "my team is part wolf, and they won't take to a grown dog. I'm afraid they'll kill him."

"Aw now, Slim," the prospector drawled, "I ain't aimin' to shuck no dawg off on ya, if'n ya don' wan' him. But this li'l old dawg o' mine ain't got a mean thought in his haid. He's like me, he git along with anybody. I'll let ya have him mighty cheap too."

Slim looked the little dog over. He was a yellow-furred Pelly River Husky, small, but well built. He bought him, and put him into harness with the team. The dogs turned on him at once, and for the first time, Slim had to use force to separate them. All the first day out, Slim spent most of his time trying to keep the big dogs from chomping choice bits of the newcomer. Along in the afternoon he passed another shack and stopped. Here was an old-timer living alone, and he had no dog. Slim explained the trouble that the newcomer in his team was causing, and that the experiment wouldn't work. He couldn't spend all his time saving the dog's life, and both he and the team would be better off without him. The prospector accepted the gift gladly. This left Slim with an uneven hitch again, but he decided on no more additions. Then with his eight dogs once more in harmony, he took the trail again.

Along the way there often was an occasional shack, some of them occupied by lone wintering prospectors, others abandoned. It was just about dark and time to make camp when he came upon a good stout one, well made, with a big drum stove and a fairly good pile of wood. This was a bit of good fortune, for although he had no thermometer, his nose told him the cold had again dipped into the subzero fifties or sixties. He fed his dogs, built up a good fire, ate his own supper and went to sleep.

About midnight pain awakened him. He never knew what caused it, but he was overwhelmingly sick to his stomach. This kept up all night. By dawn his head ached until he was dazed by the pain, and his stomach spasms continued. He was certain he was going to die, but he had no idea of staying where he was alone. He thought he would have a better chance if he could get on the trail and keep going in the hope of passing an occupied shack where he might get help.

He never knew the time, but it must have taken him an hour or more to harness the dogs. He crawled outside and harnessed one dog, then returned to the shack to rest and get warm. Then he harnessed another. He did this until the team was ready and hitched to the sled. Ordinarily the dogs were anxious for a run at the start of a new day. But these sensitive animals knew that something was wrong. On the last trip out from the shack Slim talked with Brant. The big leader sniffed a thorough examination. With a few throaty commands he instantly had the team under control. When Slim got to his feet he stood on the runners of the sled and took hold of the handle bars. It took all his strength to hold himself upright. He thought he yelled, but his voice was just a whispered "Mush," and he fell forward between the handle bars. The dogs did not lunge, there was no break into quick speed. Instead they walked slowly and carefully. Slim lost consciousness.

When he opened his eyes, the dogs were standing still and he was where he had fallen onto the sled. He turned his head and saw a cabin. At first he wondered if they hadn't moved. He shook his head to clear the fuzz. Then he saw this was not the same cabin in which he had spent the night. Smoke was coming out of the pipe, and paths were well used. Foggily, he could only guess what had happened. It was as if Brant, understanding his master's need, had followed the trail until he reached what his senses told him was an occupied cabin where help could be had. At Slim's movements, Brant turned his head and looked back. Slim tried to speak to him, but no sound came, but somehow the dog knew that Slim again could take control, and he lay down on the trail. His work was done.

Slim's head ached and he hurt inside. He tried to stand up but couldn't make it. However, he did succeed, by crawling, in tying his sled and going inside the shack. There was no one there, but there was a good fire and it was warm. It felt good. He shrugged out of his parka and crawled onto the bunk. He immediately went to sleep.

Dogs barking wakened him, and in a moment a man entered the shack. He was a big fellow, and stood over Slim and looked down at him. "So you're Slim Williams, are ye?" he said in a heavy friendly voice. "It's no' so gude a welcome I'm gi'in ye, but I'm glad ye made yersel' at home. I had a wee bit o' trouble wi' th' wild beasties yer drivin', so it's maybe best ye care for 'em yersel'. Ma name's Stewart." He stopped the soft roll of his pleasing Scotch burr and looked more closely at Slim. "Wha's th' matter, lad, are ye not weel?" His concern was genuine.

Slim told him bit by bit what had happened.

"It's no' so gude, lad, but I'm glad ye were led to come here. Ye'll be in gude shape wi' no worry. First a bit o' boiled milk to settle th' inner mon where he's upset. We'll try a bit."

Within an hour Slim was sitting up talking with this friendly Scotsman. Then he went out and cared for and fed his dogs. He spent a little longer than usual with Brant. The big fellow's answer to Slim's gratitude was a thumping flap of his tail.

Back inside Slim explained his dogs, and then he asked, "How did you know my name?"

Stewart laughed, "Slim, ye'll find ye're well known where'er ye go along th' trail ahead. Yer name is on the wind, an' it's written in the stars. It's been passed along by Indians in the way they have o' knowin' aboot things before they hoppen."

"Moccasin telegraph," said Slim.

"Aye," Stewart nodded.

Stewart was a trapper, and was glad for Slim's company. He kept him for three days until whatever deviltry had gnawed Slim's innards was surely gone.

"Gude luck to ye, lad," was Stewart's farewell.

"And my thanks to you," said Slim.

"Thanks should be to that noble animal ye got at th' head o' yer team, but ye're welcome a' th' same," the Scot replied.

Slim's next stop was a brief one at Carmacks. Here he left the rolling country of the foothills and went into the mountains. From there on the trail was rough through Whitehorse, Carcross, to Telegraph Creek. At Carcross he cut down the sled to a toboggan. This was because from then on what trail there was would be the trail he made, snowshoe wide. Sled runners were fine for hard packed well used trails, but now that he was entering mountain country the runners would be a hazard.

He located a trader who had a plane, and with that and an axe and his ingenuity he revised the runners and narrowed the sled from a twenty-two- to sixteen-inch width and added a flat toboggan surface. He also rehitched the dogs from tandem to the stretched-out single file he had used before on mountain and heavy bush trails. He left about six or eight feet between dogs, with Brant ahead by about twelve feet. This prevented the dogs from piling up or tangling if one should step off the trail into soft snow. It was such things as these, the know-how, that McDonald had meant when he said that Slim was the man for the trail outside. Without the depth of his years of accumulated experience it would have been almost an impossibility. Even with all he knew it wasn't easy, for leaving Carcross he would have mountains to cross. These were like the "upendicular" ones he had first met in the Alaska Range.

When he had his change-over to suit him, he took his bearings and set his course. He broke trail in swirling, packless snow up almost sheer slopes. Behind him his dogs, heads down, bent to their load, following the narrow paths of his snowshoes. Over each successive rise was an equal descent. Now that the sled had become a toboggan, he had no foot brake of spikes to hold it back. At each crest, therefore, he wrapped rope around the toboggan, and with this as a drag the dogs were able to keep ahead of the toboggan and on the trail. The wind, the snow, the cold were merciless, and as far ahead as Slim could see, there was another mountain and another to cross.

Going into Telegraph Creek, Slim stopped at an Indian camp, and was more than surprised to find a white woman there. Her skin was fair, her nose dotted with freckles. Her hair was red. She was apparently married to one of the Indians and had a family. She was white without a doubt, but in her actions she was fully Indian. When Slim saw her she was squatting on the ground with other squaws tanning a moose hide.

When he got into Telegraph Creek, he asked about this anomaly. A trader answered the question. "She's white, all right," he said. "So far as anybody knows a prospector and his wife came through here in '98. She had a baby here about the same time a squaw had a baby, and the squaw's baby died. This prospector's wife I guess didn't want to chance taking her baby into the North, so she give her to the Indian. An' this redhead is her. She won't talk nothin' but Indian, an' she's more Indian than white, but she's white just the same.

For the first two months, as far as Telegraph Creek, there had been trails and semblances of trails. From here on there were none. There were at least four hundred miles of wilderness travel before he could hope to see another human. Not even Indians lived in the mountains. And these were mountains. The Rockies to his left, the Coast Range to his right, mountains rugged, sheer, and beautiful that seemed to pierce the sky. Some were sharply outlined against the bluest of skies, others seemed to disappear upward in a misty halo of swirling snow. Between these two lines of mountains was the valley of his trail. All he had to do was make it as he traversed its four-hundred-mile length.

On the second day out of Telegraph Creek Slim had a visitor. He had stopped to make a pot of tea when he heard dogs. He looked back along his trail and recognized the winter trail garb of a mountie.

Over tea they visited. "I'm Constable Burns, Slim," the mountie introduced himself, "and I looked to find you in Telegraph Creek, but you'd left. Just wanted to find out if everything's all right, and if there's anything we fellows can do for you."

"Nothin' but flatten out some o' these gol-hanged mountains," said Slim. "You sure surprised me comin' up on me like this."

"Don't forget, you're breaking trail. All I had to do was follow it." The constable smiled. "But word's gone ahead to be on the lookout for you, Slim. As long as you're the guest of Canada, we want to see that we're good hosts. You've got some tough country ahead, but they tell me you're well away when it comes to that."

The constable stayed the night and commented particularly on the way Slim made his night camp, mounting his piece of canvas on poles as a windbreak, building a good fire, and sleeping between the two. "Good rig," the mountie pronounced.

The next morning, without too much more conversation, the constable said, "Thanks for your hospitality, Slim. This was just a friendly visit to see if we could be of help. Good luck." The constable took the back trail, and Slim headed south.

Day after day, uncounted days, Slim kept southward. Sometimes he made about five miles, sometimes even ten. He worked out a pattern. Each morning he left his dogs tied and went ahead, broke trail as far as he could make in half a day, and returned to camp before dark. The next day he drove the dogs over the new trail and camped where it ended. In this manner he made his slow but positive progress.

Fortunately food presented no problem. There was plenty of game, sheep, caribou, and one day he counted sixty-two moose. Also there were fish-filled lakes, frozen over, but he chopped through and caught trout. This he dried for dog feed. Nor did he waste any of the meat. He knew drying would take precious time, but he also knew from the past what hunger was. Fresh-killed meat was bulky and heavy with blood, therefore, to reduce both volume and weight, and to permit him to carry as much as possible of the food, he smoked and dried as much as his toboggan could hold. But his hardest work was not getting food to stay alive, it was to make trail. The mountie had underestimated the country. It was more than *tough*—bouldered rocks, snow, and heavily wooded. The going was worse than any he had ever known. There were days when he counted a mile as getting ahead.

There were times when he found himself following frozen stream courses which took him off his direction. This meant tedious retracing of steps, taking new bearings and getting back on his southward way. With no compass he relied on the Indian "sun compass" for accurate direction. This consisted of setting a stick to cast a shadow, and another stick at the end of the shadow. As time passed, the shadow of the first stick moved and formed a pattern which he marked by adding a stick at each new shadow's end. These sticks formed an arc. The shortest shadow marked noon, for then the sun was highest and directly south. This key shadow, therefore, pointed north. This took time to do, and fortunately he didn't have to do it every day, for time was of serious consequence. He had to reach the southern outlet of this mountain channel by spring breakup. To be sure of making it out safely he kept on the trail as long and as hard as he could each day. He had long since lost all track of day and month. His only gauge was the sun, and as it gained daily in height, its thawing warmth was felt. He worked hard but he did not hurry. Hurry, he knew, resulted only in mistaken judgment.

There were some stream channels he followed which were

almost impossible. He never knew their identities, for every one was nameless to him, nor did it matter. One in particular gave him a special brand of trouble. Its banks were sheer and rocky, chasmlike on either side. His problem there was to hold his toboggan upright and on what level ground there was along the bank. He went slowly, chopping ahead to flatten ice to make a runway for dogs and toboggan. One escape from this treacherous course was to climb out of this canyon up one of its faces and find a new trail; this was impractical because it would have taken probably a week or more to get his outfit up and over, and then with a chance of becoming lost. The other was to let the toboggan slide onto the surface ice of the stream. Slim had long since learned his lesson about this. The middle was already beginning to thaw, places were even clear of ice, so Slim did his best to keep his dogs and outfit safely on the shore. Finally, however, he reached a point where it seemed impossible to make any further headway.

Indianlike, Slim sat down to think. He looked across the stream, perhaps a hundred feet, and the bank on the other side looked clear and level and would afford a perfect trail. The problem was to get across.

Wearing snowshoes, and leaving the dogs untied, he started across. About midstream the ice cracked beneath him. A piece about six feet square broke through. With a lunge he jumped, one snowshoe broke off another chunk as it struck, but he had just enough purchase on the breaking ice and momentum to propel him shoreward in a dive. He lit belly down, half on the bank and his legs in the water. He clawed at the shore. His snowshoes were heavy dragging weights. As he grabbed chunks of ice, one would break, another would hold. Little by little, without a quick movement, he pulled himself ashore. There he sat, soaking wet from the waist down. Across the stream, watching him, were his dogs.

Here was trouble, real trouble, and the answer called for quick action. Slim would have to wait to dry out and get warm, for the dogs must be brought across what ice there was left as quickly as possible. Fast water was already chewing the opening wider where Slim had gone through the rotting surface crust. There was still one solid bridge from bank to bank, just upstream from where Slim crossed. This was his only hope. He went along the shore to a point where there was a direct line of ice between him and Brant. Slim took a tentative step or two on the ice, and it sounded and felt solid. He felt sure that it would hold the weight of the dogs and the toboggan. The dogs were so spaced in their harness that there would be no great bulk of weight in one spot, and speed would be essential for full safety. He had no thought of asking his dogs to do the impossible, and he was aware of the peril. He knew too that Brant, left to his own decision, would hesitate before leading his team into such obvious danger, so it would be up to him to *talk* his dogs across.

He called to Brant to get his attention, and then he began, his voice quiet and convincing. "Brant," he said, "you got to bring your team across. You can do it. The ice will hold you," and he talked on, watching the dog closely.

At first Brant looked questioningly at his master as if trying hard to know just what he was talking about. Then there seemed to be a moment of doubt, for he looked at the open water and the jagged edges of ice where he had seen Slim go through. Instinct warned him, and he looked inquiringly across at Slim.

Slim saw Brant going through these mental steps of doubt, but he kept on with his talking. Finally he saw what he had been looking for. Brant had understood! The dog at once became the leader. With no sense of excitement or quick action, but reflecting the firm confidence in Slim's voice, Brant uttered low throaty commands bringing the rest of the dogs to their feet, and little by little turned them so the line faced Slim and their collars brought the towlines taut with the load.

Slim watched proudly every move and tactic of this superb exhibition of leadership, and he kept talking, giving the dog all the support that he could. Slim now watched closely for the sign that would show that Brant was ready, that he had reached the point of decision. There Brant stood, watching, listening. Slim talked on. Then he saw it. Brant's head came fully up, the muscles of his big shoulders trembled, then tautened until he stood a perfect statue. At that instant Slim called with all his might, "Come on, Brant, MUSH! Come here, fellow! Come here to me, boy! MUSH!" With a full-throated bark, Brant lunged. In a single move the eight dogs jumped to action. They bounded across the ice, seeming barely to touch it, and in seconds made the bank safely with the toboggan. Brant jumped and with paws on Slim's shoulders whined and whimpered to show his happiness. Slim was near tears for pride as he roughed the big fellow's ears in affection. The other dogs, too, came in for their share of praise. He had asked his dogs to brave possible death for him, and they had accepted the challenge. Where in all the world, he thought, was there greater loyalty or courage?

Breakup was dangerously near, and Slim talked it over with Brant. "Brant," he said, "we got no time to waste from now on. This crick bustin' loose like it is, breakup's almost on us, an' if it catches us in these mountains, we're just blowed-up suckers, an' that's all they is to it. I'll get my pants dry and we'll make trail!"

The morning after his near disaster in crossing the stream, Slim started out without wearing his snow glasses. He had worn them regularly, but this one day, thinking perhaps the shadowed glare was not too bright, he left them off. About noon he felt twin pinpoints of pain in his eyes. He recognized this warning, and knew that it presaged snow blindness. He had been snow-blind before, and knew exactly what to do. By this time it was too late for the glasses. These were merely a preventive. To effect a remedy, he would have to work fast. First he tied his dogs, except Brant, and fed them. Next he built a fire and brewed tea, then he crawled under his canvas and stayed quiet. A few moments later he was blind.

·19·

I'd like to be far on some weariful shore,
In the land of the Blizzard and Bear;
Oh, I wish I was snug in the Arctic once more,
For I know I am safer up there!

The pot of tea on Slim's campfire was not primarily for drink-ing. Its main purpose was to supply wet, hot tea leaves. He made poultices of them, wrapping them in his bandanna, to cover his eyes. He kept the applications hot, and after an hour or so the biting pain subsided, but it was nearly three days be-fore his sight partially returned. Snow blindness strikes fast, its duration may be any length of time from a few hours to several weeks. It is always a thorough discomfort. As Slim lay quietly under his piece of canvas not an hour passed that Brant did not come and scratch on the canvas. Slim talked with him each time he came, reassuring him, and the dog went about his affairs of keeping watch over the camp until it was time to check up on his master again. Day and night, the dog never missed an hourly visit.

By the fourth day Slim could see well enough to go on. The dogs, after the three-day rest, were more than eager. The sun had turned the snow to slush, and the trail, now leaving the mountains, became the thick, sticky gumbo of British Columbia mud. This spelled tragedy to Slim. It was apparent that breakup had beaten him. His three-day blindness during which he couldn't travel had made the difference. However, he determined to do all he could for as long as he could. One thing he didn't know. He was almost at the end of this wilderness trail. He was within a few miles of civilization.

His first problem was the dogs. This was a new experience for them, and at first they didn't know what to do about it, then apparently they decided there was nothing to do but go on slogging, dragging the toboggan over the messy goo. To ease the burden and save his toboggan from being worn away, Slim cut saplings of green birch and fastened them to the bottom for runners. It helped some, but it was still mean going every step of the sloppy way.

To lighten the dogs' work, he packed and carried and pulled with them. There was no trail, and the gummy ground gave the most uncertain footing. There was only one thing he was sure of, he was going in the right direction. Fortunately he encountered no streams of any size. There were thaw freshets and creeks but these were fordable. A river would have caused him trouble. He and the dogs could stand only an hour or so at a time of this sort of going.

On the afternoon of the third day of this tortuous way, Slim saw a clearing ahead through the trees. When he reached it he saw buildings in the distance, and almost at his feet there was a well-worn path. He jumped sharply when he heard a human voice. Other than his own this was the first one he had heard in almost four months. He shaded his eyes. About ten yards off to one side stood a mountie.

The mountie waved and called, "Hello, Slim!" He walked toward Slim and held out his hand. "Constable Gregg, at your service," he said warmly. "I've been out here every day for the past three weeks. We figured if you got through, you ought to be here about now. I'm certainly glad to see you."

"And I'm sure just as glad to see you," said Slim.

"Just a bit over the rise is my cabin, Slim, and I guess you could use some rest, and you're welcome to use my digs as long as you like. I even picked up your mail at the post office for you." The constable was a cordial soul. Slim was fully enjoying the sound of this friendly voice. He could still hardly believe that he had safely made it through.

"You mean there's a town here?" Slim asked. "Them buildings I saw are a town?"

"Hazelton," said the mountie. "This is Hazelton, B.C."

"That's the name of it!" said Slim. "That's the town I was supposed to head for. Four hundred miles through the mountains, and I hit it! . . . . and what day is it?"

"Monday, May 15, 1933," said the mountie.

Slim slipped off his mitts and began telling his fingers, then he slowly shook his head and exhausted a soundless whistle. "Almost six months comin' from Copper Center. Four months comin' through the bush!"

The mountie's admiration was full and sincere. "That's as fine trail work, Slim, as I've ever known of," he said. "You're the first man ever to make it down with dogs."

"One of these days it'd make a good road through there," said Slim. "That was sort of one of the ideas of my tryin' it, to blaze through and see if a road would be practical. Take some work, but it could be done. Make a fine road through there."

At the cabin after taking care of his dogs, Slim shucked down and enjoyed the first bath he had had in almost six months. While he was scrubbing, the constable went into town and came back with a new outfit of clothes. Clean and freshly dressed, Slim had three requests to make.

"You name them, Slim, and if we have them, they're yours."

"First, have you got a restaurant in Hazelton where anybody can make flapjacks as fast as I can eat 'em, with maple sirup? And if there's a barber in town I've got a six months' beard and hair that I'll be glad to donate for mattress stuffin'. An' I need a pair o' moccasins."

The mountie laughed. "Fix you on all counts, Slim. You come along and I'll see to it that you're shorn, shod, and satisfied. But say, aren't you going to read your mail first?" he pointed to a sizable stack of letters.

"I'll take 'em with me," said Slim, stuffing them in his pockets.

After the third stack of finger-thick wheat cakes drowned in sirup, Slim sat back. "That was worth the walk down here. Nothin' like wheat cakes an' sirup to start a man out again, Constable."

Slim pulled out his mail. He selected a long important-looking envelope and squinted at the writing. A small slip of paper fell out as he opened it. He rubbed his eyes. "Funny," he said, "I can't seem to figure out the writin,' and it's on a type-writer too."

The constable read it to him. It was from McDonald, and the slip of paper was a check for $50.00 to help Slim defray further expenses. Slim was grateful to his friend for this added thoughtfulness. The constable obliged by reading the rest of the mail to Slim. It consisted mostly of congratulations and good wishes, much of it from people he had never heard of.

"What worries me, though," he said after the mail had been read, "is that I can't read. It must be that snow blindness I had an' was tellin' you about while I was eatin'."

"I know the lad who might even fix that, Slim. Come along." The constable led the way to an office where a doctor looked at Slim's eyes, tried several pairs of glasses, and finally found a pair that solved Slim's problem. "Just say it's a gift from Hazelton, Slim," said the doctor when Slim offered payment.

That evening in the mountie's cabin, he said to Slim, "You know, you surprise me a little, Slim. I've seen fellows come out after a long stretch in the bush alone, and they all seemed a little nuts, and it took them quite a while to get over bein' 'bushed.' But you seem to take it all right."

Slim grinned, and rubbed his chin with his thumbnail. "Feels awful good to be able to do that again," he said. "Whisk-ers is awful tiresome things to carry around. But, you see, a fellow can sort o' get used to bein' alone if he knows how to handle his thinkin'. This is pit' near the longest stretch I ever had without seein' anybody, and it's sort o' like comin' out of a vacuum would be. Funny thing, main trouble seems to be everybody's in a hurry an' all talkin' too loud. I guess it's the sound o' their voices that gets you, and half the time you don't know what they're talkin' about. Every time I come out o' the bush after a few months, it's always the same. Takes a little time and patience to fit back into things again. But it works out—gradual. For a fellow who ain't used to it, it sometimes goes pretty hard with him. I seen some of 'em too."

The folks in Hazelton had heard about Slim and were waiting for him. Their curiosity was more about the dogs than the man, and for the few days that Slim remained, the dogs had a constant appreciative audience.

Slim's first chore was to remake his toboggan back into a sled and put it on wheels. It took considerable hunting around for him to find what he wanted, but at last he located a set of Model T wheels. With the help of a blacksmith he cut the axles to length, mounted his sled on a frame, and even arranged a steering device and a hand brake for control.

From Hazelton on to the United States border, and across the States he would be on wheels, so he took every precaution that the work was well done. When he was satisfied, he took leave of his friend Constable Gregg, thanked him sincerely for his hospitality, and mushed his dogs southward over a road of ankle-deep mud for the next few hundred miles to the border. It was a weird looking but strangely practical contraption that he now put on the road, an Alaskan sled on wheels!

After a few days he couldn't decide which was worse, mud or snow. The mud clung to and jammed the wheels, it got into the sled, and spread over everything including the dogs and himself. At times he actually chopped the accumulation from the wheels and spokes with his axe. The dogs worked hard, and Slim knew that their opinion of mud was no happier than his own.

He was no longer traveling through unpopulated country. Frequent farms and villages were welcome havens, and he was received with almost royal acclaim. Invitations were waiting for him at each town with offers of a place to stay and food for his dogs and himself. Except for the mud he began to enjoy the trail.

Another heart-warming experience was waiting when he crossed the border into the state of Washington. There again was a stack of mail and a great welcome awaited him.

After he got on the highways of the United States, Slim found that he was no longer fully free to make his own decisions. The publicity that had gone ahead of him had taken hold, and he found himself a kind of progressive 'project' for chambers of commerce across the country. He was to find out that he was the property of the Great American Public. From then on, things were "arranged" for him. Each town he passed through gave him an eager welcome. He camped and cooked his meals in the city parks before appreciative and inquisitive audiences. The hospitality of the people was ample and sincere.

Slim's main concern was for his dogs. They were not accustomed to the heat they encountered, nor were they used to running on paved or gravel roads. As early as in British Columbia women along the way offered to make moccasins for the dogs, tiny canvas bootces, to protect their pads. Slim, out of sheer courtesy, tried them. One set lasted about eight to ten miles. He finally figured that the time spent in changing thirty-two moccasins every ten miles could be better utilized by driving the dogs slower. It worked.

To get away from the heat, as well as from the curious crowds along the highways which at times were traffic clogged, Slim drove nights. He camped during the day and visited with those who came to see him and his team. Slim, warm-hearted, almost faultily generous with his time and answers to countless questions, made and kept thousands of friends. He never left a town but what he was on a first-name basis with at least the mayor, the chief of police, and the president of the chamber of commerce. In the cool of the night, usually just past midnight, he harnessed up and took to the road. The night traffic was not too heavy, but he was seriously concerned about the oncoming cars. He carried a flashlight, but there were apparently no state laws governing dog teams on highways. Approaching cars slowed almost to a stop, then as they passed usually poured on the gas to get away. One motorist stopped for a chat. Slim mentioned his thought of the danger in his night traveling. The man in the car suggested that he drive ahead, turn, and come back to test the visibility. After he had driven past Slim in both directions, he stopped and laughed. "You don't have to worry about headlights, Slim," he said. "When the lights of my car picked you up, you had sixteen of the brightest, sharpest headlights I ever saw. No wonder cars slow down when they see those wolves' eyes!"

In this manner Slim averaged about thirty miles a day, and left an unforgettable trail.

On September 16, 1933, nine months and twenty-six days after leaving Copper Center, Slim with police escort lined up crowds along Michigan Avenue in Chicago as he drove his team to the Alaska Exhibit at the Century of Progress. Here he ran into rules: No dogs were allowed on the fair grounds; no fires were permitted; no hotel would take his dogs. So a compromise was made. Slim pitched his camp, with a new tent he had acquired, on the Alaska Exhibit grounds. Space was made for the comfortable staking of the dogs. And at least three times each day Slim cooked himself a satisfactory meal over the specially dispensated campfire. In one day Slim would see more people than he had cumulatively seen through his thirty-two years in the North.

He knew that he should be on his way to Washington to complete his trip and make his report. But he excused his delay on two counts: One, his dogs had just pushed about 2,000 miles of pavement behind them and it was hot hard work; they deserved the rest they were getting. Second, he was thoroughly enjoying himself. He loved meeting people and talking with them, and he never seemed to tire of answering questions and talking of his experiences. People loved him too, for many,

many of them, people of high and low estate and of every walk, came and returned almost daily to see him and his dogs. The largest crowds gathered at the time when he'd really developed an appetite and began turning a stand of flapjacks in his skillet.

Slim had to be especially careful of the dogs, to protect the people from them as well as to protect the dogs from the people. The wolf-dogs, unused to the heat and in no sense inclined to be friendly, were always under restraint. Brant was given more leeway, for he, like his master, seemed to enjoy the experience. Slim would never let anyone touch the dogs, except one person.

One day shortly after he arrived there was a lull in visitors. Slim was stretched out in front of his tent taking a nap. A growl from Brant wakened him. He sat up. Approaching the dogs was a young woman. Slim called to her to get away from the dogs, that they were not friendly. The girl stopped and turned around to face him, and smiled. "I won't hurt your dogs, mister," she said, "and besides, I like dogs, and dogs mostly like me too." Her voice was friendly and had the warm softness of a Brown County Hoosier.

This girl was small and dainty, and very attractive. Her hair was black, her eyes hazel, her skin was fair, and the bridge of her nose was freckled. He smiled. "Sorry, ma'am," he said, "I didn't mean to yell at you. What's your name?"

"Gladys," she said simply, and turned again toward the dogs.

"I'd stay away from the dogs, Gladys, they're part wolf, and nobody ever touched 'em but me."

He watched in amazement as the girl went to each dog, talked with them all, and they accepted her fondling as though it was the one thing they had been waiting for. Brant especially made a great show of friendship. Slim, as he watched this almost impossible thing, felt that he too might like to be as well accepted as his dogs.

The next day about the same time she returned. At her

approach the dogs came alert, and again submitted willingly to her attention. Each day the dogs looked forward to her coming, and on days she missed they scanned the crowds and tested the air for sight or smell. Slim also looked forward to the visits.

As the weeks went by, and even after the fair had officially closed for the season, Gladys continued her visits. She and Slim walked and talked together, and their confidences grew.

It was in November that Slim decided he had better complete his trail and go on to Washington, D.C. He told Gladys.

"I'm sure going to miss the dogs," she said. "I love these dogs, Slim, and I hate to see them go."

"Well," said Slim, somehow hoping that he might have been included, "we'll be back, Gladys. I've got to go to Washington and make a report on my trip, then we'll be coming back here, because they asked us to be at the fair again next year."

Gladys smiled. "Yes, Slim," she said, "I'd love to own these dogs. And if you don't look out maybe one day I will, even if I have to marry you to get them. Hurry back, Slim, because I'll miss you too." She turned quickly and ran toward an exit gate. Slim watched until she was out of sight. He turned to Brant. "You hear what Gladys said, Brant? An' that little girl meant it too. Now we got a errand to do, so we better get it done and hurry back like she said." Bit by bit Slim's whirling thoughts began to make a pattern.

At two o'clock in the morning, he quietly mushed his dogs out of the fair grounds and headed east.

·20·

The very best, I dare to hope,
Ere Fate writes Finis to the tome;
A wiser head, a wider scope,
And for the gypsy heart, a home.

About 30 days and some 900 miles from Chicago, and 5,600 miles and 13 months from Copper Center, Alaska, Slim and his dogs arrived in Washington. He had sent word ahead, and newspaper publicity had paved his path just as it had from the west. When he reached the city, he was directed to a place all ready for him to make camp. It was in a park, just a few blocks from the White House.

His first call was upon Anthony Dimond, Alaska's elected representative to Congress. Here he gave a full report of his trip and the possibilities and probabilities of a roadway between Alaska and the United States.

Dimond was sincere in his praise. Being an Alaskan, he knew well the dangers and hardships that Slim had been through. "You're the only man ever to make it with dogs, Slim. I don't know how many others have tried it, four or five at least, but none of them could do it. So you think there's a possibility for a road through there?"

"I sure do," said Slim.

They talked for a long time, trading news about the North.

"Proved one thing comin' out, Tony," Slim said. Everyone in Alaska who knew him called him Tony. "I proved my point about dogs. I been breedin' and crossbreedin' and rebreedin' dogs an' wolves for more'n twenty years, and I got me a team o' half-wolves now with a MacKenzie Husky leader. The wolves just don't get tired, and their feet just don't get sore. Brant, my leader, is the best dog I ever seen, but he's a dog and he gets tired, and his feet gets sore. But them wolves— they're dogs for work."

When he returned to his camp, he found a man waiting for him with a message that he was invited to the White House. He went with the man, and it was not until they were walking in the front door of the Presidential Mansion that he considered his appearance. His face was clean and shaved, but his heavy shock of black hair was in an unruly wave, and on his feet were dirty moccasins, about them a pair of well-worn, faded jeans, topped by an equally old shirt. He stopped and said to the man, "I can't go in to see anybody with me lookin' like this. But this is all I got. I better go buy me a suit o' clothes an' some shoes."

The man smiled. "Don't you worry about a thing, Slim, you go right in."

Slim needn't have worried. Mrs. Roosevelt's gracious greeting immediately dispelled his self-consciousness. She introduced him to the President, and before Slim knew it he was talking with friends. The President and Mrs. Roosevelt were keenly interested in Slim's opinion on the proposed highway, and listened attentively to his stories of Alaska.

"It must be interesting riding a dog sled, Slim," Mrs. Roosevelt commented.

"Well, Mrs. Roosevelt," he explained, "you don't exactly 'ride' a sled. Now on my trip out, I covered more'n five thousand miles, and I guess I didn't ride more'n ten. You see, the sled is for carryin' a load, and the driver is there to help the dogs. So the driver just runs along behind."

Later Slim returned to the White House with his dogs and sled, and gave the children a ride around the White House grounds. To top his experience, he was invited to the White

House for dinner. For *that* occasion he dressed. Anthony Dimond thoughtfully took him in hand and at the last moment was able to find a store which could drape Slim's six-feet, four-inch frame in suitable covering, and furnish shoes for his ample feet. Thus resplendent in the first actual suit of clothes he had ever owned, accompanied by Dimond, he dined in state at the White House.

During dinner Dimond said, "Mr. President, I'm mighty glad that Slim is here in Washington, for he's a man that I honestly believe knows more about Alaska than any man I know. For thirty-two years he traveled every trail, and where there were none he made some of his own. His experience can be of great help."

Mrs. Roosevelt turned to Slim, and said, "You love that country, don't you, Slim?"

"Yes, ma'am, I do, Mrs. Roosevelt," he said warmly. "I guess there's just no place like it. Like Tony said, I've trailed, and panned, and trapped about every trail Alaska's got, and made some of my own. Alaska's big and wonderful in every way you look at it, and it's beautiful."

Later when he was bedding down in his camp in the park, he said to Brant, "Brant, if I was ever to get to be President, you'd be just about the best-feddest dogs they is. They sure feed you good there at that White House." Slim yawned, "But I guess there ain't much chance o' me ever gettin' to be President. They're mighty nice people, though, an' them and the kids sure liked you, Brant. They liked you just fine, an' I was awful proud o' you dogs."

This praise was answered by a heavy thump of a tail against the soft grass.

Slim yawned again. "They sure are nice folks, Brant, made a fellow feel right at home. G'night, Brant."

Slim spent the winter in Washington. Dimond took the greatest advantage of this, and Slim's time was well filled in talking with senators, representatives, and many departments of the government. As Dimond had said, Slim was of great help to the Alaska Representative's office. The Washington lawmakers listened respectfully to Slim's facts, data, and sound observations on such matters as conservation, and to his authoritative opinions of Alaska's problems. Slim's main interest, however, lay in the ultimate development of an international highway, in the consideration of which he had recently contributed so much.

It was just getting dark one evening in early spring when Slim drove into the fair grounds in Chicago. The fair had not officially opened, but he had arranged for space for himself and his dogs at the Alaska Exhibit. He settled his dogs and fed them and himself. Then he started searching his pockets and pack. Somewhere he had a slip of paper with Glady's address written on it. He searched everything he owned, but he couldn't find it. She lived in a boardinghouse, and her name was not in the telephone book. He sat down to think. One night, just after he met Gladys, he had walked home with her after the fair closed. The city with its streets and numbers confused him as he tried to recall the address. He closed his eyes. After a few moments he got up, told Brant to look after things, and walked purposefully out of the grounds.

He had a mental picture of the trail. He knew they had crossed a bridge, so he walked west until he came to one. But this river was running south, and the river they had crossed ran west. Therefore, he figured there was either another river or this one had a bend. He followed it north upstream to where it turned east, and he went on, passing several bridges until he came to the one he recognized by its blockhouse corners. There he turned north along an avenue. A half-hour later he knuckled a door. Gladys opened it.

There was a fireplace in the living room of this home where she lived, and she and Slim sat before a cheery blaze.

"I'm sure glad you found the address, Slim," she said. "I was afraid maybe you lost the paper with the number and street on it."

"I did," he admitted sheepishly. "Anyway, streets and numbers don't mean much to me. I never saw a street number until I got here last summer."

"Then how did you know where I live?"

"I walked home with you one night last summer, remember? So I just shut my eyes and got the picture. We come across a river, up a wide street goin' north, hit a place where the lake is right on the east across the street, come up to a yella flat-face buildin' an' turn west. On the south side o' the street past a alley is a iron-spike fence runnin' in front o' houses. You live in the one where a corner spike is busted off."

She looked at him in amazement. "How did you remember that?"

"Gladys," said Slim, "I never forget a trail once I run it. An' when I walked you home that night I made special sure I wasn't goin' to forget this one. Like I was tellin' the dogs just tonight, maybe them and me both has reached the end of our trail, an' we ought to maybe sort o' settle down."

Gladys looked at Slim. Her eyes sparkled. "You know, Slim," she said, "somehow I just *knew* I was going to get those dogs."

Slim scratched his chin with his thumbnail, then tilting his head, squinted at her—and grinned. "Gladys," he said, "I guess you got yourself a team."

They sat quietly for a considerable time staring at the flickering flames in the grate. Gladys was first to speak, thereby pulling Slim away from his musing. "Slim," she said practically, "now that I've got a team of dogs, and you're about to have yourself a wife, have you got any particular plans?"

At the word "wife," Slim sat up straight. "That means I got to go to work, get myself a job, get a place to live—"

Gladys laughed. "Too much for you, Slim?"

Slim shook his head. "Nope," he said, "only I got to plan what to do. When they was only one of me, it wasn't too bad. But now that there's two of me, it'll take a little thinkin' to figure it out." He stretched his hands out before him, palms down, studied their backs for a moment, then turned them over. They were big hands, strong, capable hands. "Not much use in the city, are they, Gladys?" He weighed his hands as if testing the value of the experience they held. "Put 'em in the wilderness an' they'd take mighty good care of us, but they don't know much about what to do in a city."

Gladys reached over and placed one of her hands in his. "I'll go back to Alaska with you, Slim, if that's what you want to do."

He closed his hand around hers, and looked at her.

He nodded slowly. "I believe you would," he said.

"If it's what you want," she said softly.

He smiled and shook his head. "No, Gladys, it's no country for you, not livin' the way I did, on trails, in trappin' camps, roamin' the bush. It's a wonderful country. It can be a cruel country, too. It's tough." Slim paused and for a long moment stared at the fire, remembering hunger, fatigue, hardships, and the cold. "No," he repeated, "I won't be takin' you to Alaska to live. We'll work it out down here some other way."

"But you don't like the city," she said. "Ever since I've known you, you've been talking about going back."

"Makes a difference now," he told her. "You couldn't stand the cold, the months of lonely livin' when you wouldn't see anybody but maybe an Indian now and then. You couldn't stand the days on a trail—the way I lived. You see, you got your way o' livin' an' I got mine, and the two of 'em couldn't be farther apart. But somehow we'll have to bring 'em together, an' it'll be easier for both of us if we figure it out down here. Like the Indian says, 'You got trouble, you wait. Bimeby e'rything be all right'."

The promise of unborn tears glistened in Gladys' eyes.

"There in Washington," Slim said as he leaned forward to adjust the burning logs with the tongs, "I talked with just a whole lot o' people, the President and Mr. Ickes, and Tony Dimond had me sittin' in on all sorts o' political committees, and I told 'em all about the trail I blazed for a possible roadway. But the funny thing was, them fellows listened more to what I had to say about myself than they did the road. And they kept askin' me questions about Alaska an' about my own experiences up there. I bet one time I talked for more'n a hour to Mrs. Roosevelt an' some o' her friends there at the White House just about what I done up there. They was about the interestedest people you ever saw, an' they kept wantin' to hear more. An' all I talked about was me."

As he was saying this, Gladys sat forward. Her eyes were now alert and sparkled with excitement. "Slim," she said, "that's what you can do. You can talk! You've got something nobody else in this country has got. You've got thirty-two years of living in Alaska to talk about. You've got your trip out with your dogs. Nobody else ever did it. You've got all that experience to talk about. Of course people are interested in it. Why shouldn't they be? It's adventure and excitement, and it's all real and true. You can talk about yourself and be paid for it, too!"

Slim looked at her aghast. "Just for talkin'? I'd get paid? Just for talkin' about myself?" This seemed impossible.

She nodded. "You can lecture. I know there are people who take care of things like getting dates and arranging everything, sort of managers. We'll start out and find a manager for you and get you to talking!"

Slim wasn't too sure about the success of this suggestion, but he had confidence that Gladys knew what she was doing, so he agreed.

For the remainder of the Century of Progress Slim and his dogs were popular representatives at the Alaska Exhibit. At the close of the fair in 1934, Slim and Gladys were married. Meanwhile they had found the name of a reputable lecture bureau. An appointment was made, and the next day he was shown into the manager's office.

Slim started to talk, and he has been talking ever since.

Before Gladys and Slim started their lecture travels, they disposed of the team. Slim found a place in the country where the half-breeds could live out their span in freedom and good care. But the dog, his big leader Brant, traveled with his master and new mistress until age made this no longer practical.

Slim was an immediate success. He loved his subject, he was thoroughly familiar with it, and he could talk about it indefinitely. In ever state in the Union he held his audiences enthralled by the colorful tales of an Alaska no other man had seen, and of experiences that only this sourdough could tell. For more than twenty-two years under the one management he has remained one of the platform's most popular speakers.

Although in 1942 the Alcan Highway was built through Canada connecting Alaska with the United States and followed a longer, more devious route than the one Slim had taken, he lost none of his enthusiasm or interest in his trail. On their way home after one of his lecture appearances he said to Gladys, "Some day they'll build another one, over my trail, and when they do they'll find it'll be the number one route to Alaska."

"I think they will too, Slim," she said with confidence.

Printed in U.S.A.